In Search of My Soulmate

LULA KING JOHNSON

In Search of My Soulmate
Copyright © 2022 by Lula King Johnson

All rights reserved. No part of this publication may be reproduced, distributed, or transmitted in any form or by any means, including photocopying, recording, or other electronic or mechanical methods, without the prior written permission of the author, except in the case of brief quotations embodied in critical reviews and certain other non-commercial uses permitted by copyright law.

ISBN
978-1-959365-28-0 (Paperback)
978-1-959365-29-7 (eBook)

Table of Contents

Introduction vii

I Thought I Could Forget You... 1
The Significance of Meditation 16
In Search of My Soulmate, I thought it was a Man, but it was GOD .. 18
The Wonderment of His Love.. 22
The Carnal Reality – Envelops The Actuality of A SoulMates Physical Existence 24
The Ice Cream Parlor 36
Is It Sunday Morning Already? I was sleeping so Good... 42
Are You Ready for Some Football... 46
Good Morning, Monday Morning.. 58
Sweet Sleep and Peace found me... 73
Anticipation 79
The Mate to my Soul 90
Learning to Trust Again... 97
New Beginnings Just Happen 102
Dinner At Pepe's 105
After the Morning After...Gave Birth to Intimacy 114
Endurance in a Courtship is beautiful to behold 116
Astonished by the Beauty of His Creation... 127
The Bath in The Middle of The Garden 133
Good Things Come to Those Who Wait!!! 150
Life Goes On...As Time Waits for No One... 172
Tis the Season to be Jolly... 179
The Closer I get to You 199
Forgiveness Restores the Yoke of Unfaithfulness..................... 220
The Morning News, Brought Unforgettable Knowledge 230
Being Shaken by The Holy Spirit 234
If You Really Love Someone...Let Them Go...If They Come Back... 245

Springing forward into New Beginnings... 247
The Wedding Tradition Blessings..255

Introduction

This is an inspirational love story designed to touch the very essence of your consciousness...it will encourage your heart...and strengthen the spirit of love that dwells inside the dephts of your soul. May you find comfort, encouragement, strength, and the joy of laughter as an attempt is made to break down barriers that are often put up, when we guard ourselves against enjoying the simplisities in love and life.

With my whole heart, soul, mind and spirit I dedicate this book to the unfailing most incredible, uncomparable love of my life. It was given to me as a sacred gift to share with anyone that would take time out of their lives to escape from the world, to relax and allow the eyes which are the windows to our soul, to experience a beautiful excursion of discovery as we travel through the expanse of time to examine the true essence of The Lover of My Soul.

As we search for that some thing that's missing in our lives, we try just about everything before we finally hit the land of true discovery. By coming into the knowledge that what we needed was right there all along. It was instilled inside our mind, our heart, our soul and our spirit. We search and we search and we search and before we know it, the truth catches up to us and we realize what really matters. It gives us a sense of peace when we finally find or discover it. The "it" is what seems to be missing in our lives; finally finding that mate to our soul is beyond comprehension, hard to believe or conceive, it's everything you ever sensed, thought of or dreamed of. It's the heart beat that completes the beat of your heart. Immediately when you discover it, your heart will in fact skip a beat. As we wait, search, pray, and trust; we have to believe that we can really receive the desires of our hearts. We have to keep our focus on who and what we are praying for, as the truth and answers are unveiled. It's important to know and recognize what He has for us, when we trust and believe that we are worthy to receive His goodness and His very best for our lives. When we stop trying to be the answers to our own prayers and move out of the way and let God be who He is and allow him to do what he does best, by making things work in our lives as he reveals the answers to our heartfelt prayers. Prayer ultimately gives us the desires of our heart; we are tried until we can exemplify honesty, trust and love.

We are torn from one relationship to another; our hearts are riped and divided over decisions that we easily make before we are certain. After all that's been said, done and experienced we find ourselves in a lonely state of mind. Wishing, hoping and dreaming that what we feel in the dephts of our soul; is real in existance as we wait and wonder, time seems to drift away and before we know we've lost countless opportunities to trust our own innate instincts. Suddenly out of the expanse of time comes a chance to explore the essence of true love as we stumble into happiness without any effort at all on our part. Love finds us, as the winds blows its refreshing air; we inhale the breath of life with ease knowing that one day it was destined to find each of us who yearned for it's touch. As it makes its way through the search reaching to find its way to the heart and soul of where it truly belongs.

I Thought I Could Forget You...

It was cold and wet outside from the melted snow, as a chill came over me, there was a lonely feeling inside my heart. As I gazed out my window, all I could see was the evidence of the afternoon storm mixed with sleet and snow. It was Christmas Eve, my sister was on her way to pick me up. When I moved away from my window, I thought to myself; I better make sure I've got everything because one thing I didn't want was my sister, (JK) to be waiting on me; blowing the horn like there was no tomorrow. No soon as I thought about her, the horn starting beeping. (Beep Beep, went the horn on old Besty, that was the name my sister had given her very old, soon to be Classic Thunderbird, that she had not quite put her finger on the Clas-sic, just yet) "In due time" were my sister's favorite words. Everthing would come in due time, money, new exciting adventures, jobs, trips, and oh course; a good man would all come in, well you guessed it "In due time." Why she always insisted on driving is beyond me, but let her tell it she is the oldest...blah...blah...blah. (Beep Beep, the old horn beeped again, I looked out the window to cofirm the beep again and to make sure she was not coming up to get me.)

"Oh, good grief, it's definitely her, I said to myself. Get a grip girl, if he hasn't called you by now by now, after all this time he's not going to call." As I looked around my new place, with all the halls decked with decorations and lots of holly; I was so glad I purchased that huge tree it was beautiful. I pulled myself together, then I said to myself, go on girl grab your leather jacket, purse, keys and get going, life goes on, time definitely brings about a change, and changes are the best thing to happen to everyone. After all change gives birth to new beginnings." So, I held my head up, reached inside the corner of my heart and mind for a new attitude, then I picked up my keys and locked my front door. Immediately, after I started walking out I heard my neighbor call out as he was locking the door of his car, "Merry Christmas, and Happy New Year, Ms. Angell." I looked around toward the voice and I waved, "Thanks Mr. Jackson Merry Christmas to you too."

As I approached the car, I noticed the music in my sister's car was up extremely loud as usual. "My God girl, you're gonna blow our ears out? Then she shouted out, "Hey little sis, Let's go out tonight to my favorite spot? Come on girl, it's Christmas Eve." I looked at her and said, "Go out, you must be kidding, who goes out to a club on Christmas Eve?" "Girl you'll be surprised how many people go out on Christmas Eve, there are plenty of people partying tonight, all kinds of stuff is going on, come on little sis." "Well, I'm not in the mood to go out like that especially on Christmas Eve, I'd rather go hang out at mother's and just let you bring me back on your way out. I bet every guy out tonight, will either be somebody else's property, and don't forget the rejects who don't have anybody in their life; besides I don't have a date." She responded, "Oh little sis, get over it, you are such a player hater, always hoping and dreaming of old Mr. Perfect? I do believe in order to have a date, it usually happens when somebody asks you out, and if you don't have a date you can go out and get one. Come on girl, you can find a date when you get there, Mr. Hopes and Dreams may be there just waiting for you, you never know until you go. Let's go out and party till the break of dawn, come on girl I got that fever." "Sis you seem to be a bit lit already. Tell me the truth how much spiked egg nogg have you had today?" Truth be told little sis, I guess we finished off a punch bowl full, we kind of started celebrating way early this morning." "And Who is "We" suppose to be?" "Well it was about three of us we finished the whole entire bowl of everything, it was sort of like brunch without all the fancy Hoop La, tis the season to be jolly, you know!" "You look pretty jolly to me, I hope you're not too bombed out to drive straight, maybe I should take over and drive." "No thanks little sis, I can handle it, I got this, I made it this far didn't I? Besides, that was this morning I do believe, I've taken a nap since then." "You know what? You need help, Alcoholic Anonymous is always around for people like you, in need of a membership. You better be careful driving tonight, I don't need you to become another Holiday Statistic and end up getting charged with more than a DWI. I will be the designated driver tonight, come on let me drive your eyes are a little glassy right now, I don't care if you did take a nap today; I know you, I'm sure you had a little nip before you left to pick me up." "Okay, okay you know you get on my nerves, I knew you were going to say something." (After I put her on a guilt trip she moved over to the passenger's side of the car. Then I got out and took the wheel). "Thank you very much, I'm sure we won't regret it. After you sober up, go on out and let me know tomorrow if you had a good time. You just might get you a date for New Years Eve, a telephone number, or better yet a personal house call." "Yea right little sis, I don't want to go out by myself although it's never stopped me before. But back to you, I don't understand why you just can't let it go and move on."

Immediately when she said that I took a good look at myself in the rearview mirror, as I begin to question my life. (Why are you doing this to yourself, just Go on Out and get out of the pitiful zone of life; don't ever allow a man to get to you like this and make you feel down. Everything happens for a reason. When God closes one window, he opens another one for you. When one man goes, another one will come. I can't let him or anything else stop me from going on with my life. Right after I filled my mind with posiitve thoughts, the enemy flashed all the bitter memories of let downs into my mind. He's a professional at that you know, I begin to think about all the lies, the no shows, and the excuses that women are given when a man can't get what they want from you. The Jack Of All Liars Club, that's what I call them, I knew several members who had lifetime memberships. I have never been able to really understand why some people will not be honest and tell you they just don't want to see you anymore or at all. Instead people start playing the calling card game and they either don't answer or return your call. Or they use the old I'll call you right back even if they don't have your number. They just keep you hanging long enough for you to finally hang yourself; then you fail to read that stupid sign in the mirror that's stamped on your forehead, suddenly after dwelling in Stupid Ville, you finally wake up and read the signs. A man or woman can start out to really be interested in you; when we feel that instant connection, we have to be careful not to give away too much too soon. When our emotions run freely unguarded to trust too soon, it's easy to loose sight of the intrigue, excitement or interest in someone, simply because its not easy to trust someone with your whole heart. So we give away pieces at a time. Immediately after you've given away the treasures that made you a precious jem; a person's mind can and will wonder off as they move on without giving it a second thought, it does'nt take a man long to find somebody else. While we look back on the memories, the words that were expressed or the time spent together. You end up feeling worthless, used, confused and afraid to move on; hoping for a change of heart or mind. Usually there no chance of reconciliation, just a waste loveless time.

"You know, sis I was thinking I do need to go on and live my life regardless of what has happen in my past. It doesn't really matter that I've been let down, that's part of life. I have to learn to let it go. If I don't, I won't ever get a chance to experience the joy in my own future. I have to forgive myself, and him and just move on. That's really all that matters, not living in the past but living for a future. I am going to forget the disappointments of the relationships that didn't work, I guess those particular people weren't suppose to be in my life. I have a life and it begins right here with me, from this day forward, on this Christmas Eve I am going into the New Year with a new mindset. I am going to move on with my life right now. Thirdly, I will be graduating from college next year and I refuse to have a Pity Party revisit me with feelings of hurt and loneliness. I'm going to focus on having joy in my heart no matter who or what crosses my path. In the meantime, I want the past to stay in the past. I'm going out with you tonight, I'm not even going to dress up as if I'm desperate for a date with my cute little old Christmas outfit on. If I can wear what I have on, my jeans and sweater, I'll go out with you tonight." My sister, was shocked but pleased, as she replied,"I don't know whether I should say Amen or Bravo."

Even though she commented, she still looked at me in disbelief, because I have never been bold enough to wear blue jeans out anywhere except the grocery store, especially when it came down to going out to a club. Always the silks, rayon's, linen, and the beautiful 100% cotton from Egypt or Italy, it always had to be some kind of expensive drop dead gorgeous to do. Don't get me wrong, that's just how it is, I loved to look good and for my clothes to feel good on my body. My Sister was the causal girl, she would wear blue jeans to church if the Blue Laws allowed. (Only in Texas, back in the day, Remember what was called the Blue Laws? Where you couldn't hardly buy anything to do with clothing on Sunday not even panty hose. It's a long story, we have really "come a long way baby" as that old slogan use to say "to get where we got to today".)

"I can't believe it little sis, I know you're kidding, you always have to look like you just stepped out of the latest Magazine, you will have to shock me tonight before I believe it. I think I'm sobering up already on that note." As she lite her cigarette she found herself almost choking she had to let her window down so she could breathe then she said with a little smoke caution. "Okay if you're serious my favorite spot welcomes our dress attire. It's casual, they have a live jazz band and the people are so cool and laid back we'll fit in just perfect. I think that's why the name of the place is called Popsicles Toes. You'll love it, you can dance, play pool, throw darts, or watch some of the finest men walk through the door; which happens to be one of my favorite things to do. A lot of professional athletes are in and out at this club, it's the spot and trust me it's hott. You'll never know who you might be standing next to or conversating with." "That sounds pretty cool, but I don't do darts or play pool." "Little sister, I've taught you everything you know, it's not how well you play the game; it's the fact that you're up for the game." Angell replies, "Well alright then, I believe a sister is up for the game, okay sis, bring it on. But let me run back to my place and get my heavy leather coat because it's a bit too cold for this little jacket I have on; besides it's starting to snow again." So I turned the car around went back and got my coat. As I made my way back to the car, I shouted out to my sister to give her a reality check from the slight level of intoxication that I could still see it in her eyes. "Okay girl, go ahead and rest your eyes so you can get rid of that thing that's hoovering over you. Put your seatbelt back on so we can get this gift exchanging thing over with, after that, "Let's Get It On, Oh baby...with the Real Party." Afterwards, I put the car in gear and drove on to Mothers. I looked over at my sister as she seem to be nodding out. I shook my head and turned the music up, the radio station was playing some of my favorite Christmas songs, so I increased the volume. (I love Christmas Music, don't' you?) As long as I can remember, we've always spent Christmas Eve at our Mothers it was our family tradition, we would always pull names and exchange gift's. Mother said she created it that way so that as we got older and begin to have our own families we wouldn't feel obligated to drop everything to come home for Christmas. There was always plenty of Egg Nogg (two bowls' one spiked by my brother and the other spike free). The smell of mother's freshly baked hot out of the oven Sweet Potato Pies always filled the air waves, and of course the most delicious German Chocolate Cake in the world accompanied by the best hot chocolate with double squeeze of whipped vanilla cream. Afterwards there would always be plenty of inquiring minds want to know conversations, about our plans for Christmas Day and New Years Eve. It was special and will always hold sentimental memories in my heart.

When I parked the car, I turned the music up loud. "Wake up Sis, you missed all the Christmas music, the snow flakes and the whole trip, freshen up so Mother won't be tripping." "Look I'm okay why do you always have to act like you're the oldest? Remember now, you need to respect your elders and turn that music down." "Okay Elder, do you need help out of the car? Or Do you need me to get you a Walking Cane or a Wheel Chair?" "Funny, little sis, funny." As we walked up the steps to the house it was filled with the traditional decorations, beautiful as usual. Mother had all the Christmas trimming and fixing everywhere. You could smell the aroma of homemade turkey pot pies (too die for), sweet potato pies, pound cakes and fresly baked cookies all through the house. My sister and I greeted her with hugs and kisses then we put our gifts under the tree. We told mother that we were going out together and had decided not to sit at home alone, setting ourselves up for the usual holiday plans of disappointments. We told her we decided to wear what we had on, be casual, bold and beautiful. Immediately, Mother made a slight comment. "I don't believe it, but thank the Lord, that both of you are not sitting at home alone. It's about time you girls went out together and had a little fun; but be careful out there tonight even though the snow has been beautiful all day, it's still a little slippery out there. Although it's Christmas Eve lots of people will still be out and about tonight. But remember the ones who have a few screws loose after drinking too much. You girls have a good time, Angell watch out for your sister, she told me she's been having a real good time since midnight." "Mother, she told me she started this morning, I should have known." "I could tell by the way she was walking when she got out of the car, expecially when I saw you driving Angell." "Look you two leave me alone, okay let me do me, and you two; do you, besides I need some more eggnog! Where is it? I think I deserve a big huge glass." "Mother, you know your daughter, I got her back, I'm the designated driver tonight. We are driving Old Betsy tonight she has weathered plenty of storms, remember she can take a licking and keep on ticking." Mother smiled, afterwards we exchanged gifts, had some homemade turkey pot pie and of course my favorite dessert. I had two slices of warm sweet potatoe pie, and a big hunk of German Chocolate cake, and some hot chocolate with a dabble whipped cream. We finished off the evening with a little egg nogg, while we listened to some of our favorite Christmas songs. My sister appeared to be a lot more sober after eating and taking a little power nap. I was glad she put some food in her stomach, so old Mr. Ralph wouldn't visit her in the car. (You know who Mr. Ralph is right? You know that quick stomach punch you feel when you've had more than enough to drink, Ralph looses all respect drops the Mr. and punches you in your gut then you loose all control and throw up everything except your gall bladder. Mr. Ralph is never invited to the party he doesn't need an invitation he crashes everybody's party.) After the gifts had been exchanged, that Party fever started to hit us, we said our good byes gave out Christmas hugs, kisses and wishes and were off to Get the Party Started. We left for this Cool Club called Popsicles Toes, where it was so cool that you literally felt the chill like you had popsicles on your toes. I could'nt wait, we were on our way, two women about to change their world and become a little more laid back, daring and cool. Keep it on the down low, my sister was a whole lot cooler than me. But I learned how to be just as cool, and became the life of the party. It was my sense of humor and ability to warm up the crowd that became my entrance and my winning ticket to every party.

When we arrived at the club I looked around at the people that were going inside, we fit right in. My sister flashed a fifty dollar bill at the door and told the guy she was running a tab; while he took off our coats, the guys standing by the door checked us out like a radar and let us in free. The security guard greeted my sister by her initials as if she were a regular and believe me, from the strut of her entrance and flamboyant behavior she was definately a regular. After we walked past the owner of the club and a few of his friends; she greeting him and introduced me as her little sister. One of his friends shouted out, "Merry Christmas, Little Sister, you look all grown up to me; I don't see nothing little about you." Then another guy shouted out to both of us, that he would love to put the Merry in our Christmas. My sister turned and looked at him and said, "I just bet you would, Hey, Hey Now, it must be what's in these jeans. You Go Girl, With your Bad Self." The only thing I could think of that sounded remotely cool was; "That's just what this is, Gentlemen, We Do Look Good." We both laughed, then we moved straight through the crowd all eyes were on us. I must admit we were wearing those jeans.

Finally we made it over to the bar where my sister gave the bartender the same fifty dollar bill to run us a tab. She ordered me a glass of sparkling white wine, and herself a double shot of her favorite Courvoisier Cognac then we moved over by the dart board. After getting inside and checking out the scene, my sister was right, it was indeed an explosion of attractive guys in the house; tall, medium, dark, fine, yummy, handsome, and just plain delicious, waiting right in the midst of us, hovered over in line to throw darts. All I wanted to do was keep the score and get a serious eye examination of all those jeans standing in front of me. My, My, My, it made me think about the mind, it really is a terrible thing to waste, so why misuse it when you have the opportunity of a life time, to use it to the best of your eye sights ability. They certainly had quite a bit of talent to show off. You could tell my sister was a regular, she could throw darts with the best of them, I couldn't believe it, she was actually winning. She hit more bulls eyes that night than any of the woman in a long time I heard, they opened up another bar tab for us on the house; she insisted on a refill instead of taking all their money; after her windfall then she decided she wanted her christmas stocking stuffed with cash. The guys were shocked at her concentration level under the influence. Even though she qualified for a serious alcholic violation. When I looked at the score board she was kicking their butt. From the looks of things, the congnac seem to stimulate her thought pattern. She played a heck of a game with over two hundred dollars in her stocking.

When I turned around to get another glass of wine from the chilled bottle the bartender had for me at the bar, a voice called out to the bartender. "This one is on me Don, give the lady what ever she wants." There he stood, this six foot two shot of absolutely delectable, in every since of the word. This intriguing specimen with the most adorable smile, whose eyes could lead me where ever he wanted me to go. They say the eyes are the window to our soul. So I looked straight into his eyes, because I wanted his soul to open up as soon as possible. "Suppose I want something the bartender can't handle?" He looked at me and smiled again, then he replied, "Surely what ever you want, I know my friend Don here, has all the skills to make it happen?" "I don't know what kind of skills he has, but I'm sure what I'm thinking of has nothing to do with his talents as a bartender." He responded, Is that right?" "You better believe it. Tell me, TDH (which mean tall, dark and handsome) What's your name?" "TDH what's that some sort of code?" "Sort of." I replied. "Morgan" he responded. I turned and faced the bartender and said, "Tell me Mr. Don Bartender, friend of Morgan here, do you have any champagne with his name on it, if it's not any, it outa be a law against not having any Morgan Champagne straight from his vineyard?" The bartender replied, "No my lady, unfortunately, I don't have any champagne named Morgan, the only thing I have is some Morgan David Red Wine." "I looked at him and said, I heard Morgan David Red Wine is good for your heart and your blood, if that's the case I must have some of it in my system." They both laughed. "You can't mix red wine with sparkling wine or champgne my lady." Don replied. "To bad Mr. B, good looking out for me, I tell you what, I will accept your level of expertise because you've been good to me all night long. Although I would love to have had my very own rare bottle of exquisite delicious Morgan Champagne." He laughed, then he poured me up a really nice glass of champagne. "Oooh, Morgan, I just love watching those bubbles have their way in my glass." "You look like you deserve a bottle of priceless champagne," Morgan replied. But I would have to add something else to it make sure it brings out the flavor in the champagne." "And what might that be?" "It would have to be some plump juicy delicious strawberries some plain and some dipped in the finest chocolate." "Oooh now, that sounds like a very enticing invitation. Are you trying to start something, Morgan? Don't you want to know if I've been naughty or nice first? After all it's Christmas Eve and you could put the Santa back in my Claus. I would love it, if you came down my chimney, I promise you to have lots of warm homemade cookies and milk waiting just for you by my cozy lite fireplace." "Sounds intriguing, first I need to look at my list and check it twice it has always Revealed whose been naughty or nice." he replied." "We'll Santa I guess I better confess, especially since you have that list, let me see, where do I began? I guess you can say I've been pretty nice most of the year, but right now, I'm feeling very naughty." "I must agree, it appears that way doesn't it?" He replied. Angell leans over to Morgan and whispers in his ear, "But, Santa don't you have the power to wipe my slate clean, and show a little Merry Christmas Compassion or something? Especially if I confess my shortcomings for the whole year." Morgan responded, "I might be able to do something, or at least leave you something in your Christmas Stocking, it's one of the things I do best, afterall I am Santa Claus." "Oh Santa, your'e getting me all excited about your yearly duties. But you know what? I would love it if you could give me another chance by stuffing a little TLC (tender loving care) in my Christmas stocking. Would you promise me that you'll be careful because the mantle over the fireplace will be extremely hot." "Do you think your Christmas stocking is strong enough for what I might stuff in it? he replied." "I don't know but right now, I feel like a kid on Christmas morning, I can't wait to see what it is Santa, you got me craving for the element of surprise." "Hmm, after all that's what Christmas is all about love and lots of surprises isn't it." He replied." "After you finish all your deliveries, can you promise to make me your last visit I promise to wait up for you with your warm milk, hot chocolate and cookies and a nice shoulder massage. I know that bag of yours must get awfully heavy by the end of the night all you need is a little TLC. "Umm, you are going to make me park my sleigh right on top of your chimney all night long, he replied." "Oh Santa please be careful with your sleigh and my chimney. Final Question Santa, I need to make sure there is no Mrs. Claus. Is there?" "If there was a Mrs. Claus, by now I would be in big trouble." He replied. "I take it the answer is No." Angell replied. "In big capital letters." He responded "Well that sounds like Christmas music to my ears, in that case I might need to take a ride in your sleigh after all?" I replied. (What am I saying, I don't even know this man, but deep down inside for some reason I really wanted to.) "You know you're trying to start something don't you? He replied." I very boldly walked up to him and looked him straight in his eyes and said, "I don't start nothing I can't finish; however, our conversation was very stimulating, like I always say, the mind is a terrible thing to waste. But the imagination is much more beautiful, don't you agree? Exploring the depths of the mind is intriguing especially when we allow it to run away with us. Which makes it easy to enjoy the flight of childlike fantasies. After it takes you on the ride of a lifetime you'll see how incredible it really is. You know what they say great minds travel on the same frequency. Thank you for tunning into my station, I enjoyed every single minute of it."

Morgan looked at me in a very peculiar way. "Believe me the pleasure was definatley all mine. I've never seen you here before, are you from this area? he replied." As he looked at me with those very captivating eyes. I quickly turned around and thanked the bartender for his delicious champagne selection. Then I turned to Morgan again and reached for his hand, "No, I'm not! Like I said, I enjoyed our conversation, I'm guest of my sister tonight, this is my first time here." As he gripped my hand with the warmth of his, we could hardly let go. The way he looked at me, was like you belong in my arms; his lips were calling mine to his I had to hurry up and get out of his presence because our flirteous ways were totally out of control. Only one man had ever affected me like that. He replied, "Trust me, the pleasure was definatley all mine, now I see what a precious gem you really are, very classy." Then I walked away. I felt his eyes in the hollow of my back, a big chill rippled up and down my spine; so I had to add a little swagger to my walk that said what ever it takes. Oh my God, where did he come from? I said to myself. I never got a chance to tell him my name, well it didn't matter at the time, because I really needed to calm down, give myself a time out and get some fresh air; before I really got carried away I could have easily took him home with me. I better be carefully, this champagne is not playing around right now, I started feeling a little woozy as I approached the dart board my head began to pound. "Oooh, all that Champagne, I must have been out of my mind; I'm supposed to be the designated driver I've put too much Merry in my own Christmas. I could'nt drive my sister's car up to the next block in this condition. I thought to myself. Finally I made my way through the crowd and walked over to the dart board which wasn't that far away in distance but when you had a few too many every step seems like a long journey. Finally I looked for my sister, who had almost three hundred dollars by now hanging on her shirt; she had been crowned as the big winner for the night. Just as I leaned over to her to let her know I needed to get some fresh air she immediately realized I had drank too much Champagne. It had began to get pretty warm in the club I felt like I was sitting inside the furnace surrounded by all the body heat inside the club made me break out in a cold sweat. At that point I knew I couldn't afford to have any more glasses of Champagne. My sister told me where to go and that no one would bother me, she asked one of the security guards to make sure no one entered that area unless she was told about it. Then she told me she would check on me in a few minutes; after a couple of the guys got change and paid up, because she had been extremley hott all night playing darts. I walked over to the other side of the club where there were quite a few empty tables.

When I sat down at one of the tables near the back of the club, I could hear the music playing very softly. I began to develop a mild headache; it felt a lot better to be away from that loud music; the people were closing in on me. "Girl why did you drink all hat champagne so fast, you were being so silly. You know when you do that it gives you the worst headache." I felt sluggish and just a wee bit intoxicated. I was really showing off.

Thank God I left, before I said or did anything else, that champagne was talking and had a great time. I bet that guy thought I was crazy. "Ooh my head needs to be excamined because I sure would like for Morgan to be under my tree, next to my tree or just on my door step with a huge bow wrapped around him." The need to massage my temples and get rid of my headache. I looked around the area and saw the security guard standing in the doorway, then I closed my eyes. All of a sudden this mood came over me that's not easy to describe. Then I saw a few couples come in and go back out through the door. I could hear somebody trying to talk to me, but I couldn't concentrate on what they were saying. My head started pounding like a hammer on a wall, I heard my name being called over and over again, but for the life of me I really couldn't understand what was being said to me. I struggled to open my eyes but I didn't see any one there. I was alone no one was there. It was cold out back but I didn't mind because I wanted to be alone until I got rid of that dreadful headache. So I continued to massage my temples again, and close my eyes. It was definitely kind of strange, it was like being called nearer to thee, which is where I felt my mind going. I would call it, a place called there, once you go there, there is the place where God is calling you to. Once you actually get there, you sense the provisions made for you, and there is where you feel you should be, your heart is finally set free right there between you and thee. Immediately, more and more I slipped deeper into a solemn state of meditation. My head ache was being set free, there was no more recognition of the pounding as I came closer and closer to the voice that was calling me, closer and closer and nearer to thee. It seem so familiar to me, in the very depths of my soul...I was in awe the moment...I felt myself being received by this awesome power of intimacy...that reached for me inside the penetration of my heart, my spirit, my soul and my mind. It went so deep inside my consciouness, I felt as if my thoughts were all caught up in the mist of flames in the dephts of my soul. The thoughts were passing through my mind so quickly, I couldn't keep up. As I surrendered, it began to take over and begun to manifest inside this trance. I could see the figure of a man, with such a familiar demeanor. The very essence of his presence left you out of breath. Could it have been, an authentic mystical encounter with what my soul has longed for? Or was it just a glimpse into the heart of my soul mate about to set me free. Free from the loneliness that had taken root inside the dephts of my heart which taken me years to build this foundation of protection.

As I sat there I began to think through the layers of private feelings, and stirred up emotions that I had; as I listened to the anguish that surfaced into my mind. Why couldn't I be a little more understanding and just trust my heart and love for him. It's hard to understand when so many things happen at once, I went over and over it again that night. I couldn't believe, that I, Angell DiVine Summers, allowed the spirit of interference to come in and make itself at home while it totally ruined my life and my future with the man I truly loved and I know loved me. You know, when you realize how the spirit of doubt comes in to take over your mind and set you up to loose every thing that you ever dreamed of. I wasn't strong enough to let it go and move on, and just trust the heart that God gave me…that He took the time out of His busy schedule to stop by to nourish our soul and replinish our emotions, when I had no one else to love in this world but him. But we all know this to be true; everything really does happens for a reason no matter how hard or disheartening it is. The enemy always tries and will often succeed at stealing our joy if we give him enough room. The room is the space you leave in your heart to give up on something too soon. It doesn't matter what we give up on; giving up is giving up. You can give up on a marriage, a relationship, a troubled teenager, having a child, being healed from a sickness or disease, a job, your dreams, having a family, living in poverty, life getting better, believing you deserve more out of life, feeling that you are worthy to be loved, believing that you will find that special someone to love and that person will love you; the list can go on and on. After all, we must realize this truth, the enemy really does come to kill steal and destroy. All we have to do is open up and let him in our business. As soon as the door to our heart opens up he immediately tries to find a way to steal our faith, our love, our joy, our peace, our happiness, and he will try until he destroys our mind, our body, our heart and our spirit. Being aware of the devil's job description early in life puts you a step a head of his game; he only has three responsibilities and that is to kill, steal and destroy and he uses people we know and love to fight all his battles with us. Many times we lose the battle through emotions of anger and the frustrations of life when we don't know what else we can do. His purpose is to come like a thief in the night; when we least expect him. He sneaks in and out with the victory, taking away what ever we treasure the most.

The Significance of Meditation

Meditation is contemplation, a reflection of thoughts, or visualization, which is the study of, or the examination of something that is lingering on in our mind. In order for us to move on to a level of clarity it's important to learn how to clear our thoughts. Being able to reflect on our thoughts and figure out why they're surfacing in our mind is very important. We have to learn how to control our thoughts or find out what we can do to find a solution for what's going on in our head and our heart. I've learned, that if I clear my mind of the thoughts that don't make sense to me; helps me to open up a clear pathway of simplicity. I refer to those thoughts as the garbage disposal of thoughts which seem to be stopped up like the drain in a kitchen sink. When my mind gets completely stopped up, I try hard to get rid of all the garbage filled thoughts. There are times when I try to retrieve control of why my mind went off into wonder land in the first place; I realize I can't salvage anything worth while, I try hard to change my thought pattern. All kinds of thoughts can surface, that can either hinder you or encourage you to pray through it for final solution. It may take a while before you receive clarity, if that's the case, remember patience is the greatest virtue to wait on the final answer. It gives you time to make up your mind, especially if you want those emotions and feelings to heal, so you can move on with your life.

When I stop to meditate, it's always best to be alone and undisturbed where I can go into the privacy of my own thoughts. Which to me is the space in my mind, where I can reflect on the natural part of my life from a spiritual level. I have to remove myself from where ever I am; and usually I'm on a carnal level when its easy to make the wrong decision based on what you see or feel, which are emotions from the soul. Immediately, my mind, my thoughts, and my spirit seem to travel deep inside the totality of my being. And right there is where I find the seclusion I need through my own convictions and emotions. When that happens, all I want to do is examine what's clear in my head. I've noticed that when my thoughts are clear I allow the Holy Spirit to enter in and offer me true revelations. The Holy Spirit gives us free will to accept the truth that's being revealed to us. When I allow God's spirit to be revealed, the genuine aspect of my **soul mate** appeals to my inner spirit to trust and respect his divine manifestations and revelations. Meditation is so necessary and essential to the mind, it offers with it a feeling of restoration, comfort and truth.

In Search of My Soulmate, I thought it was a Man, but it was GOD

My soul is stirring...as I search deep...within my heart for my soul mate. As we go through the magnanimous channels of life, we each feel the need to balance with someone special. One who will become more than a part of our life, one that completes our life on earth. To finally make a connection with that special person that was chosen to reach inside the depth of your spirit, to pull you out of yourself. I respect love in a way that not many of whom I have come in contact with do. I understand how precious it is and how empty your life can be if you don't share the love that you possess in your own individual heart and soul. So many of us, will check out of the universe without ever sharing the love that we so desperately need to release from our heart. Some of us will even die from a broken heart of a love that we never choose to reveal; therefore it never had an opportunity to manifest or heal. We must have the inner desire to want healing for ourselves when we experience hurt in love. First, we have to make a conscious decision that we want to heal from the encounter which is number one; Second, we have to ask God to help us get over the hurt and the pain, unless we turn it over to him and allow him to help us there is no way we can be healed. Forgiving ourselves and others plays a key role in our healing. God is the only one that can heal a heart or spirit that has been broken, but we have to be willing to let the emotional attachment go and move on with our lives. When we're not willing to go on, we continue to hurt ourselves with the memories that keep on surfacing in our mind that caused the pain in the first place. We have to finally come to the realization that, that person doesn't want us or wasn't meant for us. If we continue to overemphasize it or try to make a big deal about it, it will slow down progress in our lives. We have to admit it to ourselves that we made a mistake in our judgement. But in some instances we will in our own imperfection blame God, as if God is the one who made a mistake. God never makes a mistake, we are the only ones who experience levels of shortcomings for choosing the wrong people in our lives. We invite them into our lives without permission from God. Our permission sometimes comes from financial hardships, pressure from our friends or relatives, pleasure sought from our eyes, our mind, and our own inner feelings or emotions. If your heart and mind are in doubt that may certainly be a sign that you should be. Learning how to follow your heart may help you to remove all doubt. Heartache is a familiar emotion; when it comes our way during that first instance we should notice how it grieves us. Especially when we see that blow coming from someone we really care about. Heartache and the truth hurts, we're human and we all make mistakes, nobody is perfect. Living in the truth will set you free, it can free you from hurting yourself or someone else. When a person really loves you, there will be mistakes that have to happen in order for love to grow and renew itself. In order for your love to be made new, it has to be elevated by a level of grace, these are the Five key Renewal Elements over time. Love has to be Refreshed, Replenished, Restored, Recreated, and Revived. During the course of your relationship as you grow, while you blend your lives together you will notice that many things will happen to make you want to give up and move in a different direction. But we must always remember that love is designed to be tried, tested and proven before it's strenthened. Through out the expanse of time you will ususally find that you love that person even more, remember that God always wants love to endure. After you've endured all that you thought you ever could and done all that you can do, you may find that the love you felt for that person may get lost in the space of time as you separate yourselves from each other with what ever is going on outside of your life. When you know you prayed and prayed, been counseled, and advised; God may show you plenty of signs or even speak to your heart and spirit that you need to let that person go, and go on with your life as he reveals purpose to you. He will separate us from people that we love, but don't need in our lives.

He will then use, other people to minister to our heart, because it takes time to heal and grow from that relationship, in order to gain strength and wisdom from our mistakes, misconceptions and misunderstandings. Which make us aware that we need to be a lot more careful the next time around. Memoirs help bring forth future encounters of love that we're able to share; they help us establish better relationships. Sharing memories of love can blossom in its due season we have to be cautious; there is no hurry, we don't have to rush into love with any one. We have to learn how to excerise one of the greatest virtues which is patience. The word patience has an array of definitions, it brings you the endurance to live through every kind of situation. It instills you with the tolerance to be persistent in your life and gives birth to courage which gives you the moral strength to bring forth peace in your heart and mind. People are sent to us by God clothed by the beauty of his love. He gives them instructions to share his unique and rare breed of love with us. There may only be a select amount of people that you may come across in life, that have this incredible inner spirit that shows up at just the right time to make your acquintance. Often times they come reminding us of a loved one that may have passed on. That loved one could have been a spouse, a child, a mother, a father, a grandparent, a favorite aunt, uncle, cousin or a very special friend of yours or your family. When you became acquainted with them or just get to know them you don't know what it is that made you feel such an instant connection. Before they came through your life, you may have been at a point where you stopped trusting or it could have been a time that you needed a friend, a son, a daughter, a sister, a brother, a mother or even a father figure. Some how that person became exactly what you needed at that crucial time in your life. God's wants us is to have a destiny filled with the depth of his love. He allows us an opportunity to be strengthened by his love and that love should bestow a spirit of endurance within us. To remember, or reminisce is simply being able to think back, or recall something from our past. We shouldn't become bitter or cold hearted by the mere presence of memories that are stored up our mind. We should cherish those sweet memories which turn into precious memoirs that will soon pass on. Memoirs are a part of our own personal history; they are self portraits of life's experiences. They are passed on to generation after generation; they supply us with wisdom, knowledge, and understanding. Those particular memories should be thought of as ever lasting thoughts that will continue to live on in our minds long after someone has moved on with their lives or even passed away. If you become bitter and cold hearted about the memories that rest inside your soul and your heart aches over them, they can haunt you and suffocate you. You can loose your mind over begrudging painful memories; and be broken down by a battle of resentment. In this case, its easy to end up developing bitterness in your spirit and in your heart. And that bitter taste can cause a negative impact to develop in the temple of your mind due to all the hurt and pain. The love and peace of God can't dwell inside a heart, mind, soul or spirit, that never took the time out to prepare a place for it.

The Wonderment of His Love....

God allows his loving peace to run open and free,
when we decide to remove our thoughts from all sources of negativity
We should strive to be more kind, honest and true to ourselves,
while learning how to be patient as we wait to
receive the true essence of God's help.
Ahh...The Spirit of Love
It's sent to us straight from Heaven above.
God is made up of Everlasting Love
His Spirit reveals his Love to Us over and over again
As we share Kindness, Honesty, and the Gentleness of our hand
It makes it easy by leading us into the revelation of His promised land
Making an attempt to show others that we care,
As we take time out of our lives to just stop and be right there.
When we ask God to show us the way,
Don't be surprised if it happens that day,
An opportunity is golden when you are prepared
To enter in a realm of dreams just when you dared
To believe as your hopes become a reality
Oh Yes, you might shout for joy
As your heart simmers down to finally enjoy
A love inside that's dwells deep down in your soul
God is so incredible, He makes you feel so bold
Go look in the mirror and you will see
How he reveals himself to thee.
The beauty that dwells within you,
The love that dwells within you,

The care that dwells within you,
Did you know we have the Spirit of God's unfailing love dwelling in us?
In case you didn't know He has many miracles in store just for you...
Waiting to be revealed and manifested to you,
They have been approved by God, and are available open and running free,
All we must need do is watch as well as pray how we live
It may be a channel running through the tunnel of a looking glass
while you live, love, serve, share and care
there will be angels watching everywhere.
Try to trust him with the fullest of your ability.
Just like the woman that was chosen to be your mother,
he promises to stick by you closer than a brother.
He loves us because he took the time out to create each of us...
We are as Unique as a Rare Precious Jewel...
Equipped and filled with The Wonderment of His Love...

The Carnal Reality – Envelops The Actuality of A SoulMates Physical Existence

I believe, I believe, I believe that my soul mate is truly out there, in search of the very thing that I feel inside the depths of my mind, my heart, my spirit, and my soul. Those of us who care to admit it, feel a need or desire for that special someone, who will nurture our spirit and nourish our soul. We find ourselves going through life in a time capsule looking, and searching, for the love of our life. Someone that will move us, groove us or flow with us, as we try to connect and share a familiar feeling that we hope will become visible to us when we meet someone. At some point in our lives we may have experienced some type of familiar feeling when we thought (this just feels right). Or was it just our imagination, but we never really expect in our wildest dreams how vivid our imagination could be. As you uncover the realization, you find that its so real that you can feel it as it touches the inner depths of your soul.

Instantly, my mind began to reflect on the most wonderful memories that we once shared together. I started to reminisce when we first met. Our eyes first met and they locked into a rapture of endlessness intrigue. Immediately we both knew. I felt him walk right inside my body, my soul, and my spirit. Instantaneously my heart began to become stimulated as it yearned to be closer to him. My heart raced to its highest peak. I could tell by the look in his eyes that he felt the same exhilaration too. We both knew we had to be together, I needed his love and he needed mine. Even though voices surrounded us, we both felt and heard the same call to love as the idea of infinity made it's entrance into the room.

We both were attending a house warming celebration party my sister, JK, was hosting, as he stared at me and I at him, our hands reached out as they met first. His name meant nothing, I could only feel the warmth of his touch. Instantly as his hand touched mine we immediately felt the need for more privacy. His eyes lead me straight out of the room, and we met outside to the open front porch. It didn't matter where he was leading me as long as he took me with him. My heart and body raced with intrigue, we felt the need for seclusion. My heart was beating so fast that I could hardly contain my self. I felt as if I was melting like milk choclate right in front of this guy. Which I didn't care because that just happen to be my nickname. In fact all I could hear him say was, tell me, why do they call you Chocolate? I tried to use as much suduction in my voice as I possibly could I answered in a very enticing tone, "I've always been alergic to Chocolate, even though I love it, I always have an allergic reaction." Then he responded back in such a captivating tone, "For a woman who looks as sweet as you, I can't imagine not ever giving you Chocolate Candy. So tell me, how can I make Valentine's Day sweet for you without you getting such an unusual reaction?" "Just because you asked me the question makes it sweet, besides you look like the type of man that will always be able to think of something." "You think you know me already do you?" "No but I can read a man pretty well." "We'll what about white chocolate, I'm sure you've enjoyed the pleasure." "I have, in fact it's always been my favorite, it's just as delicious." "Let me guess, it wouldn't hurt to have some fresh strawberries slightly dipped followed up with flowers, and a bottle of sparkling wine." "Huh, so you think you know me already do you? Or did my sister brief you?" "No, she didn't in fact I didn't even know she had a little sister until tonight, trust me I'm on cloud 9." I responded with a little brief musical jargon from The Temptations. "Cloud 9! Hmm, you mean, you can be what you want to be on Cloud 9, you're a million miles from reality, you know reality, reality....I'm doing fine on Cloud 9." "Oh, I see you like The Temptations, and looks like you can sing too."

"Very Funny I don't know too many people who don't love the old school classic's especially when it comes to The Temptations." "I'm loving your sense of humor, you make it very difficult not to like you. Come go for a drive with me?" "Are you sure I can trust you, where are you taking me?" "Oh come on I'm on cloud 9, remember. I promise to be nothing but the perfect gentleman." "If you're sure I won't have to spray my bottle of mace or leave your license plate number with my sister? Let me go back inside and get my purse. As you can see I'm a little old fashion, I better check in with her before I leave." "I know your sister, I don't think I would ever want her looking for me." If you say you know my sister like every one else, she'll have an APB (All Points Bulletin) put out for me, if she ever suspects anything has happen to me. You're not trying to kidnap me are you?" "Well I don't know, I just might; tell her I'll take good care of you." "You know what? You got me getting caught up on cloud 9 myself, I don't even remember what my sister said your name was?" "I'm sorry baby, it's Jon Paul, but everybody calls me PJ." "It's a pleasure to meet you Jon or PJ which ever you prefer, I'm Angell, but all my sister's friends call me Choc or Chocolate." Then he took my hand and squeezed it very gently as he moved it close to his mouth and sealed the introduction with a kiss on my hand. At that point the palms of my hands started sweating and my stomach began to churn like butter. As I pulled my hand from his, I asked him to give me a few minutes, while I went back inside to get my purse.

As soon as I walked in the door to get my purse, I thought my knees would give way, immediately I met my sister smiling from ear to ear. "You guys look so cute together, I knew he was going to like you. You don't even have to tell me. PJ is a gentleman, I trust him and oh yea, little sis, you are going to like him and then some; he's the one Choc. I never told him anything about you, I just felt like the attraction would be there once you met and the rest would be up to both of you. Just tell him not to make me put a bounty out on his head; because I do know real bounty hunters you know, and I got all kinds of connections with friends that really work for the FBI." "Thanks sis, I think we both know. He is so cute, don't wait up for me. I'll be back through to pick up my car later, if I see a familiar car in your driveway I know what to do. I would'nt want to break up the make up you got in store for your boy toys, if you know what I mean." "Listen lil sis, don't be a playa hater, after I have a few "yac's" (which is what she called her favorite cognac) show you're right, it could be any, many, mighty, moe for me tonight; I heard they'll all be coming through here as the night goes on. Hey, I'm single, living it and loving it. So you're right sis, you better check my drive way when you come back through to be on the safe side." "I know, I know; I'll see you later, you behave your self." "You're talking to me, last time I checked I was the oldest. You little Ms. Thing, need to let your hair down, let it blow in the wind and let yourself go." "Okay, okay. Luv ya." "Me too, trust me you are in good hands." "I believe you."

PJ was waiting for me outside on the porch, he yelled good night to my sister and told her he would bring me back safe and sound. Then he walked me over to this gorgeous Black Lexus Sport Coupe that was to die for, but hey I think I'll live because as we walked over I noticed the top was already down he opened and closed my door, then he knelt down beside my door and grabbed my hand and said, "Trust me I don't usually do this, but this time I have to make an exception." He kissed my hand again and walked over to his side and got in. Before he drove off, I felt the need to tell him I don't usually get in a car with people I barely know either. But for some reason I trusted him. Afterwards, he thanked me for being honest. He told me that he had just gotten his car a few days ago and that I was the first to be taken for a spin. I felt sort of special, then he started showing me all the custom details, it was equipped with all the bells and whistles. We listened to some wonderful jazz while we cruised down the highway. He had amazing taste in music, I had a love and an appreciation for all kinds of music, with a soft spot for jazz. He kept looking at me and smiling; he had such a warm smile, I was so secretly embarrassed. Then he asked, "Are you sure you didn't mind me stealing you away from the party?" I told him, "No not at all?" He responded, "Tonight was my night off, I almost didn't make it, I'm glad I finally decided to come." I responded, you know I was tired myself it's been a long week. My sister made it a special night for me as well, and meeting you was refreshing after such a long day." "JK's little sister, huh. I don't think I would stayed, if I hadn't of met you. After meeting you, I would miss you, if we had never met." "How sweet PJ, I wonder how that's possible." When he touched my hand the magnetic attraction between us was incredible. I had never felt anything like it and from the look in his eyes neither had he. We drove around to one of the area lakes for a while it was so peaceful and serene. He was such an interesting guy, we never ran out of things to talk about. After a while, time had drifted by so quickly, we both decided we were starving after talking for so long. Then he asked me if I wanted anything in particular to eat. I told him it didn't matter, Chinese or seafood would be fine. He told me that most of the restaurants in that area were closed. But there was a place that served the best Chinese fod not far from where he lived that would only deliver. Then he asked me if I didn't mind going to his place. I looked at him and answered in a very soft tone, "I'm sorry, but I don't usually go to a man's house right after I meet him. The drive was one thing, but going over to your place is another." He responded by saying, "You don't have to worry it's only for a little something to eat, I have no intention of trying anything." "Yea right, that's what they all say, but I am a woman with values, I value my selfworth and what I stand for; I'd rather not put myself or you in that position. I may be young, but I know what I want in life, and I know what I don't have to settle for. I'm the type of woman that will always speak my mind at all times, I won't ever be rude to you, lie to you or compromise who I am. If you give me your word that you can respect that and try to understand exactly that; we will get along just fine." Then he looked at me and began to slow down and pull over by the other side of the lake and very carefully said, "Look Angell, I don't sleep around, nor do I try to quickly get a woman I don't even know in my bed. I have some very high values and morals myself, I'd like to think that I exercise a lot of discipline when it comes to using my judgment for women. In fact for a few years now, I have been keeping everything on lock down. Before a woman gets a piece of this, she has to do more than look good. She needs to have just as much going for her as I have going for me. It's easy to get or find a good looking woman with a body that won't quit into bed. You didn't come across to me as easy prey, after talking to you tonight and really listening to you, I can tell you won't just accept any kind of man either. Which is what attracted me to you tonight, when I asked you to come with me tonight for some reason I just wanted you immediately off the market. I didn't want anybody else looking at you tonight, but me, I might have been a little selfish or maybe I acted a little premature, but when I see what I want, I don't waste a whole lot of time because time is too precious. What I know about you is this, you seem to be a genuine woman, no pretence, no bull crap, you're just you and from the conversation we just had you enjoy being who you are. And all I know right now is, I don't just want any woman, I want us to really take our time and get to know each other. He reached over and grabbed my hand and repeated the words again, "I want you, and I want you to know that you can trust me. I can promise you that I want ever try to hurt you intentionally, or try to ever take advantage of you. I'm a man I may do some things that you don't understand or you may not agree with, I am who I am and I grew up with morals, values and integrity and if you can live with that, you can hang with me. I just want a chance to get to know you better. I like you, I like what I see and I have enjoyed our conversation; we have a lot in common and I want to explore that. Besides that, your sister, JK would kill me! Didn't you see that look she gave me? Her eyes must have been on me and a few other guys the moment you walked in the door, I know she saw the way I looked at you. She and I made eye contact, and her eyes said, Don't even think about it, if you can't handle it with care!!! If I even tried to take advantage of you there is no telling what she and her friends would do to me. Besides I'm aquainted with a friend of hers named George who really works for the FBI." Then I said, "Thank God for my sister, and good old George, now that dude is my friend too, he is so cool. His hello's and good byes always make you wonder, he's always so serious with everybody else, but he lets his guard down with me, now he can scare you half to death. He tried to recruit me as an agent, I was literally scared to death by the whole process that he exposed me too. But getting back to going to your place, I like you too, from the moment my eyes scanned the room, I think it was something so inviting and warm about your eyes and your smile. I was hoping that we met, and I'm glad we did. I appreciate you for inviting me out for the drive, the view of the lake and your company has been more than amazing. I just want you to know that I have been living a celibate lifestyle for a long time and I admire you for being on lock down as you put it. I know, it's so easy to be in the right setting and something could very easily go down between us. The chemistry between us is almost irresistable because you have the kind of charm that will make a woman let it all go. I'm talking values, standards, clothes, and undergarments just gone; even your touch and voice is very seductive. Have you noticed how many times we've touched each other tonight, it's not that I don't trust you, it's both of us. We have such a natural flow, it would be nothing for us to start out with an embrace, followed up by a tender caress, which could lead to all kinds of locks coming off you, me and everthing else. You and I will have to be careful and stay prayed up when were together. But right now, I'm starving and I'd love for you to feed me. The next time we meet, I hope it will be soon, you can be my Teddy Pendergrass, and ask me to come on and go with you, come on over to your place when the time is right. I am feeling you, and I would love for us to take our time as you suggested and really get to know each other. Will that be okay with you?" He laughed, "Of course it is, I respect your honesty now I better hurry up and feed a sister, because I wouldn't want you to think a brother is trying to starve you to death. Let's just see what we can find." Then I said to him "checkmate." Then he looked at me and smiled, don't tell me you play chess too?" "I can play a lot more than chess, trust me I will have many surprises up my sleeves for you, just give me some time, I promise you won't regret it." Then he said," I'm scared of you, okay big girl, don't have me blowing up your cell phone later on tonight." "Don't be scared just be ready because I know exactly how to bring it." "Are you ready for this, big girl?" "Like I said I know how to bring it, I'm not a stalker, nor will I try to run you down just because I've got a phone number. I don't feel it's necessary. I think if you're really feeling somebody and the feeling is mutual he will find a way to see you. I want to keep everything fresh and make you feel the same way, every time you want to see me. We have to agree to keep prayer the center and just see if the intensity of our intentions gets stronger between us, you know like, absence making the heart grow fonder or something like that." Then he said, "What am I going to do with you?" "Just be patient, I think you'll figure out something, but first thing first; some food will help out a lot. Remember you stole me away from my own celebration that included all you can eat at no cost to me or you. You got some making up to do as far as food is concerned."

Finally we found what you call a hole in the wall that served some good old fashion tie me down and slap your brother or sister seafood. We had a huge late night feast; which included catfish, scrimp, fries, fried okra, hushpuppies, peppers, fried pickles, hot sauce, tarter sauce, and mustard (which is described as good southern style hospitality from Florida the secret condiment that makes it all taste like home.) When we saw a crowd of people standing outside the little joint we knew they had to have some good food. You know that's the secret, when you are trying to find a good restaurant just look for a long line of people or full parking lot.

It's wonderful to go out to eat with some who enjoy the same kind of food. By being upfront and honest about who you are, where you stand with no hidden agendas makes it all worth while, I call that an open deck of cards with no jokers going wild. It's a blessing to find someone you just be yourself with. Without trying to impress each other with what you have, what's important is showing respect and taking time out for each other. It doesn't have to come in one night, showing some one too much too soon can end in tragedy or dissapointment, especially if that person flips the script on you and becomes someone else overnight. Even when it comes to sharing something as personal as your home, can be misleading if its done too soon. Some can see everything a man or woman has and begin to visualize themselves in every aspect of their life. When you see yourself fixing a meal, helping with a few chores around the house, finding a level of comfort can send up a red turn off flag and push the relationship to the edge of a shutdown. It's easy to get caught up and your feelings hurt. I'm old fashion, I was taught that getting to know each other is the key, learning how to communicate and just listen, trying not to misintrepret what that person says or does for you. Learning how to respect who they were before you met them, while being able to slowly open up both of your worlds to each other, one day at a time will become priceless. Getting to a level of intimacy is easy, but often done too soon. Once you cross over the line brings on a another level of emotions. Both a man or woman can become tied to each other instantly like glue. Learning how to set boundaries, are necessary for a healthy relationship. But you have to know what you both want out it. Men and Women alike categorize each person they meet, you can sense if its going to be Short Term, Mid Term, Long Term, I Really Don't Know Term, and No Way Term. A woman may think she will be the one in a man's life and at the same time that she's thinking that, he may be trying to figure out how to let her down easy or let her go, he may not even care if they remain friends or not and vise versa. Getting involved with someone takes more than a notion, it's best to look at what you both see or can see in the beginning stages as you get to know each other. Knowing what you both want and are looking for is a beginning; trying not to play with that person's emotions is very important. I've heard that a man knows what kind of a relationship he wants from a woman within the first five seconds after they meet; that's pretty quick but very often true. Whether she's a hit it quick, a week end trick, or the one he thinks he'll take home to meet his mother. Either they care to take it to another level or they don't, most of the time a woman can feel what kind of attraction it is right off. But like a young man told me a while back, try not to ever assume anything…when you break the word down…the word is Armed and Dangerous…Assume…you end up making an Ass…(out of) U…Me…pretty cleaver huh…so if you know what's good for you and your heart…don't Assume anything else going forward.

After PJ and I had dinner, we exchanged numbers and established that we wanted to get to know each other; we realized that it would take a lot of effort, follow up and time. I'm a woman that likes to be pursued, I don't like to chase a man down for his attention, if a man wants you he will find the time for you and move right into his natural role to pursue you. He took me back to my car and asked if we could talk the next day. Before I got in my car, I checked the drive way at my sister's place and sure enough there was a car parked there, I wanted her to know that I made it back and the I was okay. We had a phone ring signal that we used…two rings meant we made it home safely and four rings meant we needed to talk. When I got home I rang her phone two times and to my surprise she rang back with four rings. I called her back expressing that I didn't want to disturb her groove and she told me she just wanted to make sure I was at home because she knew PJ was one smooth talker, who could make you get undressed over the phone. You better be careful with him, she said, he really is a good catch you just don't know how many women would love to be in your shoes and riding in his new Lex...huh you're already off to a good start. I knew he was going to be taken with you the moment he saw you, I'm just glad he was able to come by tonight. He travels a lot, but he has always keeps his word, when he says he's going to do something he usually does it." Then she said, she thought we would both enjoy the ride and she didn't mean tonight in his car. "Thanks for the 411, sis". She was just being my sister, I really appreciated her for that. "Good Night Choc." "Thanks sis, I love you too." As soon as I got undressed, I took a long hot shower finally I made it over to my bed, which I was so happy to be near. I had to take time out to pray, reflect and meditate over everything. When I got into my bed my phone begin to ring again, I let it ring four times, finally I leaned over and picked up on the fifth. "Come on sis, I'm home alone you don't have to worry." Then the response was, "I'm glad you're home alone, I promise not to worry, but I wanted you to know I had a good time with you tonight and I probably won't be able to sleep much tonight thinking about you, I had to hear your voice on the phone before I went to sleep." "PJ is that you?" "Well, I hope I'm the only one you keep up tonight." "Well, you never know, it's sweet of you to call." "Sweet Dreams, Angell." "You too, PJ thanks for calling." "I just wanted to make sure you made it home safely." "I did." "Angell thanks for your company tonight, we'll talk soon." "Looking forward to it, Good Night." (As soon as I hung up the phone I had to virtually put the pillow over my head and scream. I definitely have to stay prayed up with him, with a voice like that, Oh my GOD. No wonder my sister said he could make you get undressed over the phone. Man, oh man, oh man, was she right.) I slept like a newborn baby, thank God it was Saturday morning which meant I could wake up when I got through sleeping. When I finally dragged myself out of bed, I decided to go walking to walk off some serious calories from last night's overloaded fried fiesta. Afterwards, I needed to unload my car, get some things done around the house, and run to the market before it got too late. Just as I ran all my errands, my phone began to ring, my sister called to tell me about her wild night and all the gifts we both received. We laughed and talked for a while, then her phone starting ringing one call after the other. After about three hold on for a few minutes, I thanked her a great party and for loading all my gifts in my car, I couldn't believe how many people loved both of us. I told her I would see her in the morning for brunch, then we would meet up at church. She knows how I am, I don't like to be bothered too much on my week ends. They belong to me and when I feel the need I share them I do. I had been reading this fantastic book and wanted to kick back, chill and catch a good movie later. As soon as I got everything set up, I had my cup of tea, and my book. I checked the cable guide to find out what was coming on and there were two good movies to choose from. It didn't matter if I stayed up late, it was my night out at the movies just me, myself and I, trust me I love me some me. I knew I would get up early for brunch and we'd make our way for morning service which I loved, because it allowed me to get home in more than enough time to enjoy my Sunday.

As I sat down, I began to think about PJ and how I couldn't wait to talk to him again. I decided to look at my phone, doing the usual checking the missed calls and relooking at the received calls on my cell. When I put my book down, I noticed his business card sitting on my coffee table. I picked it up and realized he had given me all three of his numbers which brought a smile to my face. So I decided to pick up my home phone and dial his number, when I picked up my phone I didn't have a dial tone. "Hello." "Hey." "PJ is that you" "Yes it's me, I just picked up the phone to call you, were you calling me? My phone didn't even ring." "As a matter of fact, when I dialed your number I never heard it ring either. I guess we were both trying to connect at the same time. He asked me what I was doing and I told him I was about to read a book and then catch a movie." "What's the name of the book?" Then I told him what a great read it was, and he asked me to read a chapter to him. "I would love to do that." So I began to give him a little history about the book, that I had never heard of the author but the book was wonderful. Then he told me he was going to put me on the speaker phone while he got comfortable and fixed him something to eat. So we kept talking, while I read, he asked questions afterwards, we both laughed and had such a great conversation. After I finished the chapter, he asked me to read the next chapter to him the next time I read the book. I agreed. I asked him what he was eating and he told me (Batchelor Food) Sandwich, Chips, Pickles and Lemonade. He told me he wished he had some ice cream for dessert. Then we started talking about the kind of ice cream we both loved; then he asked me if we could meet for some ice cream in the middle of where we both lived. He asked, If I didn't mind him in his sweats." "No I don't mind. If you can handle the holes in my jeans and this old homely shirt I've got on, because I didn't want to change?" "Okay big girl, let's meet in about forty five minutes?" "That's fine PJ." "Until Then, Angell."

The Ice Cream Parlor

Of course I agreed to meet him, are you serious! when you get to a point when you don't even care what you're wearing, all you can think about is a chance to see that person, which is the coolest feeling. I left as soon as I could get in my car, I wasn't speeding according to all the people who put the petal to the medal; but I could have definitely gotten held up in court based on the numbers rolling around on my speedometer. When I arrived to the spot, PJ's car was already there. As soon as I parked, he was strolling toward my car to open my door. Thank God we were going in for something cold, because I would have to get a fireman from the local fire department to hose me down the way he was looking in those sweats. Now, I've seen some fine men in my time, but my God, nobody turned me on like this man, PJ. Jesus give me strength, to walk straight without my knees buckling.

"Hey, thanks for getting my door, be still my heart." "You think your heart is beating, I thought I was going to break out in a cold sweat, if you didn't hurry up and get here. I must say young lady the holes in those jeans are in all the right places, I bet you drive men crazy when you wear stuff like that, I have to tell you it's working for me right now." "Well I do believe those sweats, are doing what they suppose to do for me too. Let's get us some ice cream are we'll both start tripping and dripping right here in this parking lot, before we even get the flavor we want." "How can a woman read your mind and turn you on at the same time; I thought I had the handle on that cup. but it looks like we both got a handle on it and that is turning me on. "PJ, you need to stop it right now or you'll make me forget my favorite flavor because you are making me want to taste something that's not on the menu." "Okay, okay. Mmm mmm good, now that sounds even more delicious." "PJ stop watching my locamotion, you're making me nervous."

"Chu Chu baby, chu chu." "Boy stop playing, you are so silly." "Girl, you're makin me crazy." "Come on, were at the front door."

When we got in, I didn't know if I wanted a cone, a cup or a pint; then one of the ladies told us we could taste any kind that we wanted. We were like kids in a candy store; tasting everything we thought sounded good and exploring all the top sellers. We had so much fun, we both ended up with a cone and a pint of our favorite ice cream to go. We sat down and ate a cone tasting each other's flavor, we had so much fun then we took a pint to go. He walked me to my car and thanked me for coming. He told me he would talk to me later, he had planned to go home, chill and watch a movie or something. I told him I was doing the same, but I had already chosen two movies that I was in conflict over and didn't know which one I was going to watch. He asked me the name of both and I told him, of course he had seen one of them and suggested that I record one and watch the other. Which is what I would have done anyway, after I determined which one I was in the mood for. I appreciated him for being so thoughtful, he was such a free spirit, I loved his spontaniety. "Be careful young lady, I'll see you soon." "PJ thanks for the Ice Cream what a pleasure, you be careful too." "Always." He leaned over and kissed me gently on my lips, he caught me by surprise, but it was a pleasant surprise.

As they drove off, Angell began to reflect, "My Goodness, I keep getting this feeling in the pit of my stomach that makes me want to see him again, as soon as possible, this is crazy, God what is this feeling that's driving me crazy. Maybe I'm just excited at the newness of what this can be or might be."

PJ reflects, "That girl, is something else, God tell me, how can you feel something so strong about somebody I barely even know. Although we've talked about so much, we have so much in common and even more to discover. I can't wait to see her again."

When I finally got home, I'd made it just in time for the start of my movie, with some sweet treats to add to my hot buttered pop corn, white chocolate almonds, and my good old sour patches. I felt just like a kid at the movies, because I love me some me; and I realized years ago that I am my biggest fan. I knew how to enjoy my own company without feeling the need to always have a man in my life or somebody always hanging around. I decided to watch the drama first and the romantic comedy last. I had the best time with myself. Before I knew it, the last movie was watching me, I decided to get up and get ready for bed.

As soon as my head hit the pillow I was asleep with the sweetest dreams that I could have ever had. I kept hearing something in my sleep and I kept telling myself subconsciously, no matter what please don't let me wake up until I finish this dream. Please God, don't wake me up unless I really need to, I finally drifted off again with the same annoying sound ringing in my ear. To my surprise it was my phone ringing in the house. "I picked it up and answered it." The voice said, "I'm sorry, girl were you asleep?" "Having the best dream, did you call me a few minutes ago?" "Yea that was me, I started not to call back, I can let you get back to sleep we can talk tomorrow we're still meeting for brunch right?" "Right! What's wrong? Are you okay?" It's was my best friend, Daphine, telling me about a situation she had gotten herself into. I didn't ever want her to think I wasn't there for her; she knew that I would stop a bus, a plane, a train or anything for her, she was my best friend and I loved her like she was my sister. After talking to her for about an hour she was finally okay, she thanked me for waking up for her, I told her no matter what's going on in my life, I would always be there for her. I was glad I was able to just listen to her as she came up with a solution to her own problem. She was dating a guy that had all kinds of extra curricular activities going on. But she loved him and I knew he loved her, sometimes love is enough and sometimes its just not. When she was hurting, I would hurt too, she was my best friend no matter what. I thought about everything my best friend said and all I could do was pray for her over the phone and encourage her. I always wanted the best for her. You never want to see anybody you care about taken advantage of, period.com. I know how much she cared about this guy but his actions were not lining up with his words. Let's face it when a man tells you that he loves you, it can send you in to a state of blind heartedness. You keep looking for your heart to cover all their faults, pouring your love over their shortcomings, excuses, and disappointments.

My prayers went out to her and everybody else who might be in that same situation, because I know how easy you can find yourself in need of love so bad, that you easily search for that love you so desperately desire in all the wrong places. Trying to fill a void that continues to stay empty no matter how many times you fill up the cup. As I laid there in my bed, I began to pray for her as a tear streamed down my face for her and so many others who were probably going through the same emotional roller coaster in life. I could'nt go back to sleep I just laid there with so many thoughts climbing through my mind, then my phone rang again, I thought "Oh God please I want to go to sleep, come on now, I said to myself. I hope this girl is okay?" "Hello" "Hey, I can't sleep are you awake?" "Oh, Hey PJ, is that you? I thought you were somebody else?" "Yes, It's me, what's wrong why aren't you asleep?" "Actually I was sleeping good earlier, but my best friend, Daphine just called and I worry about her sometimes but she's okay now." "What's up, do you want to talk about it." "No not really, I'll be up all night talking about her and everything that goes with it; trust me you'll get to know her she comes with the package. And right now it's coming all unraveled." "I can respect that Angell." "Tell me PJ, what are you doing up?" "For some reason I could'nt go to sleep, everytime I tried you were on my mind. But I felt like something was bothering you that might be keeping you up, so I called." "Well I guess you must be tuned into me, Mister." "That's a real possibility, hey why don't you relax and let me read something to you, maybe I can put you to sleep." "Okay wait, let me get in just the right position." "Don't make me have to come over there and tuck you in." "No, I don't think we want you to do that, with what I have on under these covers we would never get to sleep. I would have too many problems with the touch of my tucker; which may lead your hands to do more than tuck me in. Come on PJ, don't get me started you'll have me wide awake thinking about all kinds of stuff." "Okay baby you're right, are you all tucked in, just listen." Then he begin to read. (I was astonished by what he read to me, it was some words of encourgement that were very uplifting, inspiring and simply mesmerizing to hear the comfort, assurance and strength in his voice. It was so caring and thoughtful. By the time he finished, sleep was coming all over me.) Then he whispered, "Sweet dreams." "Thanks, sweet dreams to you too." As soon as I hung up the phone, I thought to my self, "wow how incredible was that, that's what I call a midnight delight." After pondering over the words I heard, they seem to go deep inside the crevices of my mind and straight to my heart, immediately I drifted off to sleep.

When I woke up I reminisced over what was beginning to transpire in my life and I had to fall down on my knees and thanked God for everything; especially for what I sensed in my soul that was happening. I could see myself with this man for the rest of my life, learning and loving, and enjoying the wonderment of discovery as we got to know each other. He had the type of presence about him that made you want to be with him. As I thought about him, he appeared to be a man that was straight to the point and I appreciated that about him. Although, I had only received a few phone calls from him, we were at the beginning stages of building a very unique friendship which is the most important part of every relationship. It needed to be filled with respect and admiration without a hidden agenda or pressure; just allowing what we were discovering to just flow. It felt excited and different to have someone like me, who was comfortable being who they are. I was grateful and asked for guidance and direction as we moved forward into getting to know each other. It's a little scary to really want to be with somebody that you don't even know. My faith and beliefs were truly grounded, I had come a long way into becoming who was. When you know who you are and you value yourself, it's easy to wait, trust and believe that what I desired would manifest and I could receive what my heart believed in and prayed for. I didn't want to move to soon, or get caught up in a whirlpool of emotions. Where I would make the wrong assumptions. Let's face it it's so easy to assume that when you meet somebody that you're both moving in the same direction, it takes time and lots of patience, once a woman realizes that it's the man who chooses you; its not the womans job to go out and choose the man. Don't get me wrong the man makes the selection, but the woman gives her consent or approval by accepting the fact that he chose her to be with him. Then you move on to a new beginning. We can only travel on the pages of life with him; but if we don't turn the pages together it won't work if you move ahead of him to read the pages in the future. Unfortunately, we as women can get so excited that we want to hurry up and turn the page and close the deal by doing everything we can think of to keep his interest. But later find ourselves alone. What we thought we had ends up one sided simply because we turned the pages all the way to the end where we think it should end up. It's easy for the woman to move straight to the page where you find yourself in the permanent stage of planning the wedding way before the man even thinks about asking the question. At times forcing him to make up his mind and propose. When it's right, it's right. It will be no mystery, neither will it be filled with regret. One thing I knew for sure was about what I was feeling, that felt right, it flowed naturally without much effort, only time would reveal exactly what it would become. Patience was one of my greatest virtures, I knew I would wait as long as I needed to in order to receive what and who I wanted in my life. Making short cuts to get to a base hit along the way were okay as long as I got the homerun. Afterwards, I finally drifted off to sleep, dreaming of nothing but sweet lollipop dreams.

Is It Sunday Morning Already? I was sleeping so Good...

When I finally got up and I got dressed and met my Mom and sister and my two dearest friends at early morning brunch. It was wonderful, I was so glad I didn't eat much last night. Before we knew it, it was time to get to morning service. Although we had enough time to get to service on time, Daphine and I were fashionalbly late as usual. My sister always teased me about time; I told her as long as she remembered if I go before she did to make sure that my body was late to the funeral. Otherwise no one would believe that I was dead, if I got there on time. When we arrived, we met my sister in the balcony, of course she did her usual sending me notes. She asked me to look to my right and to my surprise, PJ was there. I sent her a note back...

> *Who invited Him? JK..LMNOP, (is what I called my sister when I was surprised) I'm going to kill you, Why did you invite Him without telling me?*
>
> I didn't have to invite him, because he's already a member! Thank you...
>
> *What?*
>
> Can't you read? He's been going here for ages since he was a kid.
>
> *So have we Why didn't you tell me?*

You know how you are. I didn't want you to feel like I was setting you up or something. Oh Well, looks like you'll have to get over it.

Oh Well, I'll have to get over it, is that all you have to say. I never saw him here before, I know I would have noticed him!

Well don't be so sure about yourself sis, He's noticed you for quite some time now, but didn't know you were my lsister. I wanted to feel him out first, because we went to college together. What can I say, I know a lot about him, He travels a lot with his job, etc, etc which is why you probably didn't notice him. I told him if he was interested he would have to make that clear to you not me.

Sis, I'm just surprised you let me walk into this without any warnings?

What's wrong little sis? Don't you like what you see? From the look on both of your faces, I'd say the feeling must be mutual. I don't think I've ever seen you blush before, hmm, I see he must be doing a pretty good job at making it clear to you.

WhatEver...we need to be paying attention to the message. You really need prayer and lots of it; and I'm going to pray for you too, right now that we receive the meaning in this sermon.

Oh Well I do need it, you know...Thanks Lil Sis...Now Stop Sending me all the Notes in Church...Listen to the message...

The message was heartfelt, encouraging and very uplifting. I was so grateful, it was right on time with what me and my best friend talked about last night. As soon as service was over we left the balcony; when we walked out our eyes met. Immediately he walked over and said hello, I introduced him to my best friend and he had a gentleman with him that he introduced to both of us. His name was William, who was very taken by my best friend Daphine. Who was a very attractive and always made a fashion statement, she always lite up any room with her gorgeous short and sassy hair cut, she had the most beautiful hazel eyes that changed by certain colors that she wore and a smile that could brighten up anybody's day. As we walked out toward the parking lot, my sister carried the conversation, with her usual quaint sanctified sense of humor; as if she had just received the seal to make into heaven on her forehead. We talked about the message that seem to be right on time with what we were all living through, which ended our conversation with the hottest topic that makes all Sunday Afternoons worth while. "Are you ready for some Football?" Of course the Dallas Cowboys were playing their first game of the season they were making their debut at 3:00 o'clock central time. PJ mentioned that he was having some friends over to his place and extended the invitation to all of us. By the way William and Daphine were looking at each other there was no way I could turn down the invitation, especially since I was extremely partial to the host. We agreed to go but my sister told us she had other plans, which meant the season of openers was traditional and had to be spent at my Aunt Marva Jean's who was a diehard Dallas Cowboy Fan. The game day was the key focus for her, every body knew it and if you had anything to say, you needed to back it up or bring it on. Dinner was always plentifully served and being a part of her company always had the most hilarious warm felt memories.

After we accepted PJ's invitation he gave us his address and directions. We told them we were going to get changed but could'nt wait to get there. We offered to bring something. Daphine and I decided to stop at the store to get something sweet and delicious, so we decided to take dessert. We stopped by my place and changed into something more casual, Daphine was my best friend she always brought clothes with her whenever she came to my house; even some things that she had never worn we were both into the latest and the hottest high fashions. After we got dressed I told her I would follow her to the address, but we were leaving after the game was over at the same time with no excuses no matter what took place. I was excited about the invitation for both of us and very pleased at his mannerism.

In Search of My Soulmate

Are You Ready for Some Football

As soon as we got close to the neighborhood, my cell phone started ringing, "Girl, are you sure we got the right address, Daphine screamed out in my ear, "Where did you say you met him?" "I didn't say, Daphine." "Girl, He must live close to the lake or something. What a nice neighborhood, no wonder he was trying to get you over here that night. I don't blame him, I would have been trying to get you out in the middle of the oasis too." "You know what? Daphine you are sick, you really are? No wonder you need counseling almost every night. You better watch youself with those tight jeans you got on, I hope you get a chance to breath and sit down without unraveling some seams." "Angell, I got this, you let me handle my jeans and you handle this PJ character whoever he is, I saw the way he was looking at you earlier. Don't be trying to act like the name your Mommy and Daddy gave you. Because I know you, I'm just me, like you said earlier today, we're leaving at the same time with no excuses, yea right Angell." "Girl, don't make me pull my car over and meet you in the middle of this strange neighborhood. Just keep your eyes on the road and notice which way I'm turning, so you won't need an escort all the way home later when we get ready to leave." "Okay, Okay Angell no need to preach another sermon, enough already; let's just look for the street." "I know you love me girlfriend; looks like this is his street coming up, were almost there. Oh my God, what a nice place, this is the right address right? I am real scared of him." "Remember, Angell no excuses." "I know you're not reminding me, you better watch out for this William, his eyes were all over you and yours didn't move to for from him yourself, do I have to remind you about Maurice." "Maurice who? I'd rather not spoil my appetite, thank you very much, Angell but no thank you, today I'm footloose and fancy free from all prior acquaintances and commitments, especially when it comes to him." "Okay if you say so, my lips are sealed. Can we get off the phone already?"

When we got off the phone, I was pleasantly surprised and very proud for him. After we pulled into the drive way, sitting there was this remarkable house located right on the lake. My God what a nice place, he was right when I first met him, not only did he live close by the lake he actually lived on a gorgeous piece of land on the lake. There were four other cars in the drive, as soon as I parked my car and got out, Daphine was ringing my phone again, "Girl are you sure we're at the right address?" "Yes, Daphine, we are." As she was getting out of her car, she walked over to me with the phone in her hand saying she needed to ask me one last question. "Angell, Can you tell me who Maurice is?" "Oh you mean to tell me you're going to let what you see right now affect your memory." "No, Angell but after I walk through that door it may guarantee to influence me to forget and get over a few things." "Stop tripping Daphine, before you make me look up Maurice's number to remind you about our final conversation last night." "What can I say, Angell you cured me and going to church really helped me today. He makes me sick, always pushing me to the edge, arguing over nothing, while he constanly accusing me of cheating, and making me "boo hoo" over whatever he can get away with. If I have to hurt like that everytime I love somebody, I don't want to be in love. You told me that maybe I needed to expand my horizons and get out of the rigid routine of Heartbreak City. Well I've lived there way too long, and I'm ready to change my address and let my hair down, what's left of my hair and start enjoying my life, which is something that I have'nt done in a long time." "Well Daphine, I see you were listening, just take your time and start letting everything flow naturally with a little spontaniety, give yourself time to heal and who knows maybe it'll take you somewhere you might enjoy." "Oooh, I like the sound of that; a little spontaniety, thank you Angell, I'm so tired of the drama. I know I deserve better and today I want to try to open up and give my self a chance to take a chance and just see." "What can I say, girlfriend you are sounding more like a grown woman and looks like a little wisdom is flying around in the air blowing all over your head." "Hey I like it Angell, that did sound pretty good to me; I hope we both have a good time tonight. Okay, let's do this girl; but first we have to do one thing." "And what is that?" "Go back and get the dessert out of the car." "That might help you know, even though we are probably sweet enough, we need to spread some sugar around the room to everybody else." We got the dessert and headed up to the front door. After we rang the door bell, William opened the door and immediately escorted Daphine in and welcomed us to what he called J's Ponderosa. There was a nice crowd everyone seemed very friendly and laid back, there was music playing and a very tempting aroma coming from the kitchen. PJ was on the phone giving someone directions; as soon as he saw me he walked over and welcomed us. He kissed me on my cheek, held my hand and lead us toward the kitchen. He held my hand the whole time he was on the phone afterwards he looked at the dessert and told us it was an excellent choice, an assortment of cheesecake, miniture brownies and freshly baked cookies. Then he told me what was being served to our guests and proceeded to give me a quick tour of the house. There were several plasma televisions throughout the house; the guest knew the rules where they could and could not go. He began to explain what his five rules were as if we were entertaining our guests. Then he wanted me to know how I should handle anyone if they got out of line. He wanted me to let him know as soon as possible and he or William would take care of the situation asap.

Rule # 1	*No one was allowed in either of his four bedroom's unless someone wasn't feeling well. We needed to notify William because he was a Licensed Physician.*
Rule #2	*People were allowed to watch the game in the Media Room, The Living Room, The Den or The Game Room.*
Rule #3	*No one was allowed to take Drinks into any of his Bathrooms*
Rule #4	*No smoking was allowed inside the house, they were welcome to go outside in the back yard there were two patio's one covered and one uncovered, but never any smoking in the front yard.*

Rule #5 *No one was allowed to go upstairs but the priviledged; both of his sisters, his brother Pierce who may drop by and of course William. He said we had to watch both Pierce and William when they were around, because they knew they were privileged and were known to take avantage of that which may involve my best friend. Especially since the interest seem to be on her and those jeans, a whole lot more was up, than the game.*

Any questions? "No, sir I think we can handle the rules." "I enjoy entertaining, and I pride myself on keeping a clean house if you understand what I mean, even though I may have a lot of people moving in and out especially during football and basketball season. I try to keep everything under control, while letting everybody enjoy themselves and the flow while they have a good time." "I can respect that." "Me too, Daphine yelled out, is there anything we can help with?" "No baby, William moaned, just keep walking around in those jeans and let me follow behind you like a little puppy on a leach." "Well, that depends, Mr. William, I heard PJ say that you were a licensed physician, what kind of doctor might that be?" "I'm a heart surgeon." "Sound's like just what I need, because mine has been aching all night, you think you can fix it for me doc?" "Oh I can fix anything that's got to do with the heart; it's what I specialize in privately." "Hmm, I'm just about ready for you to get to work on mine right away." "Okay sweet thing, my Mom used to say be careful what you ask for you just might get it." "Well I guess we have something in common already, because my Mom still says that same thing." They both laughed. "Okay you two, do I need to bring in the waterhose from the patio to put this fire out burning in my kitchen." "No man, we're cool, before I let the heat get that hot, I'd take her out to the lake, where we won't ever have to run out of water." "Hmm, is that what my doctor is ordering? Well take me to the water baby, it's been a long time since I been baptized." "Daphine, looks like we both are going to have to watch the two of you." "Now Angell, don't you go worrying about me, I'm a big girl I can take care of myself." "You both don't have to worry about us, we can handle ourselves, so tell me Daphine are you a Cowboy fan?" William spoke with such excitment "Absolutely, I grew up on the good old boys but I do like a good game." "Okay let's get something to eat, will you join me in the Game Room." "Sure, if that's okay with my little Momma, who feels like she needs to watch over us." "I'm okay, if big Daddy is okay?" PJ smiles, "I'm assuming that would be me?" "Oh yeah, that would be you if that's alright." Daphine spoke with such a huge smile. "Well you kids run along and behave yourselves up there and Big Daddy and Little Mamma over here won't have to tad your hide for misbehaving." Daphine screams, "Thanks little Momma and Big Daddy you guys are the best." Immediately, we all begin to laugh hysterically.

PJ guests were allowed to move throughout the house as long as they didn't leave their drinks all over the house unattended for a long period of time. He asked me to do him a favor, that if I noticed any drinks or plates left for a while if I could just pour them out throw them away. We were about 30 minutes away from game time; everyone seem to know where everything was and respected his rules. He began to show me around his place and for a minute I did'nt think my heart would start back beating. I was very pleased, he introduced me to everyone and said I was his new love interest and he couldn't wait to steal my heart. At that point I had no rhythm in my heart when he looked at me, I thought I was going to have a meltdown right there in his arms. He told me he wanted to show me the back yard then he pushed a button right next to the blinds of his patio door and the blinds opened from the middle and moved left to the right. It was mind-blowing, thank God I didn't come over there after we first met at my sister's House Warming. With a setting like that it would of have had me repenting all night, and asking for forgiviness and everything else. I was very proud for him he said he had only lived there for about two years and was loving every moment of it. "This is beautiful Jon, I love your taste in décor; your home is very lovely, warm and full of love. You have some very unique things, I really admire your eye for beauty; with such exquisite taste." "Thank you Angell, it's a pleasure to have you here in my home, I hope we'll be able to spend more time here. I have to be honest, when I see what I want I don't waste a whole lot of time. We only live once and I plan to enjoy every moment of my life, especially if I can share it with you." "Love Interest, I like that introduction you gave me." "Oh you do huh, PJ replied, then he embraced me and kissed me for the first time very tenderly as my lips embraced his." Immediately William walked into the room. "Don't be acting like nobody else is in this house but you guys; I've been watching both of you this evening and you both are looking extremely cozy to me." Then Daphine walked in behind him, "I noticed that too William, Love Interest huh? I'm scared of you Mr. PJ; now is that your given name or is there a little more to it than that?" "Now remember both of you are invited guests with privileges to move to an fro as you please. This place is big enough for all of us, so don't be trying to dip in the pool with me and my girl here. As for you young lady, being the best friend of my girl Angell here, and you William being my Best Man through thick and thin, no matter what, no matter when. We all seem to be getting a little cozy, which is pretty cool that we all hit it off; which is a first. From the looks of things we both are in good company which feels very good from what I can tell. But we better get back to the evening, now that dessert is set, all the food is ready for our guests and pretty soon everybody will be having a real good time. We are in the company of two very beautiful women in our midst, who's complaining. My advise to you Ms. Daphine is to watch your counterpoint over there, you may have to fight him off you by the time the game is over because he's got some moves, they don't call him "Will the Thrill" for nothing." As we approached the area we would be sitting in, he yelled out "Let's get ready for some Football." Jon ended up with about 18 guests; which was a nice crowd, it appeared that we had nothing but, (Are you ready for some serious Football Food)? Hot Wings, Nachos, Pizza, Grilled Chicken on a Stick, Fresh Fruit, Veggie Tray and our very own Sweet Lovers Treats. The dessert was right on time everybody had such a good time; it's nothing like being in the company of a group of really good friends. It makes a great get together, everybody was down to earth and just plain good company.

Jon was an excellent host, and the game was one of Dallas's finest games especially for the season opener; we yelled and screamed until the victory was won. We had a few sore loosers who were not Cowboy fans; and some who really didn't care who won. Which made the whole game interesting; I had one of the best times that I've had in a long time. Finally we saw everyone off, one right after the other; one of Jon's sister's told me that she hadn't seen him that happy in a long time and she wished both of us well. The other one told me that he was always the life of the party and by watching me it looks like he had met his match. Which was very sweet, Daphine and I offered to help clean up. We didn't have to do much, because I had already started collecting plates, cups and trash. I watched his eyes follow me all around his house, he kept blowing kisses at me while trying to steal a few moments away with me, from his guests, which appeared as if we were entertaining our friends. I could tell by the look in his eyes that he could'nt wait for everyone to leave so we could spend some alone time together. Before I knew it, everybody had left except the four of us, suddenly the music started really stiring us up then it happen; we started acting like a couple of kids in school at a high school disco party. We had so much fun, singing and dancing to some seriously old school music. PJ had an incredible collection of music, almost every song that came on was one of my favorite songs back in the day. Then came the slow jams, we danced, and we danced before I knew it; we were out on the patio dancing under the moon light. He held me so close I felt I didn't ever want to let him go. My heart was beating in unison with his, magic filled the air as Donnie Hathaway took the airwaves, he leaned over and kissed me softly on my lips. He smiled at me again and told me he was'nt going to keep me too long, because we both had to get up early the next morning, but he wanted to thank me again for accepting his invitation and for staying a little longer to help with the clean up. "Angell, I respect who you are and what you stand for, I won't ever try to take advantage of you. Please know that you can trust me. I would like to spend more time with you but I want to remind you that I travel pretty extensivly on my job and I've got a trip coming up in a few days and I'll be gone about two weeks possibly three. I have to tell you right now that most women can't handle the long periods of time that I may be away from them, which is why there is no one in my life consistenly right now. When I'm starting or about to close a deal, it's hard for me to focus on the TLC that a woman expects out of me. They look at what I have to offer and try to take me off the market any way they think they can, so they can enjoy it all with me. And trust me they have tried it all. It's nothing wrong with a woman feeling that way which is what we should all strive to gravitate to if that's what we want, but I want to make the choice. I believe that I should be the one to find the woman I want to spend the rest of my life with, it's not the other way around. Now I'm not going to lie to you, I have come close a couple of times but they ended up not having what it takes to keep me interested. I find you very refreshing, down to earth, easy to talk to and get along with. Your personality and your outlook on life captivates me. If you can handle my schedule, my lifestyle and me not always being around. I would love to see how far we can take this. I have watched you for quite some time and the little things that I noticed about you turned me on, what can I say." "PJ, what do you mean you've been watching me for quite some time? First let me put the conversation in rewind and we'll come back to quite some time. Why didn't you tell me that you were a member of my Church?" "You never asked, Angell." "Okay, I can live with that one. How long have you been a member?" "I've been a member since I was a kid, I grew up in the neighborhood, in fact I own a house on the street the church sits on, it belonged to my grandfather." "So, tell me this how long have you been watching me?" "For about a year now, I just never had the time to pursue you. I'd seen you come in with your friend that's here with you tonight on several occasions. I never knew that JK was your sister; I heard about her having a sister when we were in college. We all were party holics back then; I heard about her sister being on campus but never got a chance to see you. But when I did see you at church I noticed that you would leave as soon as service was over, I always ran into your sister often. After service and out at different Clubs on the North Side of town. You sister, JK does get around, and she knows a lot of people." "You know you're right, that girl knows everybody. I wonder why I never noticed you? You are definitely somebody I would have noticed." "Well, Angell the past doesn't really matter, what does matter is that I noticed you a long time ago, you always sat on the same row in the balcony every Sunday I was in town. I noticed you from head to toe, when you walked in you always looked like you just stepped out of a magazine." "Oh come on Jon." "No I'm not kidding, there were times when I would sat at a different angle just to get a different view. I wanted to apoach you but I had to wait until the timing was right for both you and me. So when your sister invited me to her housewarming, she told me that you might be there. I didn't think I would be in town but my meeting was moved to later in the week. When she called me up to confirm I would be there, she told me that everybody would be there. After I described you to her and she said she knew you very well, but like I said she never told me that you were her little sister. When I saw you walk in that night, she immediately introduced you to everybody as her little sister, I was floored. I wanted to have a few words with her about it afterwards but she can be a little outspoken, but what can I say, that's JK. But after talking to you and getting to know more about you, I see why she had the big sister thing going on. If you were my little sister I would have protected you too." "That's sweet, I wouldn't mind you protecting me, you have that way about you, I bet you could charm a girl right out of her lucky charms any day of the week." He laughed. "See, that's what I'm talking about you are so unpredictable and I love your sense of humor. I better get you back inside before you make a brother try to pour up a bowl to get some of those lucky charms." He put his hand in mind and kissed my hand and told me, "I can't wait to see you again, I'll be around until Wednesday, but after that I won't be back until next month. Do you think we can have dinner before I leave." "I would love to have dinner with you, just let me know when?" "Let me check my schedule, and I'll give you a call." "You know what, Jon, I miss you already." " You know what Angell, I would miss you even if we never met." "Thanks how sweet are you." Then I turned his hand toward my lips and kissed his hand leaving my lipstick print on his hand. "I'll have to meditate on these lips tonight, I don't think I'll wash my hand until I get ready for bed." When we walked back inside we couldn't find Daphine and William. We called out to them and they didn't answer. "Baby I told you we didn't need to leave Daphine alone with the priviledged. Just because he has the authority to go anywhere he wanted to in the house it ain't no telling where he took her." "PJ, one thing I know for sure is this, he will never get those jeans off of Daphine. She told me they were so tight, she had to peel them off to go to the rest room earlier." "Let me tell you something about quick hands William, he's my Best Man which is what we've always called each other verses best friends. You think I got that charm, now William shows no mercy if he wants something, trust me if he wants to get in he will get in. Let me remind you he does open heart surgery for a living, which mean he shows no mercy with his instruments." "Oh well okay then, since you put it that way we really need to find your Best Man." Finally, we walked into the Game Room and they both were there and it looks like they had been playing more than pool. At least we could see the balls on the table, they both had pool sticks in their hand but they were both standing in a corner doing a little more than kissing in a very heated section of the room. We both walked in a cleared our throats, the PJ spoke up. "Now we see why you guys couldn't answer, looks like you both were a little busy with more than the game." William responded, "Look we just got caught up in the music Donnie Hathaway can blow anybody's mind, we tried to play a little pool, but I could'nt hardly stand to watch this young lady parade around this table like this, man, she had me all discombobulated." (Which meant extremely Turned On). Then Daphine spoke, "Hey I think we are both two consenting adults, I was attracted to him too; it got a little heated in here and one kiss just lead to another." I responded, (Well, my Mama always told me if you can't stand the heat, then you need to stay out of the kitchen). Immediately, we all starting laughing. "All jokes aside, William, man I feel you, this young lady does looks pretty enticing tonight, no wonder you both got backed up in a corner. I'm not gone lie, Angell and I left a little smoke on the patio ourselves. We better turn off this slow music and let these ladies get home before it gets too late or all of us will be trying to put out some fires in this place." "You're right man, I smell some smoke right now. I need a fire extinguisher to hose myself down." "Down boy, I mean that literally, come on ladies so we can see you out to your car." We all agreed, then we both got our purses and walked outside. It was a beautiful night, when they realized we were in two different cars, they each walked us to our cars. "I had a wonderful time, PJ, I miss you already." "Me too, Angell." "Even though they just met today, looks like William and Daphine hit it off, pretty good." "It doesn't take much for William, he loves a pretty face, a nice shape and a woman that can wear the hell out of some blue jeans. I'm sure he'll be talking about her until he leaves in a few." "Looks like she fit's the bill, but let me remind you she is a very tender hearted person, she deserves somebody special, it's always hard for a man to trust her because of the way she looks. But she is an amazing person if he takes time out to stop and get to know her. Just let him know that, I can't tell her or him what to do, sex is so easy to do; but once you start right there, you loose the edge or the possibility of anything else happening between you. Nothing is left for the imagination to gravitate to; I'm not saying it won't bring you immediate pleasure or satisfaction; that it does, but it can lead you from one extreme to another and before you know it, the thrill is gone." "Angell, I know exactly what you mean, I have been there and done all of that and you're right. I'll advise him if you do the same, you're right we can't control what they decide to do it's up to them. I know what and who I want and right now that's you." "I'm feeling you too PJ, let me get in my car before I do something else with these hands besides driving my car." "You're right I better let you go, be careful baby, call me and let me know you made it home safely." "I will. Thanks again, for a fantastic time." As soon as I got in my car, I called Daphine on her cell phone, she yelled back at me, "Okay, Okay!" I yelled back at her to get in the car, afterwards, we both left.

My God, what an incredible day, butterflies were all tied up in my stomach, you know that feeling you get when someone that you longed for, who tells you things that you always wanted to hear. This man could really send my thoughts and feelings to a whole different level which inspired me to want to be in love; immediately I thought about one of my favorite songs by Frankie Beverly and Maze, "I can tell by the look in your eyes." Which allowed me to get caught up in the moment of their music on my way home. As soon as I got into the goove from my favorite CD, my cell rang, of course it was her. "Hey, girl William is so fine, I thought I was going to loose control of myself?" "So did I, what about Maurice? I thought you guys were going to work through your situation." "I'm sick of Maurice, I know I love him, but it's like a poison or an addiction. I've gotten use to him and I know I always let him sucker me in back in every time, because I felt like I didn't have a choice. It's different when an option shows up." "What? Are you calling William an option?" "Well yea, I like him and I think he likes me, so to me that's an option." "Only time will tell, just don't rush in too fast, make sure you got your head on straight and you're not just judging everything by that old touchy, feely thing. He is a head turner, and I understand how you must feel, just don't give in or give up to much too soon. Now Maurice is always full of drama and a few surprises that he pulls out of his hat, which is what happens when you love somebody who has kids by somebody else. But you made that choice, at the time it didn't matter, but now I know you. When you get bored you move on quickly, you may be at a point like Tina Turner "What's love got to do with it. Sometimes it's nothing, sometimes it's everything. You choose what's right for you and pray on it; I trust you'll make the right decision; when you meet somebody new it's always exciting. I'm going to support you no matter what you decide, and I know you'll do the same for me. Just think about what you really want, pray about it and pray that you'll recognize it when it comes." "Thanks Angell, girl I don't know what I would do without you. I had a great time today, I'm glad we got a chance to enjoy such good company today. Let me back this thing up girlfriend, PJ, seems like a good match for you I like him. You know you deserve nothing but the best. I will take your advice as always. I love you girl, I'll call you when I make it home be careful." "Thanks I will, I love you too, girlfriend go home, get some rest and we'll talk later."

What a night, I thought to myself as I got out of my car and walked to the door of my place. Before I could get in the shower my phone rang it was Daphine letting me know she had made it safely. Afterwards I got into shower and couldn't wait to climb into my bed. First I had to give thanks for such an incredible day. It's always great to met someone new but when he introduces you to his friends that's a special guy who is not guarded. I realize the importance of new beginnings with someone; establishing a respectful genuine friendship first is the key to an excellent start. Only time will tell where it will lead. Prayer is the key for me, because I can't really trust my own heart felt emotions; they can come over you like a rush. It can be tricky because of what's seen with our eyes in the natural; can often make us loose focus on the true essence of what we feel in our heart and our soul. It's safer for me to pray and ask for direction, revelation and confirmations. I can't live without the counselor of truth which reasons with the connection to my soul. When I got into bed I made the final phone call to PJ thanking him again for his warm hospitality, he thanked me and we said goodnight.

Good Morning, Monday Morning

I slept like a newborn baby last night, it was a Good Morning, Monday Morning. Although I was working on a special project at the office. As I got ready for work, I took some quiet time out, to meditate and think through how I needed my day and my week to flow; wisdom unveiled itself by giving me some insight on making my deadlines. Before I knew it, it was the middle of the week. When I walked into my office, people were smiling and whispering when I passed by. As I appoached my office I saw why, there were 2 dozen of red roses on my desk with a note signed with the initials of my new love interest. As soon as I sat down I picked up my phone to call him and he answered with such a warm smile. "What a beautiful way to say good morning; how did you know where to find me?" "The night I met you, I gave you my business card and you wrote your home and work number on the back of it for me to call you. I wanted to do something special for you today to celebrate our new beginning." "Thank you that's very thoughtful." "You're welcome, for everyday that I'll be away from you for the next three weeks, I wanted to give you a rose for each day. I need to see you tonight. Can we have dinner around 7:00?" "I can't wait to see you again; thank you for the roses and the gesture, I will think of you each day that you're gone. I miss you already." "I'll pick you up around 6:30 in order for us to make our reservations at 7:00." "Sounds great, here's my address." "Enjoy your day Angell, Until Then." My God, that man is something else Jon Paul, PJ whatever his name is; thank you for sending him to me. Immediately I took out my appoinment book and looked at my calendar. After the series of meetings were over I saw a window of opportunity where I could leave at 3:00. I decided to jump right through the window, bail out and prepare for my evening. When I left the office the project was 93% complete once it was proofed, edited and processed for the printer it was a done deal with the final 7% to be done; it would be Vanessa and Edgar's baby. Finaly I am off company's time; I can't wait to get home to see what he has planned, I needed to make a few stops before I got home.

When I finally got home all I wanted to do was relax my mind and get my thoughts around the evening. After sitting there I was given the sweetest idea; then I found a small box and tied a bow around it. I took a long hot bubble bath and got dressed for the evening. As the clock approached 6:15 my doorbell rang; I looked out my peephole and there he was standing there 15 minutes early. As I opened the door my heart began to flutter, "Hey, come on in. Ooh don't you look handsome." "Look at you, I don't think I'll be able to keep my eyes off you all night." "That's usually the idea." I responded. "Watch yourself now, don't be trying to start something. You have a very cozy place, it smells so good in here what is that?" "It's some scented oil the name is a little too sexy for me to reveal right now; I'll have to tell you the name later after we've been on a few dates." "Oh, it's that rated is it?" "Trust me it is." "Okay I'll leave that alone; I love the color's and your décor, this place is you." "Come walk with me and let me give you a tour, it'll only take a few minutes." I grabbed his hand and guided him through my place and he was so pleased with my apartment. I loved it, I had a 2 bedroom apartment that included a sunroom with bay windows which was my surround sound entertainment room, I also had a workspace area in my 2nd bedroom where my desk and computer were set up, my living room, separate dining room and my kitchen which included a breakfast nook. It was perfect for me and I loved the space and the earth tone color schemes in each room, 1 ½ bath's and of course my bedroom was fit for a queen. I quickly moved from the tour of my bedroom and guided him back to the living area, he asked me to come and sit next to him. He smelled so good, I could have easily just laid in his arms for the rest of the night. When he placed his arms around me, he leaned over and kissed me on my lips so soft and tender. We lingered on to that moment in time until my pleasurable kisses lipstick had disappeared. Our lips finally parted, he whispered sweet nothings in my ear, by saying "You know you are about to make me loose my appetite." "Am I now? Maybe we both are running a tie for first place?" "I'd like to be the one to break the tie." As his lips moved closer to mine, I felt like I was in the middle of a romance novel or something. Not wanting to argue with the competition; I had to oblidge him by letting him lead the way to the finish line. He had to have the most delightful lips, that really knew how to kiss a woman. Letting him cross that line was my pleasure; by the way he orchestrated his hands in the crevice of my back was a sign of a very mature lover; it was so soothing to each muscle in my body. Where did this man come from? I asked God to myself silently, over and over again. As soon as we came out of the romantic trance we both seem to be in; Jon looked at his watch and said, "we better get going we're only 15 minutes away from the restaurant. Since we've had such a delicious appetizer I don't think anything on the menu can top that." "I agree, let me freshen up I'll be just a few seconds." When I walked into my bedroom I thought my knees were going to colaspe, I better be careful with this man; he'll have me breaking all kinds of rules. Finally I freshed up and we got ready to leave. "I love your place it's so tranquil and serene I could have stayed here with you all night; you'll have to invite me back over when I get back." "Thank you, I'll keep that in mind."

When we got to the restaurant, he mentioned who he was and they escorted us to a private table in the back. It was a very nice place, I had never been there before. I didn't even care what was on the menu, but I looked anyway. I asked him what he would suggest he gave me his favorites, which all sounded delicious. Then I asked him if he would order for both of us. We begin to talk; it seemed like we had so much in common, so much to talk about it was wonderful. Finally our dinner arrived we ending up eating from each other's plate. We had a great time, he was incredible guy that I found myself drawn to wanting to get to know him. He asked me if I wanted dessert, after looking at the menu I told him, "I would love to have dessert but I'm stuffed." "Me too, why don't we order it to go and take it back to my place." "Sure." To tell you the truth I was a little nervous, those butterflies started to flutter in my stomach all over again, churning around the heavy load of food. Immediately I had to finish up my strawberry lemonade to calm it down. When the waiter came by he ordered the Key

Lime Pie which was his favorite and I ordered an incredible Lemon and Rasberry Crème Pie drizzled and garnished with fresh rasberries on top. As much as my eyes wanted to taste it right away, my stomach said hold please, as if it were communicating through a switchboard operator. After he took care of the bill, he left a wonderful tip for our waitress, Grace, who exemplified her name.

When we made it back to his place, I sat down in the living room while he prepared our dessert and some delicious imported flavored coffee and lit a few candles around the house. We talked a little more and enjoyed our dessert by candlelight. I fed him some of mine and he feed me some of his, both desserts were well worth the wait. After we finished our coffee, he hit the remote and selected some music; we sat there and relaxed I closed my eyes and leaned over toward his chest. He immediately placed a throw around us as we let go of the cares of the world and enjoyed that expanse in time. One of my favorite songs came on, I thought I would loose control, then he leaned over and kissed my hand and asked me if I wanted to dance, it was easy to follow his lead.

After the music ended we seem to dance to our own music, it was amazing we had this chemistry that makes you want to welcome a man to your world, your heart truly begins to sing a brand new song. It was a great feeling; as we continued to stand there all I could think of was how this man held my body as if it were sculpered to fit inside his arms. As he whispered love notes in my ear, he picked me up and carried me to the sofa while kissing me softly on my lips, I thought I would have a massive heart attack right there on his sofa. But I realized at that moment, how I needed to be consciously aware of every single instance. The passion between us was so strong I couldn't hardly stand it, I was wondering if he felt the same way before I went silently insane. Immediately he paused, as I opened my eyes he opened his. "Angell, this is driving me crazy; I'm not trying to come on too strong, but I want to be with so bad I don't know what to do. Please forgive me, if you feel it's too soon for us let me know. I promise to respect your feelings." "I feel the same way, Jon but before we go any futher, I need to tell you something." "Yes." "I have not ever been this attracted and drawn to a man as I am you." "I feel the same way about you Angell." "I have enjoyed being with you so much, I don't want you to think I'm playing some kind of game. But I have to tell you that God is the most important thing in my life. He is my life, I don't sleep around. Even when the mood is tight and the money is right. It doesn't matter to me anymore how the man looks or what he has to offer me. I'm not a materialistic person, I do like really nice things don't get me wrong, I try not to ever get over excited by what I see. But you have overwhelmed me, just by being you. There is nothing I would like more right now, than for you make love to me like you never have before to anyone. When I meet a man and he has got it going on, what he has doesn't cause me to immediately jump into his bed. Instead it makes me proud to see a man who understands how important it is to have something going for his self and knows how to carry the weight and be responsible. I do enjoy the pleasures that life offers me and I am very comfortable supplying my own needs. Because I know I may not have as much to offer as a man like you, but I know I got it going on too for most women my age. My career allows me to make a decent living and for some reason I've always been blessed. I haven't been in a physical relationship in a long time. Recently I've been dating only one guy, we've shared a small levels of intimacy on several occasions. But he knows I'm not going to go to bed with him just to put out his fire, I made that very clear to him when we met; he's been very patient. We talked about it, and I know he fulfills his needs elsewhere. I wanted to be honest with you about how I felt. I don't want to lead you on. The way I just kissed you really kind of scared me, I haven't kissed anyone like that in a long time. I felt something in the pit of my stomach that made me want to give myself to you totally right now. I want you to know that I made a vow to wait until I get married. So maybe we should slow down this whole mood all this kissing and touching will lead to. I'm not a virgin but I've been abstinate for a while now, which makes me pretty close to it. You see I lost my virginity by being at the wrong place and at the wrong time; it was definitely with the wrong man. It was not something planned on my part. If I could do it all over again, I would have been more careful and not so nieve. Jon, I was rapped almost five years ago. I never really told anyone the whole story. But now I feel a need to tell you, so here it goes. When I was a freshman in college, I was overpowered by this inner desire I had for this guy on campus. I had a crush on him and he had one on me. He was a senior and the star running back for our school who was saught after by scouts all over the NFL even before he became a senior. He was very popular, and didn't have a hard time putting numbers in his little black book. I learned a very valuable lesson during my freshman year in college that will last me a lifetime. My mother used to always say, what looks good to you is not always good for you. Unfortunately I had to experience it literally for myself before I truly believed it. At first, it caused a few set backs in my mind for a couple of years. You can say I'm old-fashioned because I grew up with the type of morals and values that encourged me to want more out of life. But curiosity and misjudgment of trusting someone can mislead you. I listened to some friends who continued to talk to me about how much the guy liked me. Of course the main subject was the fact that he was attractive, with a body that wouldn't quit telling you how good it looked and an excellent football player. You know how we listen with our eyes combined with what's going on in our head. We seldom stop and listen to our heart, which is what tells us the truth. I was so excited that he was really into me when I first met him. He was one of the most popular guys at school. Everybody said, we made such a cute couple. We talked a lot on the phone and he was a very likable person with a great sense of humor; he had goals other than football. Lots of women were under his spell in college all he had to do was walk by them and they would immediately be cast under his spell and his charm and go into a giggling frenzy. He told me how women would throw themselves at him, but he admired me because I didn't. He was one of those guys who was always in the know. Either he was in the mix of a party or knew where all the good ones were every week end. He and his boys really knew how to throw a good party. I have to admit, I really did like him at first when we first met at school. He would always walk me to class and carry my books even though his classes were way on the other side of the campus.

There were times when he bought my lunch and would bring me some type of unusal flower. When he came over to my dorm, I acted like I was such a bookworm and I brushed him off. He seemed to enjoy me turning him down more and more. I became very evasive to his calls and pretended I wanted him to stop calling me. After a while his calls began to annoy me. I started to play these stupid crazy telephone games or what ever to get rid of him. Before I knew it, I was pretending that I always had something else to do. I was really playing hard to get. But he loved the chase even more. The more I lied to him the more he was intrigued. He became obsessed with me. One night we had a Thursday night football game I believe he scored four touchdowns that night. He would point to me and say that one was for me. When the game was over he ran up to me and picked me up in front of everybody at the stadium and kissed me on my lips and told me I was going to be his woman. He was so sweaty and wet it scared me half to death. He put me down and asked me in front of my friends to be sure to come to the Hawks Victory Party. He told me. his partner was giving it at his place Friday night. He said it was going to be "The Bomb of the Year." He yelled out and started running toward the locker room, whooping and hollering. Then he shouted out to me that he would be picking me up around 7:00 the next night. Before I knew it, I said okay and deep down in my stomach I regretted it. I couldn't believe I actually said okay to going with him to that party. He called me after the game, but I didn't hear my phone ring. He left me a voice mail reminded me he would pick me up. I hated the fact that I missed his call. His message mentioned he needed me to help him set up the food and decorations. I tried to call him back but I wasn't able to reach him. Unfortunately, he came by the dorm around 6:30 and sent a message by one of the girls on my floor that he was waiting in his car. When I got down stairs he was standing outside his car with the door open; he asked me if I would ride to the store with him to pick up the sandwich and fruit trays, chips, dips and drinks. Even though we had everthing for a party, I had the strangest feeling in the pit of my stomach. When we got to the house no one was there yet. I looked at my watch I realized it was almost 7:30. As we walked up I asked him what time was the party starting. He told me we had plenty of time to get the food set up then we could just chill until everybody got there. After we set up the food; I noticed he wanted to set up a little private party between us. He told me how attracted he was to me and that he wanted me to be his lady and only date him. He turned on some music and told me he wanted to dance and just kick it with me for a while. Then he said he had never had the opportunity to really be alone with me; he started going on and on about how good I looked and how he had to have me. Before I knew it we were slow dancing, then he had his hands all over me. It was one of the biggest mistakes I ever made he started getting heated intimately and physically. I should have trusted my gut instincts by not getting in the car with him. While I pleaded with him to stop, tears were rolling down my face. At that instant, I took a good look at him, and then I realized how huge he was. My god, he was so tall with these stocky muscles everywhere. Before I knew it he slowly tackled me down on the sofa as if he was playing a game of touch football. He just kept laughing, touching me everywhere and pulling off my clothes. All I could hear him saying over and over again was he was going to have me right now. Before I knew it, he had taken advantage of me. He disregarded my feelings and had no respect for me. All I could do was push him off me and run to the bathroom; then he ran after me trying to apologize. I felt so filthy, used, and sexually abused. I cried until I couldn't even cry any more. I was so angry with myself for letting it happen. Afterwards, he kept knocking on the door, asking me if I was okay to come out and just talk to him. He just kept saying he was sorry and that he didn't mean for it to happen like that. He had the nerve to tell me that he was in love with me and he never wanted to hurt me. He begged me to open up the door but I wouldn't. Before I knew it a whole hour had gone by. I was too scared to open the door. All of a sudden it got so quite in the house. I couldn't hear him; I didn't know where he was or what he was doing. So I slowly opened up the door and looked around the hallway I didn't see him. Then I heard this sound coming out of the bedroom. I carefully looked in the bedroom, and there he was sleep on the bed snoring. I looked around for my purse then I called a cab from my cell phone and waited down the street. The cab arrived about ten minutes later, thank God. The driver told me he was already in the area. I got home about thirty minutes later; when I got ready to pay the driver I couldn't find any money in my purse. I was frantic, and in total disbelief that my money was gone. From the looks of my purse it looked like he had rumaged through my purse and had taken all my cash. My emotions were all mixed up I felt totally violated physically and emotionally, the fact that he had rapped me and stole my money was too much. I could hardly control myself from crying, I explained to the cab driver that the guy I went out with took all my money. He told me he could tell right off that something was wrong when he picked me up on the corner, that I looked as though it was much more wrong than I was letting on. He asked me not to worry about it, that I deserved to be treated with honor and respect. My guardian angel was watching over me that night in spite of the current events. I smiled at the taxi driver and thanked him.

The next day he boasted about it at school, not about raping me, but about me coming over to his place and sealing the deal and agreeing to be his woman. I prayed and asked God to forgive me for letting it get to that point, meaning putting myself in that position. Finally PJ spoke with compassion and anger,"Angell, it wasn't your fault that he took advantage of you." "I know, but I never should have lead him on. Eventually he got what he deserved, he was charged with seven counts of rape by several college students which included one of our college professors. Right now, he's serving a thirty-year sentence in prison for everything he did. The obsession of overpowering women superseded him. The fact that he was on trial for rape was such a shock to everybody. You see this kind of stuff on television, in the newspaper or you hear about it on the radio, but you never really think it could be somebody you know." "Wow, Baby I'm so sorry that happened to you, are you sure you're okay Angell?" "Yea I'm fine now, I've been over it for some time now, prayer and the relationship I have with God has really healed me, because I can talk about this to another a man and not feel anything but sorry for somebody like him." "Enough talk about him, he'll get what coming to him." "You're right, I believe in karma, which is the law of cause and effect. When you cause something to happen in your life, be it right or wrong you will be effected by it. If it's something good the effect will be good. When it's something negative the effect will be negative. We all reap what we sow. You know do unto others as you would have them do unto you or what goes around comes around. I'm sorry, I get so caught up sometimes. I didn't mean to tell you the gory details of my sexual track record so soon, but I wanted you to know. Jon, I don't want to lead you on; I always want to be upfront and honest with you." Then he looked at me and said, "I respect you for telling me the truth. I know that must have difficult for you, but I respect that. I'm sorry you had to experience something like that, has anyone ever made love to you?" "Yes I have had the pleasure, like I said I'm no virgin, but I'm pretty close to it." "Please don't think all men are like him because we're not. That young man got what he deserved. I'm not surprised what happen to him. To risk your life for something so worthless like sex. The possibility of having a professional career should have come first, I know he feels like fool. Listen Angell, to me you are a rare woman, not easy to find. I could tell from the moment I noticed you, that you were special and deserved to have someone that would respect and love you the way you needed to be loved. After talking to you tonight I feel as though you opened up your soul to me. It seems like I've known you all my life." Then he reached out for my hands, and placed my hands inside his. Then he looked into my eyes and said, "Listen, Angell I need you in my life, I promise I won't ever hurt you, disrespect you, or try to ever take advantage of you emotionally, or sexually. This is how I feel about sex it's not just a physical thing to me it runs much deeper. It takes different levels of intimacy to create love. I believe that you can make love to someone without intercourse. When you get to know someone I believe having sex too soon can complicate the relationship if you really are trying to build one. Shortly afterwards it can lead to mixed emotions on both ends, if its not clarified, you really don't know where you stand with that person. The heat is on and the miscommunication begins; one person or the other may want more out of the relationship a lot sooner than the other. People are so use to having sex when they meet somebody, that it's a natural thing. Sex is sex. Its addicting, a habit that's hard to break. You don't meet too many people nowadays who are really waiting or saving the best for last. I have found over the years that curiosity can get the best of you and before you know it the relationship is no longer sacred. Both the man or the man feel they just have to do it in order to keep the other person interested. You don't meet couples anymore who haven't had sex in some form or fashion. I heard people say that since they're having safe sex, using all these new forms of fancy condoms makes it different. My belief is building a strong foundation while you create different levels of intimacy. By being able to caress, hug, hold, kiss, touch, care and share your feelings with that person. You deserve that in your life, and right now I want someone special in my life that I really care about and that cares about me. Somebody that you can trust and just be yourself with. I would like a chance to share with you the best that my life has offered me, if its God will. God sends us people that we can trust who will really share his trust and love with us. I sense that when you are deserving of his will, God will pour down his goodness like raindrops and showers of blessings. Get up and come with me." He raised up from the sofa and and pulled me up. Then walked over to the patio and asked me to join him. It was a bit cooler outside than it was when we first got there, I got chill bumps on my arms. Jon noticed I was cold, so he went back inside and got us a very soft blanket. He came back out and placed it over his shoulders and pulled me close in front of him. The blanket covered the both of us. He asked, "Are you comfortable? I just need to hold you in my arms right now, let's close our eyes and just forget about the past. Do you mind?" "No, I don't." When I looked outward at the view of the lake it was the beautiful. The stars were out and a gorgeous full moon; it was so peaceful; I felt safe in his arms, it was like I was in a trance. Being with him made all the difference in the world. He was so considerate, gentle, kindhearted and attentive to what we both needed. He put his arms around me and rested his chin at the top of my head; we stood there in silence. We listened to what quite sounded like it, was beautiful. With our eyes closed, I felt as if we floated on a heavenly cloud in an oasis of divine thoughts between this intimate stranger and me. I felt so compassionate that night, that I wanted to give myself to him right there on his patio.

PJ was the type of man you could fall deeply in love with and never look back. What he described to me was what I'd longed for in my soul; and right now, I wanted to explore it with him. At that instant my heart was melting for him deep down inside; but I didn't want to disrespect my self or my vow to God. I had to remember what my grandmother use to say to me. 'Respect comes by morning; if a woman respects herself the night before, it'll remain with you both throughout the entire relationship. Once you reveal everything you got to offer a man, it won't be nothing left for his imagination. If a man is interested in you, nothing can change that, but you. Moving too fast will only make you loose what you could have. So don't disrespect yourself baby, and defile your body as soon as you meet a man, or you'll see disappointment waiting for you up the road before morning.'

As I remembered her words, I began to drift off to sleep right there in his arms by the warmth of his body. I felt so comfortable, safe and secure. I could feel my arms around him, as he lifted me up and covered me with the blanket. I had really drifted off into a deep standing up sleep. He carried me back inside to the bedroom and laid me down. I started to wake up. Then he asked me if I would spend the night, he assured me that he would sleep in his bedroom down the hall or I could trust him because he wanted to hold me in his arms all night. I felt a great assurance that he wouldn't try to do anything to me. "I'm exhausted, Jon it's been a long day I don't have to go in until noon tomorrow I"d love to stay." "Thanks for trusting me, let me get you something to sleep in; I have plenty of pajamas which is another reason they call me PJ, I've always collected pj's since I was a kid?" "You're kidding right?" "No I'm serious," then he lead me to his closet and showed me his collection, he was right" I couldn't believe it. "Oh my God, are you serious? Can I choose from any pair I like." "Be my Guest." Then he walked over to the closet and took out a robe that had the tag on it, an extra large t-shirt and the top to some gorgeous black pajamas. He walked over and laid them on the bed for me to sleep in. "Some of my collection has been things that I've gotten over the years for Christmas, Birthday's or Special Occassions. They were either too small for me or it was just some that I never got a chance to wear. I appreciate what ever a person gives me, I never tell them I don't like it or whatever, I just accept what they wanted to give me. I figured they would always come in handy when I had overnight guest. Once I thought about giving some away to charity, but I didn't have the heart since they were given to me as gifts. I'm glad I had them around because you never know when you might guest over unexpected. You're welcome to take a shower tonight or in the morning; there are plenty of towels in the bathroom closet. We both had a bit too much to drink tonight and I really don't want to drive." "I'm okay, PJ...I think I can handle the offer." So we both got dressed for bed, when he met me in the hallway, he directed me upstairs to another guest bedroom. As I walked into the room, he softly spoke. "I'll see you in the morning." Then he leaned over and kissed me again softly on my lips and we both said, good night.

After he left the room, I immediately got down on my knees and I thanked God for allowing me to be in the company of a real gentleman that was so charming and courteous. I appreciated God for permitting me to experience a man who had the kind of heart and spirit that was overwhelming me with so much joy. I prayed for both of us and I thanked God for allowing me to feel something so unique and special. For the first time I could really feel the emotions, that I sensed he felt too. I had never experienced this with any other man until that very moment, I wondered what it would be like to sleep with him and wake up in his arms the next morning. Being able to sleep with someone with peace on your mind and heart without engaging in sexual contact; can leave the door open to exploring a true connection to your soul, which is where your most private thoughts and emotions are hidden. I praised God in my heart for being the love of my life, and completed my prayers. When I got up I just wanted to lay down on that gorgeous bed it was so soft and comfortable that I couldn't hardly stand it. I realized I needed to empty my blatter from all the wine, I finally made it to the bathroom it was huge and very uniquely designed. There was a huge dressing area with two separate sinks, a black oval shaped bath tub with a separate shower the tile was black with a beautiful brass shower head. I had never seen anything like it. It was so clean there was a large selection of femine products under the counter. He told me on Sunday after I was given my first tour of the house that he kept feminie items for guest as well as his sisters who often came by to house sit for him when he was out of town on long business trip. He had new packages of undergarments and everything. I thought to myself that I had to have died and gone to a heavenly place for anybody to believe this or even do something like this. A burst of energy came over me after looking and discovering everything in the bathroom. He even had some bathrobes hanging up in the closet some with the tags still on them; I wondered why he did'nt give me one of those robes. Then I realized that I asked him if I could choose anything I wanted to wear and he gave me the opportunity to choose, which made me feel really special. After my brain finished working overtime; I felt the need to be clean and an eagerness to lay down in that comfortable bed came over me. Everything was amazing. I went ahead and took a shower it was wonderful, there was an adjustable massager on the head. I pulled my hair up and wrapped a towel around my hair and took a long hot shower. I thoroughly enjoyed everything. I became so relaxed that I almost started singing in the shower, believe me folks, singing in the shower was certainly not my forte. But when something positive inspires you or uplifts you, you just feel at ease to be free and enjoy yourself. Oh, MG, I could not believe he used the same liquid peppermint soap that I used. I loved that soap, it made me feel so at home. It was incredible. I thanked God in my heart for everything; even this not such a stranger's quaint hospitality. When I got out of the shower I dried off and got dressed for bed. The T-shirt fit like a nightshirt and the length of the pajama top worked perfect, his robe came down to a nice length. I laughed silently, I felt so comfortable, it was like a dream. As I walked down the stairs, I entered the hallway toward his bedroom to say goodnight, I noticed his door was slightly opened but I didn't see him in his room. As I looked beyond his bedroom door I began to reminisce about the whole night. Then I heard his voice, it sounded like he was on the telephone talking to someone, I wondered who he was talking to at that hour. Then I peeked further through the door of his room and saw him on his knees near his lounger praying. My heart raced with anxiety then it began to beat extremely fast. Oh God, I felt like I invading his privacy. I was shocked to see him knelt down and really talking to God in prayer the way I did. I carefully walked away from his door then I walked down to the hallway towards the stairs. The lights were off but there was a slight glow in the living room from the night light. So I kept walking toward the living room; I glanced over toward the fireplace and my mind reflected back on some very tender moments that we shared.

As I began to approach the stairway towards the guestroom, I heard his deep voice behind me. "Angell", his voice gripped my heart as if he held it in the palm of his hands. I turned around toward the sound of his voice, then he walked over to me, I thought I was going to melt, my heart almost leaped out of my chest. He embraced me and said, "Did you enjoy your shower?" "Yes I did." "I hope you found everything you needed?" "I did. It was perfect. Guess what, PJ?" "What?" "We both use peppermint soap. That's the best soap, I just love the way it makes my skin feel so silky and clean." "Yea, that's a good way to describe it. How about that we share a lot in common. This has been a special night and I really enjoyed getting to know you. I hope you have a good night sleep, its going to be awfully hard for me to get to sleep knowing you're upstairs right above my head. I hope you know that you'll be on my mind way over in the night, creeping into my dreams." "PJ, don't get me started, I feel the same way, we shared some sweet memories tonight and those memoirs of you will keep me warm and fill the emptiness in bed and in my heart tonight." "We better say good night and go to bed before we encounter memories of a third kind." He smiled. "I'll see you in the morning." Then he reached out for me and walked me up the stairs, we held hands then he kissed my hand and held me close in his arms at the top of the stairway, then we both went our separate ways. All I could think about in that bed was him, underneath me, I tossed and turned at first, before I finally drifted off to sleep; then I woke up again and couldn't go back to sleep. So I got up and walked to his bedroom he was still awake. "I trust you PJ, I just need to feel you next to me tonight." He was surprised to see me, then he pulled back his covers and I climbed into his bed then he put his arms around me and held me all night. We both drifted off to sleep immediately. His bed was just as soft and comfortable as the guest room was but there was a difference his bed was a King size explosion of paradise. We slept so well together, I had never known what that felt like, my body fit perfectly in his arms. I could not imagine what it would be like to create and make love with him. The next morning I thought I was in a trance, I didn't want to wake up, I don't know what kind of mattress he had but I felt like I had climbed up the stairway to heaven and got stuck on a cloud.

Sweet Sleep and Peace found me...

In the wee hours of the morning I woke still locked safely in his arms, I turned my body to his and he held me closer. I kissed him softly on his lips and he returned my kisses, it was incredible he gently kissed my eyes and every portion of my face then we drifted back off to sleep. When I finally woke up I noticed I was back in the guest bedroom, I never felt him carry me upstairs, there was one red rose on the nightstand next to the bed with a note attached to it with my name on it, it read...

> Good Morning, Angell, I took this rose out of my yard this morning, it reminded me of you, I never imagined that you would be here with me this morning...
>
> Come join me for breakfast
>
> It's been a pleasure having you here in my home, last night left me speechless, I feel very fortunate to have had you so close to me all night long. I have nothing but love and respect for you...See you soon...
>
> Until Then...
> PJ

As soon as I had the strength, I leaped out of bed and dropped down on my knees and spoke to God in prayer, Father, my heart is filled with thankfulness for you today, God, I know nothing is too good to be true, especially when it comes to you. I just want to say, how much I thank you again, for waking me up this morning and allowing me to spend the night.

I can't believe I'm still here. I love you so much for always being with me, being there for me, and for loving me, in spite of my shortcomings. Would you please be with us both, guide us into the direction that you would have us to go in. I ask your forgiveness for any sin that I have committed against my body, which is your temple. I know I kissed him and I even desired him in my heart, please forgive me. This was on my heart, and I hope its okay with you for me to kiss him, but I promise I will keep my vow to you. I feel so much love in this man; he touches the depth of my soul. I can't explain it other than that, I pray that you will reveal to me who this man is and who he will become to me…I bless your name Father and I thank you for who you are…Amen…

I got up immediately, went to the bathroom to wash my face; he had a new toothbrush for me on the counter. I had left my dress hanging up on the back of the door last night and it looked like it had been steamed or something. I was shocked at his fortitude to take care of my needs. I had to sit down on the toilet and take an assessment of what was going on. At first I started to conjure up a bunch of stuff in my head, then I decided to cancel all of it. I didn't want to be fearful or in doubt about things so soon. I had to learn how to believe that there are people in the world who are genuine at heart with no ulterior motives. When God chooses to bless us we have to be open to receive what he has for us. Even if the blessings are to be sent to someone else in our life that we would really care about us, share their love with us or just respect us. We need people in our lives that are genuine which means one that is true, real or better yet authentic. After changing all the negative thoughts into positive thoughts I freshen up, pulled myself together. Then I walked down the hall to the kitchen, fully dressed with a smile on my face, and a change of attitude with loving thoughts of thanksgiving in my heart.

When I walked in, it looked as though, he had just finished preparing us breakfast. Everything looked so delicious and smelled sensational, I didn't realize how hungry I was. Immediately my tummy started to growl like a starving puppy. He greeted me with a kiss; then he pulled the chair out for me. I couldn't wait to sit down. "Breakfast smells wonderful. I didn't know you could cook, can I help with anything?" "No that would spoil the whole purpose, which is to make you feel like a queen for breakfast." "Well I never had such a pleasure, thank you PJ." "There is a first time for everything." "I know I must be dreaming. Will you come over here and pinch or something, and tell me this really is real and that I'm not dreaming." He came over and pinched me on my cheek, "No, you're not dreaming, this is real, close your eyes for me. While I had my eyes closed I noticed him walking towards me. Then I opened my eyes and saw him getting out some ice. "PJ, what are you doing?" "Come on now, you're suppose to have your eyes closed. Come on close your eyes young lady, you're going to ruin your whole reality check." I opened my eyes and I saw the ice in his hands. "No, you're going to try to put that ice on me." "No, I'm not! I promise I wouldn't do that to you. Come on Angell, be a good sport close your eyes for me please." "Okay, okay, but I am going to kill you if you put that ice on me." Then I felt him lean over toward me. He turned my chair around towards him then he put his arms around me, I could feel him kneeling in front of me, what are you doing I said with my eyes closed. Then he mumbled, "Put your arms around me." So, I did. Then I said why are you mumbling?" Then he started kissing me with that ice in his mouth. It was freezing cold, then I opened my eyes and said, "boy you are way too crazy." Then he said, "Well you said you wanted to make sure you weren't dreaming, I thought I would just prove it to you. What can I say it's you, you bring out that wild side in me, then you'll turn right around and bring out the best in me. Do you see me in my kitchen fixing breakfast for you, this I only do for myself, my mother or my grandmother. Breakfast is usually made for me. I'm amazed at myself, because I don't ordinarily let my guard down for anybody so soon. But you excite me. I feel a calmness, with nothing to prove to you or myself. It's like I feel a complete something that's indescribable and you can put a period behind it; like.com; when I'm with you." "PJ, I thought I was the only one who says stuff like (.com) behind it. This is a little weird." "Wow, what can I say; you make me want to let my guard down, you ignite something deep down inside my spirit." After he expressed how he felt, I didn't know what to say; to be in the presence of someone who felt that way about me was a good feeling. He was honest and sincere which was something I had always wanted in a man. I adored him for that, I leaned over and kissed him on his lips. Then

I said real softly in his ear, "No this is not a dream, thank you for being so good to me, you are a gracious host, the roses you sent me at work yesterday were breathtaking. Jon you are an amazing man and I pray that we'll always have a special connection between us. I appreciate you for opening up your home to me and allowing me to make my self at home. You've made this a most memorable stay; its the first time I've actually spent a night with a man without feeling obligated to let things go every which way but loose; I always thought it could be special without going there so soon. The rose and the sweet words in your invitation to breakfast really moved me. Before my heart goes pitter patter, I need to let you know that I'm starving right now; if we don't hurry up and eat this food we'll start wanting each other for breakfast." "Don't get me started you don't know how hard it was for me to put you back in the guestroom this morning." "How did you do that? Without waking me up?" "What can I say, a brother's got skills. I knew I had to get dressed and finish packing for my trip. With you laying in my bed would have been a huge distraction. Besides, I'm pretty disciplined when it comes to yielding; I must say you can make it hard on a brother. The way you talk so casually about it. You shocked me when you came in my bedroom last night. When I saw you standing there, all I wanted to do was hold you close to me, looks like the feeling was mutual, I'm glad you enjoyed being my guest." "Words can't explain how hard you make it for a girl to leave, but I have to get to work by 1:00." "I know, I'll have you home in time to relax and get dressed for work; my flight leaves out at 4:15 this evening." "I wish you a safe trip, I'll miss you but I know you have to take care of business, I'll be praying and thinking of you." "Me too." "Jon come on, and bless this food so we can eat." We ate, laughed, and enjoyed our breakfast. I couldn't believe he had prepared such an elaborate feast. "You are a good cook, my regards and compliments to your mother and grandmother who obviously taught you well." "Thank you." "This almost feels too good to be true; I used to dream about somebody like you. I want to give you your props where there due. It's obvious, that you take good care of your self, and please tell me who is your housekeeper. Tell me the truth?" "Truth be told. I do have an excellent cleaning service that keeps the place up for me. I have a personal maid named Krystal. She comes in four to five times a month. She's excellent, because she comes by to check the house for me when I'm out of town. Like I told you before, I travel a lot, I like her and I trust her. However, she's happily married and they have seven children with a set of twins in the family and she is one of the best. I highly recommend her to anyone worthy of her services. She told me how much she enjoys working for me and that she doesn't want to work a demanding schedule because of her children. I admire her and I commend her for having some good old fashion morals. Her husband works twelve hours a day, Monday through Friday and some weekends for the Post Office. By her working for me it helps them out quite a bit. She told me she has only three clients, a middle aged lady, and elder couple and myself. I pay her well, because I know I can depend on her. She's kindhearted, considerate and very effecient. I admire the fact that she's been married for twenty years, and she's only thirty-eight years old. They were high school sweethearts. They have wonderful kids and they know their place, very mannerable, and they respect their elders. It's not easy to find some one who takes pride in their job cleaning a house. She does a superb job and I appreciate women like her who take pride in what they do." "She sounds amazing, she really does a fantastic job. I could tell your home had a woman's touch; you can feel the love she puts into it. It seems easy, because it feels like a lot of love is in this house; I'm sure it comes from both of you." "Thank you, Angell, I can't tell you enough how much I've enjoyed your company and just having you in my home. I feel as though I've known you for a long time right here in my heart." "Me too, I know feelings can be misleading and I don't want to be mislead by mine so quickly. I think we should take it nice and slow so our emotions won't deceive us."

We both came to an agreement, then we noticed it was around 9:30 we decided he would take me home so he could rest before his trip and I could relax before I went into work. He got me home about 10:15, I still had time to do exactly that, relax and get ready for an afternoon of long meetings as we moved toward the completion of a project." PJ came up for about fifteen minutes, then he left graciously around 10:30. As we embraced each other we both realized how long he would be gone, but neither of us let on to how much we would really miss each other. He told me he would send me a post card. Then I told him I had something for him; I reached in my purse and gave him the small box with the bow wrapped around it, that I had made him last night before he picked me up. I asked him not to open it until he got to his hotel room in New York. I had never been to New York, and there were several places that I wanted to see; so I put a special note on each day that I wanted to spend with him while he was in New York.

As PJ waited in the airport for his flight to board, he glanced inside his brief case noticing the wrapped box unbeknowned to him, that was filled with little small envelopes inside. He smiled and wondered with anticipation what was in the box. Just like a kid, he opened the box and scanned through the group of envelops and noticed that each envelop was enscripted with a date, the first one said I knew you just could'nt wait, so open me on the plane to New York as soon as the seat belt sign goes off. He put the envelop on top and smiled. As he boarded the plane he sat down and waited until the appointed time for the first of ten envelopes.

> ***Envelope #1*** *– I knew you Couldn't Wait...(smile)*
> *Open me on the Plane to New York*

> *When we met, I never thought I would feel as high as I imagine your plane is soaring across the sky, every time I'm with you, you make me laugh, as I close my eyes and sigh; in the hopes of us enjoying each passing day, I look forward to the nights together as they go by. I'll smile while you're away, with memories of you on my lips, that I'll cherish the thoughts of you each day. JThank's for the amazing flight last night, I'm finding it hard to land especially when I reminense of the touch of your hands caressing my body, it gives me the assurance that you are more than just a hot toddy. While you gaze into the window of my soul; I can still feel the presence of both of us not loosing control. As you open me up while you're on your Plane to New York, please take me with you. When we meet again on the next pages of my heart...have a safe flight and a successful trip...My Darling Jon...until we meet again, I can't wait to see and be with you Angell*

Anticipation

Three weeks passed by so quickly, the project I was working on took up all my time and energy, I didn't have time to really reflect on anything else. When I glanced at my appointment book I realized that it was time for PJ to return. Although I couldn't wait until he returned but out of respect I realized that he needed time to recooperate from his business trip. I had planned to finally get by the grocery store and pick up a few things then I would get to relax and enjoy my Friday Night doing absolutely nothing. When I got home I stopped to pick up my mail and finally made my way up to my place. I was so glad to get home to run myself a nice bubble bath and chill completely out. I did just that. I fixed myself a light dinner then I climbed into my bed and drifted right off into "NeverLand," you know the land that children never want to leave. "NeverLand was where I spent many nights, I was especially grateful to have a 3 day week end as we were approaching a National Holiday, Labor Day, oh yea, I love America!!! "Sweet Dreams." I said to myself.

The next morning I slept late, after arriving back from my own personal trip it was always difficult to come back no matter what age you are, but I relutantly returned. When I woke up all I wanted was a glass of orange juice, my pillow and my blankee. I didn't realize how exausted I was, I could imagine how PJ felt. When I climbed back into my bed, I realized I had a ton of mail after reading reports going over and over presentations I didn't want to read anything. Finally, I pulled the covers back over me; closed my eyes once again to find that space in time of release and let go of all the cares in my world. What a feeling to go back to bed and find rest. The month had drained me. I subconsciously thought about PJ, his life was a lot more upscale than mine in business; the responsibility he had was totally overwhelming. As I slept I thought of how he must have been just as exhausted as I was. Although my heart couldn't wait to see him again, I knew we both needed to rest. It was three thirty when my eyes decided to open; all I wanted was a hot shower and a cup of tea. After dragging myself around, I finally got around to going through my mail and to my surprise I had three post cards from PJ. He had sent me one for each week that he was away, how thoughtful was he. The words he wrote were short but very sweet.

The 1st Post Card

Angell,

Your presence was evident on the Plane to New York,
Missing You this Week was obvious,
Although I felt you here with me every day...
It's been meeting, after meeting, after meeting;
Can't wait to see you again...

Jon Paul

I couldn't wait to read the next card, the first one made me hungry as I was filled with anticipation, then I realized I had eaten anything all day. So I put down my mail and made me a tall glass of milk with a warm blue berry muffin with lots of butter. As soon as I demolished it, I picked up my mail and continued to read the next card. I did'nt want to be too anxious for anything

The 2nd Post Card

Angell,

The museum and the play were incredible...
And so was that dress you told me you desired to wear for me last night!
I enjoyed the morning getaway you planned for us at the coffee shop; It was just what I needed...and so are you...
I don't know what else to say, but thank you for being you.

Jon Paul

How adorable was Jon I thought to myself; I am so glad I wrote those notes and most of all I'm thankful they meant something to him, too. Hmmm, I can't wait to see him again, now what is he saying to me. I mumbled to myself as I began to read the last card.

The 3rd Post Card

Angell,

Thank You for being thoughtful enough to send me Words of Encourgement for each day that I've been away from you.
It Was Hard to Honor Your Wishes, when you said;
"No Phone Calls Please" (You were right we needed to stay focused, we'll have all the time we need) I have 2 tickets for a Jazz Concert on Saturday Night at 8:00...I'll pick you up around 6:00! Don't worry about what to wear! I have a special gift for you from a personal friend of mine, who's one of the top designers here in New York.
I'll call you between 4:00 and 4:30 Saturday Evening...

Until Then,
Jon Paul

Thank God, I picked up my mail and looked at it, my God it's almost 4:30 pm. As soon as I glanced over at the time, my phone began to ring, I thought my heart was going to jump out of my chest. Immediately, I took a deep breath and answered the phone. "Hello" "Hey, I've missed you; can I come up stairs." "I'm not dressed yet, actully I just woke up about an hour ago, I've barley washed my face and brushed my teeth. I look a mess." "I find that hard to believe; I just want to see you, I slept all day yesterday and pretty late this morning. When I woke up all I could think about was seeing you." "Jon did you say you were downstairs?" "Yes I am." "Can you give me about 15 minutes to at least brush my hair from having a party all over my head and just throw on something." "Okay, okay but I'll be knocking on your door in 16 minutes, I do need to make one phone call and I'll be right up." "Thank you I can't wait." Jesus I hurried and clocked myself. I was filled with a huge amount of anticipation, I could not wait to see him again. Finally, I had to rebrush and floss my teeth from all the buttery blueberries, finally I jumped in the shower, brushed my hair up and slipped on something comfortable. Before I could get lotion all over my legs and body, Jon was knocking on my door like clock work he was so cute, he had given me an extra 10 minutes, I appreciated him for that. I turned on a little jazz to enhance the mood for the upcoming night.

When I open the door my heart was beating so fast, I felt like he had been away at sea or something when I gazed into his eyes. He looked at me as his eyes began to pierce the inner parts of my soul, immediately we embraced each other and our lips found each other. He picked me up and carried me over to the sofa seizing the moments that we had; as my hands held his face in the palms of my hands, his hands caressed my body gently in the most sensual erotic way. I thought he was going to make my body parts explode; finally he began to kiss me gently on my face as we began to just hold each other as if we would never let each other go. "I've missed you, I don't know what you're doing to me, somehow I can't control myself." "Jon, it's so hard to believe, but I can't help but feel the same way!" "Me too." "Please tell me, how was your trip? I just got your post cards out of the mail last night, in fact I didn't even look at them until I woke up a few minutes ago. It has been such a long week that I hadn't made the time pick up my mail less known read any of it." "I can relate to that; but I'm glad you read it before I came over this evening." "It was so charming, thanks for thinking of me." "Angell I couldn't stop, the whole while I was gone, the notes were very thoughtful they made me feel you with me every day. Before I forget, I have a surprise for you." "Oh, I wouldn't want you to forget that." "I'll be right back." "Okay" "As soon as you hear me come up the stairs I need you to close your eyes." "Your wish is my command." I was so excited, just like a kid at christmas, waiting for my Daddy to say with this huge smile on his face, "Sweetpea go ahead and open your gifts!" When he walked in he asked me to open my eyes, to my surprise he had a garment bag, and a large gift bag with two medium size boxes and a small gift bag with some gorgeous yellow roses bursting out of the bag. "Oh my God is all this for me?" "Yes, I hope you enjoy it." "Jon, Where do I start?"

"Let me suggest the garment bag first." I did exactly that. It was a gorgeous black dress remarkably like the dress I described in one of my notes to him. "Sweetheart, go try it on." "Absolutely." The dress was a perfect fit, my God he had such excellent taste. "Oh Jon this is beautiful, I love it. It looks like the dress I saw in that magazine the night I wrote those notes to you. I didn't own the dress it was just the perfect description for the occasion." "And so it will be tonight, turn around and let me see it; oh yea that is exactly the way I hoped it would fit. Here open this one next. While I put your roses in some water." "Thanks there's a vase in the left corner of my counter you can use." Oh my God, there they were some spectacular black and bronze shoes with a price tag that you Hear about on the show, Sex and the City. While roaming the streets of New York; you have to be a fan of the show to know where I'm coming from with that line. "How did you know what size shoe I wore?" "The night you spent a night at my place, I was admiring some shoes you wore and I noticed the size. Come on sweetheart open your other two gifts." Immediately I thought of my Dad and smiled. The next box had this amazing bronze purse to match the shoes. Finally I opened the gift bag and there was the most astonishing jewerly. All I could do was put it on to show him the finished project. His eyes lit up like a christmas tree; I couldn't wait to thank him. Immediately I sat down beside him and kissed him softly as I whispered thank you in his ear. "Baby you're killing me softly, you look amazing. I can't wait to take you out tonight, look it's almost 5:30 I need to go back home and get dressed, the show starts tonight at 8:00. Do you need more time?" "No in fact I can walk right out with you right now." "That's my girl, in fact can I walk behind you and just watch you walk." "Oh be my guest, but first let me touch up my face with a little makeup which will take about five minutes. Then I'll need to grab my purse it'll fit right into this gorgeous bag that you gave me. By the way I absolutely love it, how did you know?" "Oh I have watched you long enough and I know how you like to have it going on from head to toe, but I ain't mad at you, because the pleasure was all mine." "I have to remember to give you a special treat for being so thoughtful and observant. Thank you so much, I'll never forget what you did for me. By the way who are we going to see tonight?" "The master himself, Michael Franks." "You are kidding me, I heard his concert was sold out. I had forgotten all about it was tonight. When did you get the tickets?" "They were a gift from one of the partners in New York a while back." "I am so excited I've been wanting to see him for a long time, he is one of my favorite jazz artist." "Mine too."

As soon as we walked out the door my neighbor came out when he heard me close the door, trust me he had already been watching PJ's car since he drove up. Mr. (nosy) Dixon everybody needs one in their neighborhood; he always watched out for me, he was so inquisitive, always up in my business and everyone else. He pretended he had to come outside so he could see who was driving up to see me or anyone else for that matter. It seems whenever someone came by my house; he would always be the one who shouted out something to let everybody know that he knew me. He was kind of like my little guardian angel, he protected me too, he always let me know when someone came by while I was away from home. "You two kids sure make a nice looking couple, have a good time you hear." We both said thank you to Mr. Dixon, and asked him to have a nice evening too." I kept walking toward the car while PJ watched my every move. Then he moved in front of me and opened my door. Then he leaned over and kissed me, as he watched Mr. Dixon looked on. "Come on baby let's give him something to think about, we giggled." Then I put my arms around him real tight while he leaned into me more, oh boy what a show we gave." Then to my surprise Mr. Dixon yelled out, "that's what I'm talking bout." That dirty old man, what can I say we encouraged him. We both laughed then PJ pulled off. When we got to his place he jumped in the shower and got dressed. He wore a nice black suit with a gorgeous goldenrod colored silk shirt. "Oh don't you look handsome." "Thank you, baby, you are the one whose a knock out." "I can't believe how well this dress fit's its so silky and sexy, oooh, I feel like a million bucks and you are bonus check that a woman wants." "Thank you, baby the feeling is mutual. Come on let's get going before you get something started in this place."

The jazz concert was wonderful, our seats were amazing, Michael Franks was unbelievable, we enjoyed every moment. We held hands, talked quietly, and shared some tender moments while we were there. I felt so excited like a teenager; the concert finally came to a close, we decided to pick up something to eat on our way home. We were both famished, we wanted fried fish and scrimp again; we knew exactly where we could go to get the best seafood. It was the same place we went after we first met; afterwards we went back to his place to eat since we were closer. The fish and scrimp was seasoned to perfection, we drank some delicious refreshing rasberry limeade everything was just as yummy as the frist night we ate there.

After dinner we sat down in the living room to relax while we finished up our drinks. We starting talking about the concert then we went over the details of his business trip. He told me again how pleased he was with my little notes of encourgment and excitement while he was in New York; he said he looked forward to opening them every day. Then he asked me how my project went and I told him how well things worked out and he was happy to hear it. He moved closer to me and removed my shoes; then he began to rub my feet. Thank God I found the time to go get a pedicure on Thursday his hands felt so good all I could do was close my eyes. I could see us start to struggle for words, after the end of each sentence. Our conversation started to come to a close, then he got up and washed his hands and sat back down, I had my eyes closed, then he pulled me closer to him as he stroked my shoulders softly then he started running his fingers through my hair. "I've never missed a woman as much as I missed you; the funny thing is it wasn't like I missed you. I felt a level of anticipation, and this uncontrollable eagerness to see you again. I think I'm falling in love with you Angell." I was shocked, I never expected him to say that so soon. "Jon, I don't know what to say, you know you make it hard for me not to feel the same way about you. It's easy to love you, you seem to be everything I've ever dreamed of and prayed for." "Angell, I think you're more than a dream and an answered prayer, I'm grateful to God for giving us this chance to get to know each other." "That goes for both of us."

Angell Silently Reflects,

> *(You know, when you are single and waiting on that special person that God has in store for you, you have to trust him and wait. I always wanted God to remain in control of my*

life, I knew I had to exercise discipline and a lot of self control. No matter what the weather was, or whatever the situation was, no matter how it felt. We have to cling to our faith, and believe that our turn will come, and there will be a time and a place for every thing, there no need to rush into everything. We have to wait on the Lord, and be of good courage. It's hard to maintain the spirit of discipline, but we have to for the sake of our soul and spirit. When we desire to receive the greatest reward that he has in store for us, is an amazing thought. That alone carries me through to the level that I have to remain on.)

You know it was so hard to contain myself, after hearing the way he felt, we both were so candid. Our eyes continued to meet; all our hands wanted to do was touch, suddenly his lips began to make contact with mine in the most sensual way, then the telephone began to rang. (like the old saying, "I was literally saved by the bell" it was really true in our case). Even though he just kept making these moves on me; it was about eleven forty-five, so he decided to let his voice mail answer the phone. But the phone rang again, I asked him to please pick up the phone, in case it was an emergency, since it was getting late, you never know who it could be. He said, "Okay, baby, all right, since you insist I'll answer it but don't forget where we were." When he walked over and answered the phone his eyes were fixed on me. Then a big smile lit up across his face, then he said, "Of course I'm here, I made it back safely. Yes she is, she is the one who told me to answer the phone, I almost just let it ring, again, you know me; but you know how much I love you too, I wouldn't ignore you, you would never let me. I'll see you tomorrow evening, of course I brought you something back I always do. You know you are the love of my life and always will be. I wouldn't ever forget you for the world, I'm glad I answered the phone. Hold on let me let you say hello to her." I looked around the room to see if any one else was in the room, then he said to me, "Telephone!" I said, "For me?" he said, "Yes you!" I said, "Who is it?" He said, "The love of my life." Immediately, I realized it must be his Mom. So he handed me the telephone, "I said, Hi," Then she said, "Hello, how are you", my son has told me quite a bit about you, I bet he didn't tell you who I was, did he?"

"No he didn't." "He always calls me the love of his life you know, as you can tell this is his Mother, thanks for making him answer the phone, I hate leaving voice mails, I usually just hang up and call back," I laughed as a sign of relief, then I told her, "I know exactly what you mean, I usually do the exact same thing. I don't like leaving messages either, I would rather call back and get a real person to go with the voice. To me voice mail is for people who really need to leave you a message because they can't call you back." "Exactly, she said." I told her that it was nice to meet her over the phone. Then I told her how much I had enjoyed getting to know her son, and that he was the perfect gentle man. And I complimented her, on the way she raised him. Even though I had just met him, I felt like we had known each other for years. She told me in confidence that he called her from New York and told her some very nice things about me, which is why she called him to find out how the concert was and she wanted to make sure he made it back safely. I told her it was wonferful, we had a very nice time. Then she told me she was glad we had a good time, then she asked me to take care and that it was nice meeting me over the phone. "I'll look forward to meeting you real soon, if he's not too tired tomorrow." "Whenever he gets back on track, I'll look forward to meeting you, thanks for calling." Then we both said goodnight. The most peculiar feelings came over me, I thought wow, it's always good to see men who have a unique relationship with their mother. It was also rare to come across the kind of man who displayed morals and integrity that he obviously had been taught to live by and respect. That really turned me on, but not in a sexual way at all, but in a humble and considerate way for him and men like him. When we hung up the phone, I sat back down on the sofa and watched him place the phone back on the hook, then he came over to me just like a little boy, and sat down on the sofa right next to me. "That was my love, you know, she's my best friend, who I tell just about everything that's going on in my life; even when I don't tell her she can always tell when something is happening in my life. No matter what it is, she always seem to know it all and call." I responded, "That's called having a great relationship with your mom. You know she has that mother's intuition, all real mothers that are tuned into their children have it; but a lot of women who bare children are really not tuned in to it; because there is no bond between the mother and the child. It really does depend on the closeness of the relationship that a mother builds through that bond with her child. Mothers will ask you a question when they want to know something; and some mothers can feel when something is wrong, and they just know when something is going on." "Come here." Then he reached over and put his arm around me, and he held me real tight, then he kissed my hand, whispered in my ear, "Baby, I'm exhausted, but I couldn't wait to see you. My mind, my thoughts and my whole body was about to collaspe we may not make it to church in the morning, but I'm grateful for the extra day off on Monday." Then he whispered again in my ear, "Can you stay with me tonight? I just want to hold you in my arms tonight and fall asleep." I turned my face towards him and asked, "PJ why are you whispering in my ear?" "I know my mother is probably still listening. I thought I would whisper just in case she was trying to tune in to what we were doing right now." I started laughing, and I said, "Boy you are so crazy, do you know that?" "Yes I know." Then he raised his voice a little and asked me again if I would stay? I told him, I would. But first I have a surprise for you, remember I told you I had to remember to give you a special treat." "I'm intrigued, what is it." "You are going to have to get undressed, just get dressed for bed and remove your shirt." "Girl, don't start getting me all hott and excited." "Come on, get your mind out of the gutter, I promise you will enjoy every single moment. By the way I need to get changed too, I'll meet you in your bedroom in about fifteen minutes." When I knock on your door I want you to have your eyes closed." While he was getting undressed, I lit some candles and placed them all over his room; then I heated up my scented massage oil and poured it in the empty plastic squeeze bottle that I brought with me from home. When he walked into his room he was amazed at how quickly I had pre-set the atmosphere. After I knocked on the door I had already changed into a nice pair of pajamas and a robe I thank God for my ability to create all types of levels of intimacy. I asked him if his eyes were closed as I walked in, then I asked him to open his eyes. "Hey, my name is Pleasure and I am here to bring you a level of relaxtion that is going to make you forget all about this little young thing named Angell. But I'll need your full cooperation tonight." "Yes maham, do you want me to lay down or roll over like a little puppy that you got me for Christmas." "Oh if that's the case, roll over boy, and close your eyes and relax; while Pleasure takes over your entire body." "Yes maham." I began to pour drips of hot massage oil onto his skin as the muscles in his back began to flinch, then I began to massage each muscle until I felt the assurance of pleasure, ease, release and relaxation enter the room as his back begin to yield to my touch. I listened attentivly as he moaned and groaned while making gestures of pure satisfaction; I soon heard the sound that gave me the most pleasure. He began to snore, and finally he drifted off to sleep. My certification in the trade came in handy, thank God for the course and that special gift that he blessed my hands with. As soon as I finished I placed the massage bottle right next to him, washed my hands, and blew out most of the candles. I left two burning that were safe to leave lit then I layed down right next to him. The aroma therapy from the scent of the candles were amazing, that scent always did exactly what it needed to do. I didn't realize how tired I was until I laid down next to him; his bed felt like a little slice of heaven, that you could never get enough of. As we slept we found stillness, peace, and silence between us as we reached another altitude of intimacy in our relationship.

The Mate to my Soul

The next morning, we laid together face to face I could still smell the scent of the massage oil. It was an aroma theraputic scent that was sensual on his skin, which made you sleep well as you inhaled it. This was the first time I was able to put the scent to the test, we both slept like a new born baby after you bring it home from the hospital. Suddenly I felt his eyes fixed on mine, as I began to open my eyes we both gazed into each other's eyes. Then he said softly, "Good morning." "Good morning." "Pleasure huh?" "Well yeah, How was she? I heard she was here all night, I thought she would never leave, looks like she gave you exactly what you needed, from the looks of her, I had a feeling that she wanted a little bit more!" "You think so huh, Well would you thank her for me?" "Absolutely." "You are so beautiful when you wake up." "Hmm, thank you, did you sleep well?" "Like a baby, how did you learn to massage like that?" "I took a class that lasted about 8 weeks during the summer; but my girl Pleasure, has that special gift with her hands you know." "Yes she does, thank you the candles, the scented oil and those hands made me feel like a new man. Come closer to me." As I moved closer to him, he held me tighter in his arms; then we both closed our eyes again and drifted back off to sleep. I felt so safe in his arms it was amazing. When we woke up again, I felt him kissing me softly on my lips. Finally I began to embrace him with my morning breath as we engaged in a very passionate kisses. I felt weak in my body as I began to remind him that as much as I wanted him to do everything he could possible dream of to me at that very moment; I couldn't go back on a covenant that I had made with myself and with God. (A covenant is simply a promise, an agrement or a pledge that I had made to myself not to settle for nothing less than best.)

It had been five years of grace, since I had made that oath and I did'nt want to go back on my word. Although it was absolutely evident that he would be the one, nothing was more clear to me than that. But I wanted it all, it was a part of my covenant; the admiration, the chivalry, the courtship, the ring, and the license to do everything he desired for me to do and I refused to settled for anything less. I felt I was worth it and at this point so was he. It was apparent to me that he was indeed the mate to my soul, I knew it after the first time we were alone together. Now over this period of time I never felt so sure of anything. You see the soul is made up of emotions that are ignited by a force beyond anything you could ever conceive or control in the essence of your spirit. No matter what you do that mate will stay inside the depth of you inner being, which is the very core of your heart until eternity; you never forget them neither do you ever really get over the love you feel for them. This man had the credentials of someone whose love would go the distance and I truly believed that we had what it took to live that happily ever after aspiration. "Angell, I want you to know that I would never try to force you to do anything you don't want to do. I respect the fact that you desire to be celibate in your life right now, not many people would stick to a vow they made to themselves less known to God. As much as I want you right now, and trust me I have the know how to turn a no into a yes by nature any day of the week. I'm a man, and let me tell you, we love to conquer the prey and a man is always up for the challenge when a woman says no; but we do know how to wait until the right time. What can I say we know how to hang in there until we get what we want. But I want more with you, you are a rare find and I promise to do everything within my power to love you and cherish you. I've never felt this way about any woman. I can say that I have been in love before, but its never really felt like this. What surprises me is your level of maturity; you never cease to amaze me and that is what turns me on. I promise I'll always respect your vow, and if it's God will that we take this to the ultimate level; know that I can't wait to find every way that I can to satisfy you." I was shocked and speechless, but I cleared my throat and spoke up. "Wow what do I say? I appreciate you for saying that, you don't know how frustrating its been being a single woman with my christian values, because there are so many people who are proclaiming to be Christians, but still fornicate with whoever and whenever they like until they find that perfect fit. What they think is that "it" then before they know the "it" is gone. Then they ask

God to forgive them and really believe that everything is okay after they repent countless times; afterwards they feel they have received a clean slate which gives them permission to go out and start the process all over again if "it" doesn't work. They believe that God, will simply cast their sins in the sea of forgiveness and everything will be okay; suddenly they got "it" their new beginning. It's so many different STD's (sexually transmitted diseases) and serious deseases out there it's scary. People are just fooling themselves if they believe that they have a healthy relationship with GOD when they keep putting themselves in unhealthy siuations especially with no protection. The sad part is that they use "it" as a shield to protect their inner sexual desires. It's unreal to me, what people will do behind their Christianity. What they don't realize is that while they are hiding behind what they think is a shield of protection which is the actual word being a Christian; we have to have enough respect to protect ourselves and our significant others. God sees all and he knows all that we think of and do. We do have to continue to repent and ask GOD to forgive us daily its very important. But we must know that after we repent, it takes time. sin has to die in us every day, if we don't try to be more considerate with our own inner thoughts and secret desires our uncareful actions and quick reactions will consume us. If we want to be saved by his precious grace we have to repent and really mean it to be blessed to receive his mercy. Rebellion, which is simply being disobedient, will not allow us to continue to be under his grace, which will prevent us from finding out how sweet his loving grace and mercy really is. We have to trust to be comforted by his sweet tender mercies and grace every day of our lives.

PJ, listen to me, I'm sorry I told you I can go on and on. I do feel such a strong connection to you and would love nothing more for you to take me and make love to me until we both are consumed by total exhaustion; but my vow important to me. I want you to understand my commitment and my relationship with God. He is the most important thing in my life and I have a level of joy and peace in my soul; and the love I feel in my heart for him run circles around the dephts of my soul like a shield of protection and nothing can ever take that away. Even if I loose you because of it; I believe that if I have to let you go and if we truly found love with each other true love will always come back to you. See, here I go again, getting carried away, I'm sorry PJ as you see I told you I can go on an on." PJ just looked at me and carefully responded. "No really it's okay, I could listen to you talk all night it makes a lot of sense; and I respect you because of your beliefs. Are you okay?" "I'm fine just a little stiff I probably slept wrong, trying to protect my "goodie bag" all night you know." "Your goodie bag, huh." "Yea, my goodie bag, I know you want some of my chocolate treats in here." "You better believe I do, I want the whole bag, baby!" Then he laughed, "You are something else." Tell you what! I'm going to return the favor. I'll be right back, I need to run to the bathroom and I promise to give you a sweet treat." "Before you do that could you put your pajama top back on, that chest of yours is driving me crazy. I might be saved but I'm not dead; every part of my body and my senses are up and running. Don't make me crash like a computer, you'll screw up my mega bites and it'll take me forever to reboot my hardrive." "Okay, but I must tell you, I can fix any kind of computer I been known to be a wizard with any kind of system whether it sits on your lap top or on that desk top of yours." "I just bet you can! Come on now, I can feel my gigabites about to loose their gigs. I think I need you reboot me right now, do I have time to go use the restroom?" "Absolutely, just be right here before I get back. I'll race you to the finish line which is back in my bedroom." We took off running like a couple of kids, when I made it back he had lit candles just as I had. There was fresh orange juice, some sweet rolls and some fresh strawberries next to the bed. We enjoyed our morning snack in bed as he feed me lite kisses between each strawberries and danishes.

Then he asked me to remove my shirt so he could return the favor from last night. I looked at him, and said I know you know how to tune up my whole system, so be gentle, please try not to move it up to high speed internet, I like dial up much better. Its slow and keeps me on the speed I need it to be on. As I removed my pajama top I turned my back toward him and gave him a little show that I'm certain thrilled him from my back. Then I laided down on the softest body pillow in the world that he laid down for me. He begin to drizzle my back with my warm silky massage oil, which smelled incredible. While my senses were heighten, his hands felt like warm butter gently being churned at a homemade dairy factory. He was incredible, I moaned and groaned with sure pleasure and delight. I could not believe I had finally met my match. He was indeed the mate to my soul and the gentlness of his hands soothed the essence of my total being. Every crook and cranny that was hidden in the crevice of my bones were touched by his hands. Then he gently removed my pajama bottoms and began to massage ever muscle that existed in my legs all the way down to my feet. Then he asked me to turn over, my whole body felt like it was in a pleasure boat of paradise floating around to be rescued. The he turned the pillow and placed it under my head; I was scared to death because of the sensitivity of my body. No one had ever touched my body the way he did; I opened my eyes and watched him as he closed his eyes and allowed his hands to massage every muscle and joint in my hands, my shoulders and the core of my breast. I can not believe I trusted him in such an intimate way. But some how I felt he would'nt hurt me or try to take advance of me. Afterwards, I certainly had to repent after watching him do that; I could have easily let him take over my entire body and do with it what ever he wanted to do. I never closed my eyes, I watched the look on his face as he continued to touch me with his eyes closed. I thought I was going to explode, and just give in to this erotic passion that I had never explored. It was unbelievable. Then he asked me how did I feel, I couldn't tell him I was about to burst into flames and only he could put the flame out! I think he knew that. "Your hands felt incredible, so gentle...how did you learn to touch like that? You know what?" "What, baby?" "I have to be careful with you, or you'll make me break all kinds of rules, laws, vows, commitments or what ever." "Baby you won't have to do that, trust me when I get a chance to cross over to that side, the feeling will be mutual and legal. Your skin is so soft and silky it was a pleasure. I love touching and kissing you, then he leaned over and kissed me again." As his lips touched mine there was so much desire in the room, you could have lit three dozen candles with it. He held my body in the palms of his hands I felt my heart rest inside his, my body slowly began to tremble then I pulled away and asked him a question. "PJ, I need to put my pajamas back on before my body ignites. Please give me a few seconds?" "I've already started exploding like fireworks on the 4th of July, if you don't want me to turn into one of those rockets bursting in mid air, hurry up." "Trust me, I will send your rocket to the moon; when the time is right for us to cross that line. I promise you won't regret the moon, the rocket or me. Don't tempt me man!" Afterwards we quickly climbed back in bed we embraced and kissed each other with a different level of passion in our eyes. I thought I would melt, there wasn't any tennsion left in my whole entire body. This man knew his stuff and knew exactly how to work all of it too; timing was everything and he was surely becoming everything I ever wanted and needed in my life. What a morning, night and evening as I looked back on everything, not necessarily in that order.

I'd become totally moved by this man, for respecting me in a manner that I had never experienced. As my mind rested at ease, I somehow felt more than admiration for him for not seizing the moment to try to see how far he or any man could or would usually go. He knew I wasn't trying to lead him on, but what he didn't know was I could have easily gone where ever he had taken me. Then I began to reflect on his eyes when we first met; and the conversations that we had about what we were both looking for; we expressed that we wanted and needed more than just a casual platonic affair. (I have always thought of these incredible love songs when I was growing up. This one was a classic by a group called Enchantment...listen to the lyrics.

> *(Here I am, there you are, we been sitting here for so long, you and I touching each others eyes, and wondering if we should get it on, Should I just walk away with nothing to say or just take a chance on romance, Oh Girl tell me where do we go from here. Here we are, all alone, finally got together to see, if you and I can share a love affair; to find out if we were meant to be, should I just turn my head like nothing has been said or take a chance on your love, Oh girl tell me where do we go from here.)*

As I laid there I began to fall asleep with the hopes of being blessed to fall in love. He made it so easy to love him, we were both open in our mind and our hearts which seem to beat as one. What an incredible feeling; sleep began to come down on both of us. So I took heed and followed its lead believing that this man had to be the mate to my soul, hoping and believing that there really was such a thing. As I began to ponder trusting a man again with my heart; each beat in my spirit began to wonder into an expanse of La La Land. Oooh, love it is incredible when you find someone that seems irrestible to love or simply deciding to release your heart to learn to trust them, as you let go and finally take that chance on love and share. Where do you go from here, straight into what dwells inside the desires of your hearts sharing a love affair that you know in your soul is real, true, spontaneous, open, free, full of hope, commitment, communication, respect, dreams, wishes, faith, belief and prayer where you can truly have it all.

Learning to Trust Again

The next day we got a late afternoon start, Jon took me back to my place to change. He took me to meet his mother, at first I was a little nervous because its an event that a woman encounters when a man really cares about you. A man wants to get the voice of reason, a final approval of wisdom on whether you may or may not be the one. Mothers, grandmother, sisters, brothers and best friends all given the right of passage that will either eighty six you from a mans life (which gives you your exit papers and before you know it; you've struck out before the ball comes flying across home plate). Strike three and you are out. You may get a couple of balls that may walk you to first base but trust me with the mother or grandmothers approval if you are fortunate and they're both still living you may hit a home run. So ladies, batter up and get ready when the statement is made that a man wants you to meet the important decision breakers in their life; whoever they are, you need to listen up very careful so you'll know who that person is. If you can past that test you will be batting a thousand and might just score the victory. You have to trust yourself and who he's going to trust for their connected intuition.

When we met the meeting went well, respect, honor, good manners and grace gave me favor with his mother. She watched us interact with each other with a very keen eye and before the evening made its appearance; she openly told him what a nice looking couple we made and that she could tell by his behavior that I was different than anyone he ever talked about or met. When the stamp of approval came, he told her he was in love with me, she looked at me for my response. And before I could say anything he grabbed my hand and looked in my eyes, I became touched by my emotions, that I whispered to him how much I loved him. Although his mother was sitting there, our eyes brought us closer to our lips and we embraced with a very tender kiss, it was at that moment that I had truly learned to trust again.

After a wonderful weekend I was home alone, thinking to myself of how I got here in such a short period of time it seems like a life time ago of change that I had begun to welcome with open arms. I reflected over the value of keeping your word, which helps you realize the importance of integrity. The dictionary describes integrity as honesty, virtue, honor, morality, principle, uprightness, righteousness, and goodness; now that's a lot to think about.

My mind reflected over the last guy I was dating during the time of my graduation from college, which was like a nightmare on Elm Street... especially after my car broke down literally on Elm street downtown. Brannon, had agreed to drop me off early if I my car was still in the shop. He told me that he wouldn't be able to stay for the entire graduation, because he had meeting at 8:00 p.m. that night; he asked me to page him if I needed to be picked up later. He was an attorney who was always being paged; definitely a ladies man. He was a lot of fun and I enjoyed being with him whenever. He wasn't good for me relationship wise, but there are times in our lives when we want what we can't have or worse than that, who and what we don't need in our lives. I let my guard down, and my standards were a relaxed with him. He was extremely attractive, well dressed, and had his choice of women. It seems like we all took turns sharing him, he always let me and everybody else know he could have any woman he wanted, but chose who he wanted to be with. Those kind of men are always on the run in a hurry gota to go, gota run; you know the type. The signs are there that point us to a meaningless relationship that we often ignore just have somebody. Although he was all of that and a bag of groceries, forget the bag of chips; with him you needed salsa, something to drink and definitely something sweet. He simply had it like that. But, I gave him a run for his money with change for a hundred dollar bill...that carried with it some dignity. We had a see-saw relationship, sometimes we were up and sometimes were down; lets face it we all like a challenge with benefits. I've matured since my see-saw, merry-go-round relationship with Brannon and a few others in between. There was a point in my life when I was a little nieve; I did some silly things that I thought I should do to keep the man. Even though it would end up not working out, I enjoyed my life. Brannon taught me a lot about life and how to advance in my career.

As I looked around that night outside the University's Campus, I realized I was at the auditorium alone. That old saying crossed my mind, (friends are never around when you need them.) Instantly, my cellphone died...I was so caught up I had forgoten to charge my phone. So I began to walk around looking for the nearest phone booth, I remembered seeing a maintenance man, locking up the building near the back; he was about to close the doors when he noticed me walking around, thank God. He asked me if I was okay, I told him my phone was dead and I couldn't find a phone booth anywhere, he offered me his cellphone. Immediately, I called my mom and several of my friends but there was no answer. Finally I dialed my sister, I knew she would be home because she was having her house warming party after my graduation. She came to the ceremony but left early to get everything set up for her party, she was sure I had a way home with "that guy" that's what she called him. I hated to call her to hear the old "I told you so speech," instead she told me she would send somebody to pick me up right away. She was a little upset with me because I hadn't called her sooner. Well I really wanted to feel all grown up, after all I had just graduated, but it was really stupid to wait that long. After paging Brannon, before my phone died, I was disappointed and embarrassed, anything could have happen to me while I was out there by myself. It made me really thankful I had a big sister; who was always there when I needed her. She immediately sent a car to pick me up, thank God, Joe the maintance man, waited with me. I was very grateful again, that my guardian angel was watching over me. Just as everyone screamed out happy graduation, somebody popped the cork of a bottle of bubbly; a few cups surfaced quickly and the celebration was on. What I didn't know was my sister was planning a surprise party for me all along, using her house warming as a cover up. She had some great friends, balloons were hanging in the sealing all over the house that's said, "Congratulations." They all expressed how proud they were of me, which immediately lifted my spirits. Several of my friends were already there, including my best friend Daphine, tears of joy sreamed down my face with a huge element of surprise. Although my feet were killing me softly, my high heels were accusing me of foot abuse, I was overjoyed through the pain. It was amazing to feel and see all the love in the room. It's awesome how God can shift your life from one extreme to another. It hard to realize many times that he really is watching over us…I realized that he was sparing me of being in the danger zone of a relationship that had become toxic. It had run into a cycle of repetition. After the thought freed my mind I decided to release my heart right back where it belonged, I trusted God to handle it with care and help me move on where he desired me to be. I felt as though my life was just beginning, I reached inside myself for that inner peace, I forgave myself and embraced the newness of life. At that moment, I silently surrendered to his love in my heart as it comforted me. Knowing that God always wants the best for us, all we have to do is trust and believe it's true. As he closes a door or chapter in our lives he'll place us in the path of exactly where we need to be. All we have to do is take a leap of faith, as we step out there and trust our instinct. As I looked back on it he was truly placing someone that I needed in my life at just the right time. Having a broken heart is not so bad, because the beauty about God is that he's in the business of mending, repairing and fixing anything that's broken in our lives; he knows exactly who and what he'll use to do it. With time comes age, with age comes maturity, wisdom and understanding are right there to gain as you move on to another phase in your life. As we gain enough wisdom and knowledge to recognize the type of person we need and want in our lives, chemistry which is mutual attraction is what connects us. Instantly, when I took a look around the house there were so many gifts everywhere in the living room; with a beautiful bird cage filled with cash, gift cards and envelopes. I was filled with tears of joy; to think for the entire time, I thought my sister was having a house warming party; as the date got closer she complained that she wanted to cancel it. I kept encouraging her to have it; I even gave her money to help out with the expenses. It was crazy…because of her party she made reservations for us to attend a champagne brunch with our Mom and two of my friends the next morning to celebrate my graduation. She had really surprised me this time, she made such a big deal about the party and the brunch. We agreed that I would come by her place for her party after the graduation and we'd go to the brunch the next morning. There I was, standing there a little embarrassed, suddenly I couldn't stop the tears from flowing down my eyes. I hate the fact that I get so sensitive sometimes, it just irks me. At that intance, my mind told me to look across the room; I felt someone staring at me. Immediately this gorgeous specimen began to walk toward me offering me his handkerchief. "Congratulations, big girl this must be a big day for you, what an accomplishment! You look a little overwhelmed! Were you surprised?" "Yes I was, thank you." He took his hankerchief and carefully wiped away the tears from my eyes and gave me his hankerchief. "If you need a shoulder I'll be in the next room." His aurora left me mesmerized, the scent he was wearing could make a woman say take me I can be yours for breakfast, lunch, dinner, supper or for snack time in between. After coming out of a mini trance, I got a chance to run down the hall and change clothes. When I walked in the bedroom there was an adorable gift bag from my mom; with a note that said open me first. The card read, "To my beautiful daughter, I'm so proud of you. Enjoy Your Party...See you in the morning. "Surprise" Love, Mother." My mother was so sweet. I really was surprised...afterwards I freshened up and changed into this gorgeous blouse from my mom with some faded glory jeans that were perfect for the occassion. Immediately, I fluffed up my hair, touched up my makeup and pulled my self back together. I remembered purchasing a pair snake skin shoes for my sister that were soft as butter in her closet. After finding them, I realized my feet were going to live after all, I took a deep breath feeling the sweet comfort of pleasure as they embraced open toe shoe paradise, I exhaled. My whole body was relieved. Although my sister told me I would probably wear the shoes before she did, and she was right, I had to wear them at least once. I remembered smiling as I left her a note on the empty box, that said, "Sis you were right, Thanks in advance!" Immediately I went back down the hallway to join the party; I wanted to thank the gentleman for being so generous and looking just as good. On my way to find him, I thanked my sister for being able to pull off such a surprise; then I showed her the shoes and we both laughed. She looked down and said, "You, Heifer." We laughed again. Which lead me straight to destiny

New Beginnings Just Happen

When I finally found that gentle man in the den, the party started to come to life for me. I told him how much I appreciated him for extending me his handkerchief. I apologized for getting make up all over it. He asked me not to worry about it, since I was shedding tears of joy. When he said that I felt a warm sensation come over me, I started feeling a little faint all of a sudden, I thought I would break out in a cold sweat. Immediately I began to get dizzy, I thought I would pass out right in front of him. He took my hand and lead me to the kitchen and asked me to sit down for a few minutes. "Let me get you something." I remembered I hadn't eaten all day. He brought me a bottle of water and small plate of fruit. I felt so much better. I thanked him and made my way around the room giving out hugs and kisses. My brother walked up to me and gave me an envelope with my keys and three one hundred dollar bills. "Sis, you own the night, your car is running good, I had it detailed for you and that's your money back for the expenses. I took care of it as a little graduation present from me to you. I know how pissed off you must have been when you didn't have a way home, it was the least I could do." "Thanks brother, for everything." We embraced each other. As I walked around the house there was a lot of love in the house for me and my sister; it turned out to be a really nice night. But there was one problem, I couldn't shake the vibe that kept coming over me whenever we came near each other. Then this long time favorite song of mine came on by the Isley Brothers...entitled "I want to groove with you." It goes a little something like this...

> "Oh I been thinkin of you, and you've been thinkin of me, Oh I'll give love that I have, if you give all that I need, And Oh...let's be fair, I think its time we cleared the air. You been watching me, I been watchin you, you know I been wanting to groove with you. Groove with you...Girl speak your mind... Groove with you...you've been thinking all of this time... Groove with you...Oh baby, what I wouldn't do? (Groove with you) It's spending my day with you...Oh, love is all in your eyes...Love fire's burnin for me...You stay in my mind... Oh woman, it's easy to see...

All I could do was get in the mood and groove to the music, that is one song that everybody has to stop and relate to. I knew he had been watching me because I certainly had been watching him. It was like our body chemistry would ignite like electricity or some thing each time we got anywhere near each other. Just as things began to unwind the music was flowing our eyes kept meeting in the midst of each song and they would dance to the music. We couldn't take our eyes off each other. It was one of the strongest feeling I'd every felt around a man. Eventually that connection let us outside and rest of the story remains to be told.

Behold, that's where I am right now...feeling like I've been struck by a lighting bolt of cataclysmic (earth-shattering) love beam or something... because it happen so quickly, feelings toward what's now a cherished stranger. A stranger that I was beginning to care for and wanted in my life. Life is so funny, just when you think you've been dealt the worst deck of cards in your life. God comes through with the best hand you could ever encounter. But we have to recognize that the best hand is always his hand. Asking for his divine guidance, counsel, and direction allows him to cover and protect you. When we allow him to guide us, he won't led astray. The struggle comes when we go in our own direction that leads us to making horrible mistakes that take us years to correct. At a certain point in my life, I asked him to prepare me to be the best woman I could be. His precious holy spirit gently prepares us to become our very best, all we have to do is trust what we ask for, believe that we will receive it, and be patient that he will give us the wisdom to achieve it. Whether we ask for a career, a vision, a plan, a dream, or as simple as a husband or wife or the mate to our soul, we must go through the preparation period filled with teaching us endurance, determination and persistence while he equips us with the fortitude to believe. Understanding that he grooms us privately for success and failure, while he test our faith until we are tried and true to him and ourselves. Then finally he will send us exactly what we need, if its that special someone that we've been groomed for, he gives us that innate spirtual discernment to recognize our mate, because God speaks to the heart first, we have to pay attention to what our heart is saying. He will give us confirmations to reveal the answer. A confirmation is the evidence, the proof, or the verification of the truth. It comes directly from God, he gives them to us in dreams, visions, or they can come to us verbally through friends, a relative or by a complete stranger because you never know when you might be entertaining an angel unaware. In spite of what we may think or believe, God does speak to our heart. We have be still to seek him, tune in, and the answers will come; in due season as we mature and are prepared for the answer to our prayer.

Dinner At Pepe's

Beep, beep...Oh my God, I almost forgot where I was, there I go again, day dreaming. P.J. is downstairs, oh my goodness, I looked down at my watch, it was 7:15 p.m. Beep, beep...I wondered how long I had been stuck in my thoughts. "I hope he hasn't been waiting long, then I got up and checked myself, then I decided I wanted to put one of the roses in my hair that PJ brought me the night of the Michael Franks Concert they were blooming so beautifully. What a night that was, I took a deep breath as I remembered the gentleness of his hands all over my body bringing me such soothing pleasure in every touch. So I reached over and took a rose out of the vase, then I cut the stem off and I put it in my hair with a hairpin. That night, I wore a long tight blue jean skirt and a canary yellow silk blouse with triple spagetti straps, and my short sleeve blue jean jacket with some gorgeous shoes. I walked out, locked the door and I went downstairs. There he was, standing outside his car in a pair of jeans and a nice long sleeve olive colored cotton shirt. He looked so adorable, my, my, my, I thought to myself, "why did he have to wear those jeans?" I don't know why I'm so crazy for a fine man in some jeans, but hey we all have our weaknesses and so there you have it, that one was mine.

(Then I started having flash backs on the way to the car, of that guy who was'nt worth a dime...the heart throb, the gigolo, the guy who never wanted to belong to just one woman. He hid himself behind all those women, but what he didn't realize was he had a problem and the problem was he didn't like to be alone. Running from true intimacy, which is the closeness of warmth and affection that stops you from developing the spirit of genuine passion. At that instant, I was thankful that I finally let him go that night, if I hadn't closed the door of my heart to him, I never would have been open to meet PJ. As I looked at PJ, while I approached the car, I began to feel sorry for him and many others, who simply don't want to take the time out from roaming from one woman to the next to stop and experience the discovery and beauty of love.) I thanked God for the fact that things change, nothing stays the same. Only God and his wonderful grace gives us countless opportunities, as we seek his face and his amazing grace to make changes in our lives as he creates the circumstances for them to take place in our lives. Then is when we can be moved to another place in time in our hearts and in our mind, to receive his precious gifts; all we have to do is to give him our time.

The spirit of comfort touched my heart as I came closer to P.J.'s car, we greeted one another. Then he took my hand in his, and kissed it gently, and he placed the palm of my hand on his face and closed his eyes, and said, "Finally, the woman who makes my heart skip a beat. Angell, you look amazing." I looked at him and said "Thank you so do you, how was your day." "Full of thoughts about us. I'm thankful to be right back here with you in my arms." Then he kissed me softly on my lips." "Honey watch the lipstick!" "I don't mind, I love that sunkist orange lipstick. It makes me want to kiss you even more." "Does it really, now?" "Hmm, absolutely." After I got in the car, he closed my door, and we left. I told him how much I adored him for bringing me the flowers and the gifts, they were absolutely over the top, then I kissed him on the side of his lips and I wiped my lipstick off, he asked me to leave it on because it was mine. He smelled the rose in my hair and told me, "It smells sweet like you, it looks really nice in your hair." "Thank you, I love yellow roses with the brunt orange trim around the edges." "I remembered how much you loved flowers, it's my job to please you, you know." What an incredible feeling it is to have someone who you truly feel in your heart and soul loves you…Everyone should want a love of their own…As soon as we drove out of the parking area…one of my favorite old school classic's came on by Average White Band…"A Love of your own"…it goes something like this…

> *"The sooner you give…the sooner you get to have…a love of your own. The longer it takes the better you get to know a love of your own…Don't you be afraid to give your heart…you never know til you try it…don't you be afraid to walk right on*

in...the door is standing open...you know I'm always hoping... Oh....the sooner you give...the sooner you get to have a love of your own...as far as you go...its never to far behind...A love of your own...don't you be afraid to shoot the moon...never know til you try it...don't deny it to yourself."

Wow that was music back then...with so much love and meaning in every lyric...PJ grabbed my hand and told me how blessed he was to have found me...I leaned over and kissed him on his lips and whisped "me too...I love that song...It make me want to fall deeply in love with you..." "Me too, baby, me too." I smiled at him, while he held my hand inside his. PJ told me that he wanted to take me somewhere special, we went to one of his favorite authentic Mexican Restaurants named Pepe's; where the food was homemade by the owner's family. He told me that his friend Pepe owned the restaurant and that the restaurant had been in his family for over 35 years, it was a small place that was named after his father Pepe Rodriguez Sr. The restaurant had been converted and totally renovated from the house that Pepe Sr. and his family grew up in. Their house was a corner lot years ago, now the whole neighborhood has been reconstructed into a very lucrative business district. PJ told me that he went to school with Pepe Jr. and that they had been friends for a long time. When PJ became an architectural engineer he helped Pepe Jr. renovate the small restaurant in honor of his father; they turned it into one of the finest restaurants in town. The neighborhood is called Little Mexico City located near what we call Midtown. I had never gone to any of the stores or the restaurants in that area, but I'd heard about it for years. The neighborhood was very nice it was literally like being in another city, the people were very friendly. When we pulled up and got out of the car every one was speaking to us in Spanish and PJ spoke back to them in their language, he was amazing, they began to ask him how he got so lucky to have a date with such a beautiful senorita. He told them not to be so jealous to go out and get their own senorita that I belonged to him. I whispered to him in an undertone, "Mucho Gracias, then I spoke back something to him that was real sweet in Spanish. "Baby I didn't know you could speak Spanish, did you hear what they said about you," "Yes, I heard everything all the explict details and everything. Then he smiled and told me something extremely beautiful in Spanish; I thought I would melt, he was so fluent. I was a little rusty, it was obvious I hadn't spoke Spanish since I had advanced Spanish 202 in college but I could hold a conversation whether it was business or pleasure. After we got settled for the dinner, I noticed how quaint and scenic it was; Pepe's family was very attentive they treated us like we were a guest in their home. They worked very well together; I got a chance to meet his whole family. There was an area were they made homemade tortillas in a glass area, right in center of the restaurant. The restaurant appeared to be small on the outside but it was extremely spacious and very crowded, people were waiting as long as 45 minutes to an hour. Thank God we had reservations and PJ knew the owner. They told me that although the place was always completely booked around the clock; reservations were made three days to a week in advance. Every table in the restaurant was full, people took a chance and waited in line for last minute cancellations. The food at Pepe's was extremely delicious, it made your mouth water in between each bite, it was certainly one of the best authentic Mexican Restaurants I had ever gone to. Pepe's whole family worked there, his gorgeous Wife, his Mother and Father, his stunning identical twin sisters, and three of his brothers ran the entire restaurant. There was the traditional music played there by a Mariachi Band that would come out of nowhere to entertain you as you dinned, the whole surrounding gave you such a wonderful warm feeling of their culture and heritage. PJ and I ate so much that I thought the buttons on my blue jeans skirt were going to pop off. When you have to unbutton any part of your clothing after you eat; you know you have really ate good folks. After dinner we decided to go by the video store and pick up a few movies and go back to PJ's place to watch them. We picked out three new releases, we chose a comedy, a love story, and a serious drama, it was really interesting that we liked some of the same type of movies. When PJ got home from that long flight he had't even took time to unpack all his luggage. He always made me feel special no matter what; it's a good feeling when you know a man wants to see you and spend some quality time with you, but I could tell that he was still kind of tired. I felt the need to get him to park his body right there on his sofa or just dump pillows on the floor and fall in. You have to have enough common sense to know that being a woman, besides that I had a lot of respect for him and his profession. It was finally time to get comfortable and relax on the floor, we added a couple of throws so we could watch the movies before they started watching us. We laughed a lot, and whispered to each other through out the movies. It was really great watching a movie with a man who was interested in the movie too and not just trying to make a move on you right away. I was thankful that his mind didn't wonder or try to undress me with one hand while he ate popcorn with the other, we respected each other. The setting was very comfortable; we continued to enjoy each others company, we watched the love story last. I got a little emotional; it was definitely a tear jerker. He just stared quietly at me, we didn't say much while that movie was on, he just moved a little closer to me in between the scenes. Before I knew it, PJ got a handkerchief out of his pocket and wiped my tears away. I turned to him and said, "Are you always gonna wipe away my tears?" As he put his handkerchief away he said, "Remember that's how we met, whether I'm with you or not, I just want to be there for you and love you through each tear. My heart belongs to you, I carry you right here, inside it. Whether your body is with me or not I'll always feel your spirit with me. I think when two people are meant to be, you can feel their presence in your soul. You have to have someone that will not just love you, but cover, comfort and protect you throughout the relationship during the good times and the bad. Promise me, you won't ever forget that Angell, will you promise me?" He said it with such a serious level of authority, he looked straight into my eyes waiting for me to answer him. "I promise, I want forget." Then he kissed me softly on my lips. We laid there together for a while, long before the movie ended we begin to drift off to sleep. I felt a slight chill in the room and heard PJ snoring, I reached over him and pulled both blankets over us. While we laid there on the floor snuggled up as we drifted off to sleep. When I finally woke up, I noticed the television was still on, I looked at my watch and it was about two-forty-five in the morning, yikes, I thought to myself. I looked over at PJ and he was sleeping so peacefully, I didn't dare wake him up to take me home I knew he was still exhausted from his trip. As he held tightly onto my arm and his pillow, I reached over to get the remote, oh my gosh he was way too heavy to move, but I finally got it and turned off the television we cuddled up again and sleep entered the room. Somewhere around three-thirty, I felt the warmth of his touch slowly rubbing my arms and holding me closer to him. Then I felt the moisture of his lips touch my face, it seemed as though he was trying to kiss me, but his lips were no were near my lips. It was so weird, then all of a sudden he started talking in his sleep, and yet he was calling my name. I reached over and touched him as my eyes opened a little bit more, "Honey, I'm right here next to you, I whispered to him. You must be dreaming?" He seemed as though he was still in a deep trance, he never opened his eyes. He must be talking in his sleep, I thought to myself; so I closed my eyes again. Then he started talking to me with his eyes closed, he started telling me how much he wanted to see me and make love to me; he said that the first thing he wanted to do was come over to my place and kiss me as soon as I opened the door. "What? Honey, I'm right here with you, PJ, are you awake?" "What is it baby? Angell, I'm sorry, I must have fallen asleep on you. What time is it?" "I guess it's almost four o'clock or somewhere in between. Baby why didn't you wake me up, I'm sorry you want me to take you home." No, honey I wouldn't ask you to take me home this late, remember it's a holiday were both off. I know you're still exhausted from your trip; we've been knocked out for a while, you were talking in your sleep." "Sweetheart, I'm sorry what did I say?" "Not too much, just sweet little nothings, like wanting to kiss me as soon as you saw me today." "Oh really! You think you can make that possible?" "Always." He leaned over and kissed me as if butterflies were landing all over my face, it was so adorable. "Baby do you mind if we get up off the floor and get in the bed, I've been longing for my bed and you, seems like for months. Let me help you get up, I don't want to be stiff in the morning, I need to use the bathroom and get changed; baby you know where everything is, get you something comfortable to sleep in; I'll get you home as soon as we get up. Come by and kiss me good morning before you go to bed." "I will." When we got up, I put all the pillows back on the sofa, folded up the throws and finally got changed for bed. As soon as I got to his room he had already started to fall back to sleep, so I leaned over to kiss him good morning, he told how much he missed my touch and the way I smelled. Then he asked me if I would lay behind him, he said he wanted to feel my body next to his again. I couldn't resist, I had missed him so much, so I climbed in behind him and immediately fell alsleep as soon as my body laid on his incredible matteress, my face found comfort on his pillows I felt as if I had been dropped off in front of the gates of heaven. It did'nt take long before we were both calling down some serious zzzzz's Way past the crack of dawn, I felt his body turn toward me as his arms reached around me and squeezed me. Then I heard his voice, "Good morning baby, did you sleep okay?" "Hmmm, I'm still there, I can't even open my eyes where are you?" "Right next to you, may I kiss you?" He began to turn me over toward him where I laid under his arm, with my eyes still closed, I whispered yes, please." Immediately, I felt his arm go under my neck as he begin to kiss me softly on my lips, then we both slowly opened our eyes, staring at each other for a few moments in time in complete silence. Then he begin to touch my face with the back of his hand then with his fingers as if he were drawing my face on a canvas, he carefully traced my eyes, then my nose, then my cheeks, then my forehead, then my ears, then my chin, then he carefully ran his fingers across my lips, his touch was mesmerizing, the more he touched me, the more I wanted him. Our eyes were filled with the most indescribable level of innocent passion filled with erotic desire. Then he leaned over as his lips moved closer to mine and mine toward his, his kisses started; they were very tender and pleasing. Inside my heart it felt two dimensional like snow cone ice so soft that it starts melting as soon as you eat it, then like cotton candy dissolving in your mouth as the pleasure of it touches your tongue. He kissed me all over my face with such affection and kind hearted passion. Once on the left side of my mouth, then the right side, then on my left cheek, then my right cheek, then on the top of my nose, my forehead, my left eye, and then my right eye, then my lips opened up as they touched his. Our rhythm was so well executed that my lips were willing to be gently loved on by his, then my kisses became open and totally free. The rhythm went on for a while, they were definitely pure moments of loving pleasure, finally we came to a stop, and he whispered in my ear, "Can I hold you closer to me Angell, I promise I want go any further." "Honey, I trust you." He held me in the warmth of his arms, then he spoke very softly in my ear, "Thank you for trusting me, I love you baby, I promise I want ever hurt you." "I believe you, I've missed you so much." Then he closed his eyes and just held me closer to him. My heart was beating two thousand miles a minute some how the rhythm in his heart beat caught up with mine; oh my God he said he loved me again. I'm sure he meant it in a very caring way, so I closed my eyes and asked my heart to slow down.

It was different not to be pressured or asked over and over again by someone nagging or lusting after you all night long, trying to pursue you just to get what's in your cookie jar or cracker jack box, to get the ultimate prize. My experience with him was something I had'nt ever felt, it was different, the tenderness of each moment touched the depth of my soul. We both were held captive by feelings that had built up inside our hearts. When you feel a level of comfort, an at easement with someone that you know you can trust, its an amazing feeling. Finally our eyes opened, we looked at each other, then PJ mumbled, "Angell you are incredible, this feels so right almost too good to be true; it feels too good to let it slip away. God must have made you for me." "You think so, huh?" "Yea, I do." Then he started to tickle me, I started laughing uncontrollably. Come on it's too early for this PJ, stop it, please!!! I'm sorry I can't stand for people to tickle me, it makes me crazy and it's like I'm out of control or something. I usually start running like a three year old." "Is that right?" Then he looked at me and before I knew it, he was chasing me like he was out of his mind. It was so crazy. Here we were at about six thirty in the morning acting like teenagers. Finally he trapped me in the corner of the den, then he actually picked me up and carried me back to his bedroom and closed the door. He laid me on his bed and we started kissing all over again, then he told me that he cared a lot about me, then he asked me to be more than just a part of my life. "Angell I promise I'll always respect and honor you, I won't ever pressure you into doing anything you don't want to do. I missed you a lot while I was out of town, I've never missed any woman the way I missed you. Then I kissed him softly on his lips, I missed you too, I feel the same way about you." We sealed our feelings with the sweetest kiss. "Baby after all that running I'm even more tired, you think you can keep your hands off me long enough so we can go back to sleep." "Me keep my hands off you? Huh, well I guess I can, if you can stop kissing me, man." "I'll try to keep my lips off, you if you stop touching me." "You are so silly, lets see if we can go back to sleep?" "Come on let's watch my bed do what it does best; all we have to do is lay here and give it a few minutes, while it sends us into what you call never land, where anything is possible." Then we pulled the covers over us and watched his bed do what it did best; as soon as I laid my head on his chest it wasn't long before we both drifted back off to sleep. I was very appreciative to God and my sister to have met this man, I didn't want to make any mistakes that I would regret later. It appeared that feelings of passion and desire were building up deep inside both of us, for the first time I was totally overwhelmed. As we held each other that morning, after we had cuddled, touched and caressed we had developed the kind of affection that love should be built on. It was astonishing to feel the presence of love with out making love. We rested together in his bed locked in each other's arms. With our eyes closed, we slept in peace, comfort and inner satisfaction. We developed one of the most unique relationships that I had ever had with a man, we created our own level of intimacy which included an emotional closeness that could only come by what you hope for which is something you can't have without faith. After all, faith is the substance of the things you hope for, the evidence of things you can not see. It was hard to believe but it was real.... it felt even better than that, to know that it was possible.

After the Morning After... Gave Birth to Intimacy

The noon hour, begin to dawn and draw near as we consciously awoke on his bed as we lay there next to each other with my head on his chest and his chin at the top of my head. Then I heard him chuckle...and I said, "what's so funny, so early this morning," he said, "so early...in the morning... is that what you think?" We'll I don't know, what time is it?" "It's early in the afternoon baby...I'm laughing because after all that tender passion, the running, the tossing, the turning and hard core sleeping from the floor to the bedroom this morning, you still have that flower in your hair." "You're kidding?" I said...feeling around in my hair, then he placed my hands toward the direction of the flower, we both laughed, and I said, "I can't believe this rose is still in my hair," "Well it is, it's still has a beautiful scent too, can you believe most of the petals seem to of held together too. That's a sweet blessing, it's kind of like us, we didn't get too carried away as much as we wanted to. The flower is still arrayed with part of its splendor, just like you, that makes you very special. You know what?" "What, honey?" "I love your face in the morning; you look beautiful when you wake up." "Thank you, you're sweet and sticky just like honey; that's why I call you that." "No baby, you're the sweet one, and thank God you belong to me." Then he planted more butterfly kisses on my lips and a few that lingered on, with my Mexican Food morning breath an all. It was a tender moment, I felt like I was in a movie or something, I wondered what my next line was going to be; instead I got another sweet kiss which was much better than being in any movie.

Everything was so easy and natural with him...I loved being with him, talking to him, touching him, and sharing a piece of myself. It was an unbelievable experience, he was so patient and good listener. I really wanted to make the most tantalizing creations of love, that I could make with him; I could only imagine in my heart what it would be like. But there was one problem; I had to remember every time we got close; that I made had a vow to myself and to God; I wouldn't settle for less. Which sounds corny and old fashioned; but I was going to save myself for him or who ever was truly the one chosen for me; by waiting until I got married; having the ring, the date and the man who loved, honored and respected me. It meant a lot to both of us to do it right, we didn't want to regret it later; by making that move to soon. It felt great for someone I cared about to really want me for me, and not just for my physical appearance.

After the morning after, came the most exhilarating feelings that the two of us shared, it left the warmth of emotions and intimacy inside our hearts. When we got up, we freshened up with a long shower on both our parts; we met up over an afternoon breakfast. We didn't say much we just sort of stared at each other; as the incredible essence of love filled the air. When you finally meet that special someone that you feel you belong to, it's an awesome feeling in the very dephts of your soul. Soon after we enjoyed that quiet afternoon; we finally came to an agreement and decided to develop a lasting relationship to find out if it could nurture the love we both felt. With faith, patience and endurance; we would focus on building a foundation on what we found in each other an take it to another level. We agreed on three months which is 90 days for sort of a probationary period of compatibility. Which would give us the time we needed to withstand whether or not we could endure the course of a meaningful relationship, mentally, emotionally, and physically without yielding to the heat of the moment. We wanted to explore what was really going on between us, the real attraction, and be capable of sustaining the relationship without crossing the line. Because we both wanted more than we ever had in our past experiences; we agreed that we had something special and felt it was worth it. Now it was on like popcorn at the movies...like...let me tell you bout...the birds and the bees, and the flowers and the trees, and the moon up above...(you...know)...that's the story of a thing called love...you remember that song...right?....Ahww...there I go again...pulling you back in time...but you have to admit that was a nice one...but those are memories... like the corners of my mind...misty watered colored memories...of the way we were...see what I mean

Endurance in a Courtship is beautiful to behold

The courtship began, it was beautiful, no one could believe we were not having a physical hard core "I don't have to tell you what" in our relationship. But we knew the truth, which gave us an awesome sacred kind of love, that was held together between two friends. During the course of building our relationship, PJ traveled quite a bit, the more he traveled the more we discovered the endurance of love in our courtship, it was harmonious, yet vivacious (which a high spirited sparkle of inner joy) filled with a charming level of innocence. We saw each other every opportunity we had when he was in home. It was very difficult for us to part but we withstood each departure. After all the comings and goings; we became extremely tolerant of the foundation of love and the life we were beginning to build together there was strong bond between us. We attended church together; either we met up for dinner afterwards at his place or mine, or at times with friends. I really got a chance to get to know his Mom and I adored her, she was upfront, honest, and easy to talk to, which made her such a dear to me. I meet his grandmother and she told me she thought I was special and that she saw something she hadn't seen in a long time in our eyes. PJ told me that he had only taken a few girls to meet her and that she had not told anyone some of the things she told me. He said I should take it to heart because she was very hard to please when it came to him; she was a little bias on who she thought was good enough for her grandson and she made no excuses for it. I was honored by her compliments. PJ had become very fond of my mother too. There were no ill or negative vibes between us or our families which was truly a blessing, I thought to myself, if we all ended up in-laws I wouldn't mind it at all. I may be jumping the gun before the broom, but I thanked God anyway.

P.J.'s mother invited us over for dinner one evening, while we were waiting outside her door; I was standing directly in front of him and he put his arms around me and squeezed me real tight from behind. I closed my eyes and it was as if we went to another place in time. Kind of like the first morning I spent with him on his patio. As I stood their reminiscing about how much I loved this man; as the door began to open, he whispered my name in my ear and when I looked up at him he leaned over me, and kissed me. We stood in that position like a couple of college kids, it was so romantic and lovable, I didn't think we would be able to stop as the locks on his mothers door began to open. He caught me off guard, but I loved his spontaneity, he was a romantic. I always wanted to be in love with someone who had that kind of impulsive behavior and he knew how to be exactly that at just the right time. We heard his mother's voice calling out to us through the door; I was so embarrassed because just at that instant we realized we almost got caught just like a couple of kids. My lipstick had done a number on his lips, "Good Evening Maham, your son is something else, I know you know that?" She laughed, and said "I can tell, looks like I almost interrupted something?" "Looks can be deceiving, you know, Mom, it wasn't me it was Angell's fault. The girl can't keep her hands of me." His mother responded, "I see, it appears that you can't keep your lips off her." Then he took his handkerchief out of his pocket, wiped his lips off and gave his mother a big hug and a kiss on her cheek. Then we walked inside. "What can I say...Mom...What's for dinner? I'm starving." Whatever it was had the aroma all over the house. We had a delicious meal with a great time, his mother was an exceptional cook.

Through all the phone calls, letters, short notes, poetry, post cards, which were the little things that kept our relationship interesting. We became intrigued by each other and just the excitement alone strengthened our love it was fascinating. We were always surprised by what we both would say or do. Looking forward to keeping the relationship full of life became enthusiastic, free flowing, compassionate, and filled with significance. Before we knew it a hundred days had passed us by, during our courtship, we had totally over looked the 90 day goal that we set. While we were waiting on the trial period to be over we actually lost track of the days that had gone by. We discovered the real delight of creating the meaning of a courtship that a man and woman should both explore together. During the developmental stages we established in our love encounters were definitely mind-blowing.

After all the long trips and the hard work that PJ had put in to the clients that he had been working closely with came to final completion. PJ's boss gave him a week-end trip with all expenses paid for two to one of the companies beach houses. They gave him a choice of anywhere he wanted to go, he chose something local which was in Crystal Beach near Galveston Texas because it didn't take long to get there and he thought it would be a nice short get away trip for the both of us. He definetly wanted me to go with him to celebrate us making it through our trial period, he promised he didn't have an ulterior motive. He simple said, whatever happen would happen, but he planned to enjoy himself doing practically nothing and if I came along; it would only sweeten the trip. I had never been on a trip with him before, it was a sweet way to end our trial period. I asked him to let me think about it and I would let him know in a couple of days. It was a small vacation for him from what he was used to; to just kick back and relax on the beach was what we both needed. I knew deep down inside my soul that I wanted to go and just relax and totally let go, I knew he really wanted me to go just as bad. After all this time of getting to know him, I felt very secure in our relationship because he had bent over backwards to assure me of that. I was a bit nervous after all, I had these beach fantasies with him in my head, which is what I was worried about. We had written each other lots of letters and I remember how much he told me he was intrigued by the letter I wrote him about loving him from midnight until the crack of dawn on the beach and how I wanted to be soaked up by the warmth of his chocolate kisses in the early morning sunlight. He was a romantic, and I knew he had not forgotten what I said in all those love letters we had written to each other. I thought to myself, what should I do God, he was the only man in the world that I wanted to pledge my love to.

A week had gone by and it was approaching day one-hundred and ten, his boss told him that every thing had started to slow down at the office and that the following week would be the perfect time for him to get away.

The company could arrange his travel accommodations the following week end if he was up for it. He told his boss he would go ahead and book the reservations to leave on Thursday evening through Monday and that he would be back in the office on the following week either Friday or Monday. He came over to my place that night and told me that he was exhausted and burnt out and really needed to get away and do absolutely nothing. Which he deserved it. He had been working extremely hard, for the past six months and he definitely needed to go. PJ reminded me that he told me from the beginning, that he would not pressure me into doing anything I didn't want to do. I knew that he wouldn't, I prayed and trusted that in my heart. I wanted nothing more than to be with him for the rest of my life, because deep down inside I wanted to be the ultimate choice, his wife. PJ was going with or without me, he told me that. The week was here, I knew he had packed his bags just as he usually did the night before his trip. I picked up the telephone but I couldn't call I'd dial his phone number and hang up before it rang. This was so silly, I was so nervous. It's Wednesday I could hardly concentrate, I stayed home I didn't go anywhere when I got home from work, I could just feel him thinking. My phone never ringed, I picked it up to be sure it was still working, and of course, it was. I can't believe he didn't call me at all for the past two days. He's making me think. Oh God, this is making me sick; I do not like this I am tired of thinking, maybe I should just call him so I could hear his voice. No, I'll just go to work and maybe he'll call me to see if I'm still coming; surely he'll call me tomorrow. Girl go to bed, try not to think about it. (You know how we are as women, always trying to play that role, sometimes we do stupid things just to see how much a man cares about us.) I could hardly sleep all night, I tossed and turned and turned and tossed. My heart kept saying, Why are you doing this to yourself, girl you know how much you love him, but my mind just ignored the voice and tried not to think about, so I decided to go on to work the next day.

The next morning I got up, got dressed and went to work. I looked at my morning schedule, I couldn't believe it I had meetings scheduled all the way up until noon. My goodness, I hadn't even thought about my appointment book or what my scheduled looked like for today all week, I was preoccupied Monday through Wednesday, with the "Should I Blues," you know should I, or shouldn't I, should I, or shouldn't I. Over and over again ringing around in my head. I just kept listening to my mind over and over again. My heart never entered into the Blues Contest; it just sat there inside my chest where it belonged, motionless. To tell you the truth, I don't even remember it beating. I guess it had to be pounding, because I'm still alive talking to myself. There I was feeling like a little girl picking up a daisy; and doing the "He Loves Me, He Loves Me Not" game, as you remove each petal, you remember the little flower game that was played when we were kids. (Ooops, I maybe telling my age...) Now here I am at work, all morning my mind just kept playing tricks on me, while I was in my last scheduled meeting, PJ called and left me a voicemail message, to let me know what time the flight was scheduled to leave and what gate it was leaving out of. The message ended with, "I love you more than words could ever say, I wouldn't love you any less, if you decided not to go. Your ticket is paid for in full, I'll leave it for you at will call, no matter what you decide, nothing will ever change my mind about the woman I love. I love you, baby." The message hit me straight in my heart like a bow and arrow, and it left me wanting him even more. Why are you at work Angell, when you know that you want to be with him. That voice spoke to my heart and totally convicted my spirit then my conscience started to bother me. So, I finished up everything on my desk, then I went over to my bosses office and told him that I had to leave for the day. I had already taken off Friday and Monday and I reminded him that I would see him on Tuesday. I told him if any kind of emergency came up to leave me a message on my voice mail or better yet hand it over to Destiny Jones my assistant, she was my right hand and could take care of what ever came across my desk. I walked away and told him to have a good week-end. I don't even remember everything my boss was saying, I think he asked me, if I was okay. "I remember saying, No I'm not okay but I will be in a few hours." I commented, "I was almost insane, but I really need this time, then I thanked him." I went back to my office, spoke to Destiny briefly on my way out, got my purse and left. I stopped by the beauty salon on my way home, as a walk-in, got my hair done, a manicure, and a super delux pedicure. I felt absolutely gorgeous. Then stopped by one of my favorite stores and picked up a naughty and nice things for my trip and two gorgeous pairs of sunglasses for some fun in the sun. Afterwards, I went straight home packed everthing in my bags, took me a hot refreshing bath, got ready and left for the airport on the shuttle from my place. I didn't call PJ back on purpose, I wanted to surprise him.

When I arrived at the airport most of the passengers had already boarded the plane. I stopped by will call and picked up my ticket and my boarding pass, checked in my luggage and boarded the plane. I marveled at the fact that our seats were in first class, as soon as I got on the plane I saw him. He looked so adorable, sitting there with his sunglasses on, reading the Wall Street Journal. I acted as though I started to go pass his seat, but he never looked up he just kept on reading. So, I decided to lean over him and take his newspaper out of his hands. "Excuse me, I want the direct pleasure of sitting next to you, you look so yummy and delicious sitting here, I hope you're not married!" "Fortunately, I already taken." "My name is Passion, I'm lost without you." He looked up and smiled. "Me too, baby." Then I took my glasses off and said, "No more Wall Street or any other business while were on this trip." "Yes Maham!" "Did I surprise you, baby?" "Pleasantly Surprised." Then I sat down beside him next to the window, and I kissed him softly and very passionately on his lips." "Passion huh...you taste dangerous...are you sure about this?" "Yes baby, I am armed and dangerous." "Fully loaded are you?" "Absolutely." "Thanks for coming, baby, you just don't know what you do to me, girl." Afterwards, our love seem to fill the air, it was in flight and predestined; for much greater love to be birthed. We held hands all the way, and stared at each other most of the way, he whispered in my ear and I in his. The airline stewardess kept coming by and smiling at our love for each other, she asked us several times if she could get us anything, we spoke not a word, PJ nodded to her and just kept his eyes on me during the whole flight which said a lot because she was a very attractive airline stewardess. I noticed several people in our section starring at us and they actually told us we made a handsome couple. They said it was obvious that we were in love and that it was radiant; several people asked us if we were just married. One couple evem told us that they admired the beauty of our love; can you imagine, love being beautiful, they told us that it was obvious that we were newlyweds; we just smiled soaking it all in. PJ told me he wanted the week-end to be special for both of us. The flight didn't take long at all, it happened so quickly before we knew it, we were landing. When we arrived PJ had already made reservations for a rental car to drive down to Crystal Beach from the airport. He rented us a beautiful candy apple red corvette convertible, I was beginning to really get excited. We loaded our bags into the car, got in then we took off, we couldn't wait to get to the beach and wake up to the ocean the next morning. PJ told me that the place we were going to stay was at one of the companies Luxury Beach Houses; his company owned several condominiums and townhouses all over the world. As we soaked up the breeze while we were leaving the airport we noticed it was sort of muggy and very humid in Houston, all we could think about was getting to the beach.

When we finally got to Crystal Beach we noticed it was somewhat secluded, there was a wonderful breeze in the air; it wasn't muggy at all, it felt absolutely amazing. We saw a fruit market on the way to the Beach House, so we stopped and got some fresh fruit. The season of Fall has set in which made the weather both perfect and beautiful with cool mornings and nice warm afternoons; which is the perfect season to fall in love. The Beach House was right smack in the middle on the beach, in the perfect location it was private and very secluded. PJ told me that he had never been to that location before, he said he found out about it when he got the accommodations from the companies travel agency, the agent suggested to him that he would really enjoy his stay if he wanted both privacy and seclusion. This was my first trip with PJ, I had taken a few trips with some friends, but, I had never been to Crystal Beach nor had I even heard of it, most of my friends lived in the surounding areas in H-Town, Big D or Funky Town in Texas which are all nicknames for Houston, Dallas and Ft. Worth. (Almost everybody that lived in Texas near Galveston Beach had been there at least once in their life. PJ had been to all parts of the world just about, and had much more experience of travel than I did. (I had just begun to really travel, I had barely been out of Texas. I'd gone on a busines trip to Corpus Christi where I barely got to see the sun come up or go down, and taken several pleasure trips to Houston, San Antonio, Austin, Oklahoma, and Hot Springs Arkansas. I was looking forward to a trip I had planned to go California which was gift trip from my Aunt Laura; to head for the Beach, enjoy fishing in the Mountains and of course shopping on Rodeo Drive in Beverly Hills where we would shift our gears and experience the lime lights of Sin City, Las Vegas. Which would be coming up soon for my vacation where I was looking forward to spending some quality time with one of my favorite Aunt's, this was the college graduation present that I received from her.

I had also visited the Windy City, a couple of times when my Uncle Hollis and wife both were extremely ill unfortunately they both ended up passing away in Chicago. As memories of the Windy City surfaced in my mind…I remember it was exactly that, it was so cold that the freezing temperatures rapped around my rib cage and almost totally sucked the life right out of me. People use to tell me about "The Hawk" in Chicago, they were very clear that once I got there I would met him head on. I thought back to when we first met, my plane had just arrived at the O'Hare Airport in Chicago; I was a real Texas Cuttie Pie you know. I had my little wool coat on across my shoulders and my scarf around my neck, sun glasses in tact, because the sun was out and I thought it was the kind of cool like it was in Texas when I left. When I checked the weather before I left town, it was about the same as it was in Texas, I knew about the wind chill difference I had been warned by a few people; but it dropped severly while I was on my flight. As I got off the plane I observed the People who were in the airport, I noticed that most of them had on jackets, thick sweaters and all weather coats. What I didn't realize they had on layers of clothing; I thought Oh, I can handle this weather. I picked up my bags and I went outside to catch a cab, when I met the hawk he jumped all over my body; like I was fresh meat at the meat market that needed to be in the deep frozen section of the meat market. I was totally instantly frozen with frost bite on my lips. I know the chill went straight through my flesh and said good morning fooooooool; if you don't get that coat on your body, it's going to take you a week to recover from the freeze alert that I'm about to cover your body with. I immediately ran back into the airport I remember shivering like I was at the north poll, my legs feeling like popcicle sticks. With my hands shaking and all the blood drained out of my body, I realized that was definitely the Hawk and I did'nt like him very much, he did not play no games about himself or his reputation. Immediately with my hands shivering, I put my coat as if I was almost paralized, as quick as I could; I found my fur hat and one of the smaller hats that I had in my bag and put it on under my fur hat then I wrapped the scarf that went to my small hat around my neck and added my fur collar around the top of my coat and immediately found my black leather lamb skin gloves. I was almost shaking to bad to walk I had to stay inside until I fully warmed up. Then I got back up and walked outside and it took only a few minutes for the taxicab driver to get my bags loaded into his cab as I waited for him to get into the cab my teeth were chattering, I could barely tell the cab driver where I needed to go. Thank God, he knew the city very well, he knew immediately that I was not from Chicago; he gave me some windy city tips and told me the secret to building the best relationship with The Hawk, which was lots of layers of clothing. I was so cold the next couple of days while I was there, my body temperature barely went up to normal. I slept with about 5 quilts on my bed, three pairs of socks on, a pair of long johns, and a thick flannel gown and the warmest robe that owned. I still get chills when I think about it, If you don't know who The Hawk is... when you get to Chicago it won't take you long after you get there. Trust me you don't have to look for him, he will find you. You know The Hawk has to be a man, because I don't think a woman could be so cold, but you better take my advice...honey...dress with layers of clothing on and make sure you own a real heavy wool coat. Now after my season of being dense, I know exactly how to greet him now.

After the chills came over me, I began to realize where I was right now at that moment, as the warm air blew across my face, it was exactly where I wanted to be. I was so excited to be on this trip with PJ, the beach was remarkable. He said he really wanted everything to be out of the ordinary, over the top for both of us. (I thought to myself, I'm so thankful that we decided to wait and not rush into having a physical relationship. I knew deep in my heart how much I wanted to wait on God's timing if we could help it, in all the things that really mattered to me in my life keeping my vow to him was the most sacred. Searching my heart always helped me to find the true answers and I trusted what I felt deep down inside my gut which hold the emotions to the soul. It's true that the heart never lies, God knows the heart and he will give you the desires of your heart when you wait on him. Our timing is completely off the mark, I believe in my own thinking that it is much more rewarding when we hold on to our own heated desires. When you don't hold onto them you loose control and they can leave you walking around with all those carnal thoughts bouncing around in your head, your bed or anybody's elses bed for that matter. And sooner or later they will follow you as often as they can as the temptation grows into yearning then those desires will start burning inside you and those feelings are very hard to shake and depart from your thoughts, mind, actions and reactions.

Now a days we live in a sex craved society, inspite of the risk, some wear all types of intriguing sounding raincoats and some don't. (If you don't know what a raincoat is by now at your age…it's the grown up term that prevents you from what can transpire from getting your self all wet.) If you don't get it now…it may take a while…It's hard for that cycle to break. The cycle can rotates over and over in our mind, it can and will have those same thoughts and actions going in circles, round and round they go leaving them strung out over their deep rooted tantilizing desires. If the man has not chosen you for his wife, but chooses you to be the one who use your rain to put out his fire. That fire usually comes through stimulation by many types of arousals. Most often you're not the only partner that may be choosen to come in and out of their bed. Remember many times it works both ways, it's not gender specific. He or she will have as many as it takes, to satisfy the hunger that lingers on deep down inside the loins of their body that will curb the appetite of their desire. It's dangerous out there, no matter how many raincoats, better know as condoms you use…you see what that term really means now, right? You can have a trunk, purse, briefcase, drawer or pocket full of them, but nothing is a 100% sure to protect you from that quick burning sensation.

Trusting God is the only thing that is a 100% sure thing if you allow him to be; you can count on his enduring love and protection to be there for you every time. Through all the hurt, the pain, and the short term love affairs, putting forth a commitment to close the door on our own over heated desires, and trust me they can be over the top...in order to help us cross over from yielding to every Tom, Jane, Dick, Mary or Larry. In order for our individual sinful desires not overtake us, they have to be replaced with an inner desire for spirtual discipline; its always our choice. We have the key to lock or unlock the door to our own heated passions. It's up to us individually, if we want to ask God to help us keep that door closed until we have a partnership that will take the relationship to another level...if thats what we're looking for...if not it will just keep raining...so I say if its rain you enjoy...don't forget the raincoat its only a temporary fix of comfort; but its nothing like the real comforter. The comforter comes to do exactly that, to comfort us, as it calms us down and brings us up to a whole different level of peace of mind...joy creeps in as we recognize that God's spirit truly is holy, sanctified, blessed, sacred, consecrated, glorified, anointed, and dedicated to being true to us...which makes his spirit absolutely perfect to keep anything in our lives under control.

Back to my own Reality Check...

Speaking of control, my whole existenence was running out of everything that it was made of, totally spiraling out of it's jurisdiction into a completely different territory. As I feasted my eyes and intimate thoughts on the view of what was before me, The Beach House, the only thing that came to my mind as I returned back to my own reality check...was the wonderful experience that we were about to indulge in.

Astonished by the Beauty of His Creation...

When we stopped the car to get out at the beach house, I could not believe how gorgeous it was. PJ told me he would get our bags and take them inside. After I got out something came over my total being, I took off my shoes and placed them and my purse and totally abandoned it and left it on top of the hood of the car. I just started running toward the beach, like a kid with newly found discoveries of aventures. It was easy to be in awe of the ocean, within walking distance from the house, truly it was a beautiful site, incredible to behold. PJ may have thought I was crazed or just totally out of my mind. But he just let me go and be free honestly, I felt just like a child. Being in awe allowed me to be astonished by the beauty of his creation. I finally sat down, and gazed upon the expanse of waters, it was more of a divine experience. After a while the waters became very calm, filled with serenity, then a tranquil spirit came over me. I looked down at the ground and couldn't believe all of the different shapes and sizes of seashells that were lying in the sand which was nothing abnormal. They were so plentiful, I started picking them up one by one from the sand, putting them inside the pockets of my capris.

I looked over toward the beach house and saw PJ walking toward me, I was sitting on this huge rock moving my feet in the sand. When he walked up to join me as we starred out at the water, I had become still, into a deep meditation. I felt like I was in a trance or something. "It's beautiful isn't it?" I turned to him and looked right up at his face. "Beyond words." "May I sit with you." "Absolutely." I reached over and grabbed his hand, honey I'm sorry, I've got a true confession to make to you." "A true confession, huh! What might that be?" "Well, I'm a little embarrassed to tell you this, but when I saw the beach, I lost it." "Baby, you lost what?" "No, honey, I don't mean I actually lost something…to be honest with you, I've only been to the beach on one and half occassions…which really felt like half of a second, once it was too crowded during a holiday and another time it was promising rain when I was at a training convention. I know you could tell, truth be told, I was acting like a kid in a candy store." "No, I didn't think that Angell! Are you serious? So this is your first real experience, I had no idea!" "You don't mind that I'm sort of a beach virgin, do you?" He started to laugh a little. "Honey, I'm not kidding, look at all these seashells I collected." I stood up and took the seashells out of my pocket and threw them all up in the air. We both looked at each other and started laughing hysterically, I felt like a kid who had never gone on a summer vacation. "Baby come here." he grabbed me and pulled me in between his legs and said, "Look we're just in time to watch the sunset." Just as he spoke those words, oh my, the glory of the sun began to seek rest upon the expanse of the waters…it was one of the most beautiful sunsets. As the sunlight glowed across the deep you could see the most brilliant bright orange color that actually sparkled over the waters like an orange crystal reflection of light. I had never seen a sunset over the ocean before, I will never forget it, it was so magnificent, as the waves in the water bowed down to the sun the exist gave way to its splendor of what God's creation makes visible…it made you speachless PJ looked at me and said, "That was incredible!" "Yes, it really was." "That makes it all worth while doesn't it, baby?" Then he kissed me on the side of my face, oh…how I had longed for the warmth of his lips in a setting like this. "Honey, I have another confession." "And what would that be." "We'll, I was kind of nervous to come on this trip with you, this is my first trip out of town alone with a man, but I had to remember that this wasn't about just any man it was about my man. When you told me that you decided to go to the beach, the excitement of going on a trip with you to the beach was really something I had only dreamt about. I wanted to tell you how uncertain I was." "Uncertain about what, baby?" "I guess, because you've traveled half way around the world and have experienced all kinds of different places, things and even women. I know, I'm young and inexperienced, I'm 25 years old and I haven't done half as many things as you have, you're 30 and you've seen more in the past six years of your life than I'll probably see in my entire lifetime and I was'nt sure I could measure up." "Measure up to what, baby?" "Well, to what you're use to I guess. Sometimes for the life of me, I don't know what you see in me, you could have your pick of women around the world. I don't hold a candle to any of those type of women you've met or even been with. What can I give you besides the genuine love that I have for you?" He looked at me and said "That's all I want, give me you and I will have what no other woman can give me, you Angell! I only want you and nobody else, none of the well traveled, highly educated, career oriented or experienced women I've ever met or been with have ever made me happier than you do. You know, earlier today, I was on my way to the airport without you, a sudden emptiness came over me deep down inside. A part of me was missing without you, I didn't feel right, but my heart kept telling me, she loves you just as much as you love her; just trust your heart. You don't know how much I wanted you to show up... the moment I saw you on the plane, the part of me that was missing came back to life. I knew then, just how complete you make me feel when I'm with you, you fulfill my needs far beyond any physical need that I have ever encountered. You're right, I have been with several different types of women, but none of them hold a candle to you or the love we've found in each other. Angell, you are the candle that lights my fire. Its in your love that I find hope and in my true existence with you, I find all my hidden desires." "PJ you're making me all hott and bothered...now you got me melting inside like a candy bar." "Good, because I want to love you, take care of you, be there for you when you need me, I believe you were meant for me, in spite of what you think. I want to embellish you with my love and cherish the love we have together. You make my life whole and complete I've thought about this for a while now, Angell, I love you, and I want you to be my wife?" I couldn't believe what I was hearing, I looked at him and said, "Are you serious, you want me to be...your...wife?" "Yes I do. Angell, I have to admit, I was a little nervous to take this trip with you too. I felt that if you touched me the way you usually do, I was afraid of what I might desire to do not once but over and over again. I didn't want us to just end up in the bed, then all kinds of crazy thoughts about you were going back and forth inside my head. I didn't want what we had taken all this time to build together be destroyed by my hunger for wanting you, don't get me wrong I want to make love to you so bad I could taste the sweetness of it. But at the same time, I don't want it to take away from what we have, I want to marry you and make it right." "I know what you mean PJ, I want it to be right too, I desire your touch and your kisses make me crave you even more, but I didn't want what we had destroyed either. Your love for me is so incredible, it has been such a precious gift to me, I love you so much. You make my life complete too, without you I feel my heart aching into misery. I can't think, and I have to find a way to be with you, I had to come here with you this week end or I would have been miserable. When I got your message this morning, my heart ached for you even more and that fear I had of being with the man that I loved no matter what, totally left my body I wanted to be where ever you were. I began to trust myself and you and have faith in our love. I was no longer nervous about the trip, I became very bold, because of our love. Immediately, I went to my bosses office and asked for the rest of the afternoon off even before I was scheduled to leave. I left my assistant in charge of some pending projects I was working on. Then I left. I got my beauty thing on; then I went shopping you know me, I wanted to look cute and sexy and pleasing to you. When I got home I packed my bags took a long hot bath and got ready to head to the airport. All my life I believed that I would meet a man who would really love me and want me for me and really mean it. I knew in my heart that God would not let me down, I trusted him to work everything out. It makes a big difference when you allow God to work in your life. He will reveal himself to you and show you what he's truly all about and that is love." "He's all about sharing and exposing us to what his love truly is, in rare form."

PJ picked me up and cradled me in his arms, then kissed me tenderly on my lips while he walked with me in his arms down the seashore. "PJ stop you're going to drop me, come on put me down?" He didn't say a word, he just kept walking and kissing me gently on my lips, it was like we were under a magic spell or something, secretely I really didn't want him to put me down. The level of intimacy became so strong and intense, it captivated both of us, we felt a sense of joy fill up our hearts. The mood flowed between us in moments of time, my arms were around his shoulders caressing his arms. We were the only two people out on the beach that evening, as if God intended it that way. There wasn't one soul in sight, we were in unison with one another and the creator. The ocean was extremely beautiful, the water deep blue; instantly my eyes became a little glassy. He looked down at me and held me closer to him while he carried me in his arms all the way back to the beach house my stomach started growling. "Wooee, from the sounds of that outcry; we better get that tiger something to eat." "Hmmm, That's the best thing this tiger tummy has heard all day. I'm craving some huge jumbo scrimp, grilled or steamed with lots of garlic butter a giant baked potato and a salad with all the trimmings." "Honey do you think I can get away with no shoes on?" "For now baby, you can get away with anything by me." "Oooh, I like the sound of that." So I jumped in the car and he closed my door. When we got in the car, we found the greatest carryout place nearby, they had the most fabulous grilled lemon pepper scrimp drizzled in a tangy garlic butter sauce on skewers with and unlimited baked potatoe, with a tossed green salad. There were several types of greens, with cherry tomatoes, cucumbers, shredded carrots, sliced mushrooms, sweet onions, and black olives, with an delicious Italian Vinaigrette, topped off with homemade garlic buttered parmesian bread sticks. When we got back to the beach house with dinner, PJ had unloaded the bags we got from the market and put everything in its proper place in the refrigerator and on the table. He had placed the fruit in an exquisite crystal fruit bowl. It was a good idea to have fresh fruit in the house while we were there, it made it feel more like home.

As I took a look around the kitchen it was remarkable, filled with just about everything for our convenience, a toaster, refrigerator, a built in microwave and double oven and a built in grill and of course a huge bar complete with a blender to make unlimited smoothies. We took a tour around the house, and it was nothing short of the flair of the lifestyles that seperates the have's from the have not's. It had three bed rooms and three baths; it was charming. The living area had a double fireplace; there was an incredible deck out back with a jacuzzi, an outdoor grill. I could'nt wait to eat so we could enjoy the entire setting. I was starving, we finally finished our dinner, which was delicious. After dinner I wanted one of PJ famous frozen drinks. Immediately he got started and made us a blender full of his famous frozen drinks we turned on some music and got totally relaxed. I noticed the time; I couldn't believe it was ten o'clock; time had flown by, here we were getting our little weekend vacation get away on, at this gorgeous beach house. We both got a chance to completely unwind while we checked out the entire setting, talk about exquisite, it was like being in one of those vacation spots in a magazine, I couldn't believe that we were actually staying there for the weekend; very tastefully decorated. PJ told me that the travel agent informed him the decor was changed three times a year. I loved it, it made the trip all the more exciting, we were going to be there for 4 nights and 5 days. The master bedroom's bath had a round white marble oval shaped Jacuzzi. The name was written beautifully in calligraphy script on the wall outside and framed in a oval shaped antique framing the Jacuzzi outside on the deck was even more breath taking because there was a direct view of the beach with plants it was unbelievable...labeled perfectly to fit the occasion.

The Bath in The Middle of The Garden

It was so awesome. The second bedroom had a bath with a separate shower and the third was the regular combo, there were so many beautiful plants in each of the bathrooms. It was like being inside "The Garden of an Arboretum in any city." If you can go there and imagine with me the beauty it must have displayed. The master bedroom, was enormous with a plush love seat and two large incredibly luxurious chairs that you could sleep in for days. We both sat down and closed our eyes they were so comfortable, it was like we were in another world that neither one of us wanted to come back from. They each faced the patio allowing you to gaze through the inviting translucent drapes, which allowed you to view the most spectacular outlook of the beach. PJ pulled the drapes back and opened the doors to the patio then we walked outside and gazed out at the beach. We took a deep breath and stood there for a while. The furniture in the living room was just as embellished and refined, the dining room was just as pleasing to the eye. It really was breath taking, we were definitely in another world, we had every thing that you could dream of at our disposal in that beach house; including each other. I felt like I needed to change my name and address and move down to Crystal Beach and never return back to my former life.

PJ told me he wanted to run a hot bath in the bathroom, after we finished the tour of the house, he asked me to put on my swim suit and join him. That Jacuzzi was impressive but never had I seen an oval shape like this one, it was huge. I got so excited I changed, and unpacked the scented candles and my candle holders that I brought along for the trip. PJ fixed us another pitcher of smoothies, and melted some milk chocolate and took the strawberries dipped them and set them aside. Then we found some beautiful crystal goblets to place the strawberries in. We turned the lights off, and allowed the room to be illuminated by the candle light. The Jacuzzi was filled with hot bubbling water, it was so soothing and relaxing it gave our bodies just what we both needed. We drank our strawberry smoothies and feed each other those huge delicious chocolate dipped strawberries. After we relaxed, PJ started sharing some of his private thoughts with me, then he said something really strange to me I could hardly believe my ears. "Angell, he said," "What is it?" "You really look stunning in that swim suit," "Thank you, PJ," "I don't believe I've ever seen you in a swim suit before, that's funny." "What's funny?" "Can we have true confession?" "Always." I was so nervous while I was waiting for you to enter the room with your swim suit on. It seems odd, that we've been a part of each others life for well over six months and I've never seen your whole physique, especially in a tiny bikini, that looks mmm, mmm, good. I have to admit, I did imagine it several times, but my imagination could have never conceived of how incredibly gorgeous you really are and mmm, mmm, your body structure looks tasty and delicious. I have got to be the most blessed among men. Its been such an experience to be with someone that you really wanted, to know what it would be like to make love to; and at the same time how intriguing its been to not really know yet. I wanted to wait until the time permitted us both the right opportunity; not yielding to temptation has given me a lot of inner strength that I didn't know I would have, it introduced me to a level of patience that I needed to have confidence in loving you. No matter how much the desire of wanting you burned deep down inside me, I know I'm only human. I wanted to respect you because you were the first woman who I felt, was worth waiting for. You and I both wanted to see if we were compatible and worthy of each other's love. It was great to be able to go beyond communication, and just trust our instincts about creating the kind of love that we both wanted. I've never experienced this before, it's been amazing. Being in tuned with each other's love, was something that I always believed in and prayed for. Being able to talk to you about everything, learning to trust and be honest with you, has helped heal me from the person I use to be. Becoming the best of friends with out engaging into physical intercourse was never common for me. When people see us together they don't believe its true. You know what?" "What?" "That turns me on even more about you, because we stop ourselves from giving in. The self-control we have is scary to me sometimes, I mean being with you intimately, because I know deep down in side how much I want to make love to you right now. But by being in this relationship with you it has taught me that you don't just make love, you create it. I'm glad we found each other. When I first laid eyes on you, I could tell it seems like you had a spark in your eyes or something, that made me feel that I was going to fall in love with you. I just knew it deep down inside that you could be the one for me, it was the way you moved, the way you talked and walked. Instantly I wanted to be alone with you, just you and me." "Trust me baby the feeling was mutual, it looks like we both got our wish." "Yes, we did and then some. I want us to stay on this level if we can, I want it all, the totality of your intimacy when we become one. I want the innocence between us, to remain with us, until you have become my wife. Then he turned and got right in front of me, on both knees, and whispered in my ear, Angell, I want you to marry me next year on the first day of Spring? Say yes, I want to pledge my love to you right now?" As he spoke those words the door of my love opened up for him even more so, I couldn't believe what I was hearing. Tears begin to roll down from my eyes. "It's nothing more I would love, than to be married to you." This was something I'd been asking God for every since I could remember as a little girl. The emotions of passion filled up the bathroom, the long anticipated venture of long awaited love now existed. We shared the most incredible explosions of sweet intimacy and tender passionate kisses that night. The emotional closeness was so genuine for each of us. We chose to try to reframe from entertaining the thought of engaging in intercourse, there wasn't one question lingering on our mind. We both knew we were about to receive something much more rewarding than a feeling of erotic release. So we became emotionally satisfied with our kisses as the candles burned through each flame so did our love.

I was very assured, that I could wait for him as long as he wanted me to, and I knew that he wanted me and would wait for me. As the seasons in our lives turned there would be a time and a season for everything under the sunshine of our love. That was the most extraordinary night that I had ever spent with him...before it was genuine feelings, pure and full of innocent desire. (My thoughts drifted off, I couldn't believe I bought that tiny bikini, but I knew that it would really turn him on, so I took a chance and looks like it worked. Although I purchased three, two for his eyes only and one for being out in the open on the beach.) We caressed and touched as though it were for the first time. The heat from the water was so soothing; with our eyes closed we flowed together in unison; listening to the rhythm our love made. As my mind pondered, I began to feel a sense of honor given to me by a man who respected me and the request I made to God, that was beyond anything I could ever measure. PJ wanted to be with me while learning and discovering how we desired to love each other. My relationship with God was very dear to me, I had learned to respect and trust what we had and shared together. It was very unique and special. As I sat in the bubbling water with my eyes closed, tears started to fall from my eyes, and PJ leaned over to me and started kissing my tears away, then he kissed each one of my eye lids. I felt the intensity of passion that he had for me; we were both content that we both decided to intensify the love that we were creating, and build a stronger foundation for our future together. I wanted to spend the rest of my life enjoying him and making the best love that we could ever discover.

After the most tantalizing experience that I have ever experienced in a Jacuzzi, I felt exhilarated with a tenacious need to lay my body down and just rest in the safety net of his arms and go to sleep. I knew that I would treasure that whole encounter in my heart forever. After we got out of the Jacuzzi, he dried me off and suggested that we hand wash our suits and toss them in the dryer and get ready for bed. I took a quick refreshing shower to freshen up my body with some peppermint soap, it felt and looked like a wrinkled set of clothes. Finally I got dressed for bed, brushed my teeth, and put my hair up. When I came out he was praying, and looked as though he was finished, he looked up at me from his knelt down position and ask me to join him as he finished his prayer. I knelt down and listened as he spoke to God with thankfulness, immediatley I felt another level of closeness to him that I had never felt before. I hadn't ever had the pleasure of praying by his side before. He thanked God for me as an answer to his prayer to become his wife, and he prayed that our unity would be blessed. Then he presented me to God as his wife, I got a little emotional because I couldn't believe he did that. I really didn't know what to expect. I was honored for the respect he had for me and most of all the reverence he had given God. I loved him for being a man after God's own heart because he sure did have mine. After we finished our prayer he kissed me on my forehead and told me he was going to take him a shower, and wanted me to go ahead and go to bed and get some sleep. He told me he would join me a little later. My heart started beating a little fast.

While he was in the shower, I knelt down and thanked God in private and told him how much I loved him, for loving me and giving me to him as my husband. I finally got in the bed and started falling asleep, the bed, the sheets and the comforter were so comfortable and the pillows were just as wonderful. Once I got completely in that bed; I tried hard to stay awake for PJ but my eyes just kept closing in on me. That king size bed in the master bedroom suite made you feel as though you had gone straight to heaven. I was so relaxed that my mind, heart and spirit traveled to the land of infinity. I finally felt him come to bed, I felt the warmth of skin form right next to mine. His body was so well toned and his physique was in excellent condition, he seriously had it going on. I felt just like his queen, he treated me with such respect, he never tried to fondle me or make any sexual advances. When I woke up about 4:15 by the digital clock on the night stand, I turned over and saw him lying right there next to me, I kissed him gently on his lips then I turned all the way around and faced him, then I drifted back off to sleep. I heard him talking in his sleep a while later, I couldn't make out everything he was saying, but I heard him say the words trust and honesty. Then I thought and reminiced about what my grandmother used to say about people who talked in their sleep. She told me that lots of people commune with God in their sleep, if they are speaking and you get an opportunity to hear what they're saying and they do more than mumble they speak clear words that sometime describe the nature of their own character in the likeness of God himself. That person is truly blessed and the spirit of God and his angels hover over them as they sleep and slumber. I smiled at him with a warm feeling in my heart of my Grand Mamma, then I went back to sleep.

My eyes were barely opened around 7:00 in the morning, when I began to feel the covers next to me I noticed he wasn't in the bed. As my eyes began to focus, I raised up and looked around to be sure of my surrounding and that I was still at the beach house. I checked the time on the clock it read 7:05 a.m. I thought to myself where is he? Maybe he's in the bathroom or something. So I laid there trying to pick up where I left off in my dreams, then I noticed that the blinds were still drawn back from where we left them last night but the patio door was slightly opened as my eyes began to slightly close again I could still see and smell the ocean. Then finally, I caught a glimpse of him sitting outside on the patio soaking up that magnificient view of the ocean. As I drifted back off to the land of milk and honey; I could feel a gentle breeze that was very soothing to my skin. All I needed was a time capsule to capture each moment so I could take a piece of it back home with me. If only it could fit in my luggage my thoughts seem to drift away while they got tangled up and became even more ridiculous by the moment; finally I made it back tucked away in my own bed of oasis. The excitement of being in the lap of luxury just kept trying to wake me up. "No." I kept saying in a soft repetitive voice, finally yielding to my inner self I got up; after the bed had given me a superior plush hangover from that redicously comfortable mattress. I walked over toward the door of the patio, then I turned around toward that bed and had a "Terminator Movie Moment, when Arnold Schwarzenegger say's in that deep voice "I'll be back". I could have sworn the bed was expecting me to feel that way. I got up and walked to the bathroom and washed my face, brushed and flossed my teeth. Then I shook my hair and pulled it up in a ponytail. As I walked out onto the patio, PJ looked up at me and said, "Good Morning, baby, did you sleep as good as you look?" "So good that I just had a counseling session with that bed in there; I have to take me an afternoon nap, I may fall in love and become addicted to that bed." "You are silly, come here, I'd rather you become addicted to me instead." "Hmm that sounds deliciously tempting, I just bet you would, you keep that up and you'll both be running a tie, and we'll just have to use the bed to make our final decision." "Oooh, I don't know if I can handle a combo meal like that." He started laughing, then he said, "I'll give you a combo meal alright then he started chasing me all over the deck until he caught me. "Baby come take a quick walk with me to the beach?" "Let me just throw on something first." "Come on baby, don't worry about that, just take my shirt, I got on a T-shirt under this shirt." I threw my robe over the patio chair, then we walked toward the beach; he put his arms around me while we gazed out toward the sky watching the brillance of the sun rise to the occassion. As I looked across the extent of the ocean it was phenomenal as the waves seem to celebrate the light as it hovered over the waters. "God is so magnificent in all his splendor and glory which helps me understand why people love to bath under the rays of the sun, especially on the beach." "And why is that baby?" "Well its like bathing in the wamth of his love all over your body." "Hmm baby, that sounds kind of sensual." "Exactly, after the sun finishes, you receive an atonishing glow all over your body that no love on earth can give you " He looked at me in an incredible way, then he kissed me softly on my lips "that's what I love you about you." "What?" "Listening to your heart, how you rattle things off sometimes...I never know what to expect...Then he started to sing this song, entitled "You are so beautiful to me." He was so endearing, he always knew how to make me become more enchanted by his love for me. Afterwards he ask me if he could have a real good morning kiss. "Do you really need an answer?" I turned around towards him; we shared tender moments of morning sunrise kisses. He knelt down and got in a position for me to get on his back; when I got on board he carried me down the beach toward the beach house, then he began to spin me around like we were a couple of high school kids on Spring Break.

When we got back, we showered and went out for breakfast. We ate at a charming place out on the pier, where we sat and shared some very private thoughts about our future together, places that he wanted to take me, the places that he loved to travel to during certain seasons, and some of the different beaches that he had seen around the world. I was ready to go with him where ever he wanted to take me. We felt so free to talk to each other about each and everything, I loved it. My travels were very limited, but his were both extensive and fascinating. He had gone every where just about, except Germany, Australia, Brazil and The West Indies, just to name a few, his conversation always took my mind traveling on a journey into places I had only dreamt of, but I longed to see them with him. I loved how he could reach into my thoughts and elevate my mind. He told me he had a wonderful weekend planned for both of us and wanted us to enjoy every single minute. After we got back from breakfast we took a drive around and did a little shopping. We found one of the most exclusive little antique market; that had some lovely pieces. He purchased me some really nice things, and got some things for both our Moms, and even my sister and had it shipped to his house. He said if it weren't for my sister, we probably wouldn't have met the way we did. Which was very thoughtful of him, we got her something that she would adore for her house. Then we drove to the Galleria mall in Houston where he picked out a gorgeous dress that he wanted me to wear for dinner. On our way out we stopped by this very exquisite custom design jewerly store where PJ inquired about buying me this beautiful yellow diamond necklace to go with the gorgeous dress that he had just purchased for me. I felt like a fairy princess or something…fortunate and blessed. As we were leaving out, the jeweler inquired immediately about when the big day was…and straightway convinced us to take a look at some rings. Of course PJ encourged me to try some on; they were all gorgeous, but there were two that stood out; we both were drawn to one in particular it was one of the most exceptionally designed cuts that I had ever seen; that weighed in at 5 carats. I thought I was going to pass out with a need for resuscitation. Immediately I had excuse myself and walk out to get some air; I literally could not breathe; nothing had ever had that affect on me. PJ asked me if I was okay. I told him I was fine, just a little overwhelmed at the cost of his suggestions of generosity. Then he told me he would be right out he wanted to get me the the yellow diamond stud earrings to match my necklace. When I walked back into the store PJ handed me the bag with the diamond studs in them. "Sweetheart are you sure you're okay?" "Yes, I'm okay; I don't know what came over me. Baby you didn't have to spend so much on me." "I love you, sweetheart, money means nothing to me if I don't have you to spend it on. Besides, I want you to have nothing but the very best." "I have to admit that ring was breathtaking. I probably would have felt the same way if I were a woman it was worth everything to see that look in your eyes. I loved every moment." "It was incredible honey, the experience was priceless." "No baby, it's you, youre the one that's priceless. I love you so much." "I love you, too honey." Then he leaned over and kissed me right there in the jewelry store. The people in the store were so sweet they honored us with such excellent service. After we shopped, we went and picked up a few more groceries for the beach house, then we went home, to a place where people only dream of, a dwelling where not many people would ever even get a chance to travel to; but just knowing nothing is impossible is all that matters. When we got back we were exhausted from all the walking; we both decided to put everything away and take a short nap because we have gotten up so early that morning. We got comfortable and fell asleep, when we woke up it was early in the evening. I was grateful that we could really sleep together.

(There are many men and women who can not go to bed and sleep together unless they try to enter into a little recreational foreplay. People nowadays don't give each other a chance to really get to know each other and be friends. They get use to the each others bedtime manners and the thought of it becomes habitual. Its easy to get hooked on an addiction from a person's sexual abilities. When the gate of emotions are opened up, the mere thought of it can become addicting. After you encounter qualities you're looking for in bed the body will make you crave and yearn for that feeling over and over again. It's easy for your emotions to spiral out of control when you open yourself up to a person intimately, its not just your legs...your mind and your heart opens up too. It's like a head on collision when you stop receiving that level of satisfaction; like running out of love...sometimes you want to do whatever it takes to feed that need or desire. Sooner or later when you recognize the feelings are not mutual you end up with a broken heart or spirit. Getting close to someone else to replace that feeling to soon can backfire on the person that you use. The replacement has no idea that your're afraid to share that level of love and trust with them, because that previous addition is not so easy to let go. The heart, mind and soul needs time to heal. When you don't have a personal intimate relationship with God it makes it very difficult to heal and have a relationship with someone else.

A healthy relationship is not always easy to maintain, the upkeep is filled with hard work, dedication, consistency, loyalty, and faithfulness. The need to be on the same page and working toward the same goals is essential; if not it will be easy to loose interest in that person and awaken your curiosity to be aroused by a sudden desire from a perfect stranger. The desire will turn into a hot mouth-watering enticing love affair that can overtake you to engage in more than your mind or body can wrap itself around. The temptation is guaranteed to peak your couriosity; it can tempt you into getting tangled up into something much more than you bargained for. Whether you're in a relationship with someone you thought you cared about or if you're married the tempter will come. Knowing it may be a test of your character is one thing, or to see how strong your level of self control and perseverance is is quite another. It doesn't matter who's tempted the man or the woman, after a while if you're not caeful one or the other may yield for a short moment of pleasure yielding a lifetime of regret. It can happen at a very crucial time when you're both at vulnerable turn in your relationship or marriage, it can turn into a dangerous sinful hunger that won't ever completely satisfy your appetite.

There are many people in life who are addicted to something in their life, from prescription drugs to over the counters, head ache tables, to any controlled drug related substance, alcohol, beer, cigars, cigarettes, even over eating, to too much meat, sweets, ice cream, chocolate candy, or just plain junk food, to the television, the computer, the telephone, the cell phone, to texting or sexting, to any obsession, to the doctor, a job, a counselor, spending too much money, or gambling money, to sexual promiscuity, to having an affair with someone else's spouse or a friend's lover, having more than one lover, to cars, trucks, boats, clothing, even weight loss and crash diets or wanting to be too thin from anorexia. Lets face it, people in our society love things vehemently like flames of fire behind their hidden desires, which leaves their passions burning deep down inside their being. Some loose their life because of any one of these different kinds of addictions. If it were more people addicted to God, in a healthy spiritual manner, we wouldn't suffer so much loss financially, because when you think about it...all of these things cost money, he doesn't cost us one dime all he requires is that we spend time learning how to get to know him, ultimately there is a cost when we give our all to him. His love is free just as Salvation is free. Man is the one who charges us the fee for everything under the sun. When we pay our tithes we have to understand that when we freely give God our 10% it in turn allows him to protect the other 90%. In doing this, it allows us to develop a deeply rooted relationship with God which is what he desires for us to do, being addicted to him, not to all the things that the world has to offer us. We've probably all experienced some type of addiction in our own personal lives or someone we know or love is going through an addiction right now. When people have been over taken by certain addictions they don't realize that they are wrestling with, the principalities, and the rulers of darkness, those are the ones who become overtaken by what they believe in and end up in the news with a life that's no more in existence. They are over taken by a belief which can be strong enough to kill or destroy them or anything they have, we have to learn to be more careful. God is a loving God, he is love he would not ask us to take our lives or commit suicide, he gives us the breath of life, he can give life and take it away. We have to be careful for nothing, and learn to trust him through all things. He doesn't want us to condemn each other, judge not that ye be not judged...in life there will always be someone that we know who are struggling with some type of addiction on a daily basis. There will come a day in many of our lives when these addictions will pass away they will not be part of our lives, because the former things can and will as we know them pass away. The word addiction can be placed on a spiritual level and turned into being addicted to love for God; not to a religion, or a particular church or its prominent leaders. The greatest commandment in the word of God is...for us to...Love the lord your God...with all your heart, soul, mind and strength. Because it doesn't matter where you go to worship...as far as the building is concerned, he wants us to feed, and to assemble ourselves among other believers because it gives us strength. We must know that the building up of our faith comes by hearing and hearing by the word of God. What matters is that we learn how easy it is to develop a relationship with God, as we honor him and keep his laws we will find the most precious gift of all and that's his love; which covers and protects us with his loving favor.)

My Soul Mate
would be the one who was chosen specifically for me, the one who could reach down inside my heart and create an explosion of love inside my spirit....

Later, that afternoon we got up from resting and decided to get out for the day. The day was filled with lots of merriment, exhilaration, and feelings of our oneness. We laid in the sun, went horseback riding on the beach, played in the water, then we just had to take on a childist fetish by building a sand castle. I couldn't believe what we came up with, we were both very creative, I must admit after all the oohs and aahs from the other people who were out on the beach; we must have done pretty good. Afterwards we let them stand and trusted that the waves would reach the shore by sundown and wash all our sand piped dreams away. The waves were incredible as they washed across the shore, we chased the waves and took advantage of the water. Before we knew it, the sun was setting and nightfall would soon be upon us, we headed in cleaned our body of all the sand. We decided to stay in and fix a home cooked meal in that phenominal kitchen; we took advantage of everything in the kitchen that only chef's dreams are made of. The deep fryer conjured us up some "Cajun Styled Butterfly Scrimp" spiced up with a few Blacken Filets topped off with some homemade potatoe chips. Dinner smelled delicious; we made a great team in the kitchen together. We listened to some music and ate our dinner by candle light out on the patio; we had the most extraordinary view of the ocean, the mood was commendable and mellow. We didn't talk much, we listened to the music as we ate. We had one of those, he looked at me while I looked at him moments; afterwards PJ asked me to dance we had a great time. While we were out on the patio we sat in those comfortable lounge chairs for a while before we knew it, hours had been spent watching the waters in the ocean as we continued to listen to more music it was great to just sit and do nothing but relax.

The next morning, we got up and had some fresh squeezed orange juice, fresh blueberries, french toast and a delicious cup of coffee. After breakfast we took another drive back to Houston, PJ told me he wanted me to meet his cousin Jacquelyn and her husband Bernard he said they were both more like his sister and brother. He and his cousin were very close and he admired and respected her husband a great deal. We were scheduled to hang out with them and have dinner at their home. They owned a Boutique of Elegant Wear at the Apparel Mart near the Galleria; filled with some of the most gorgeous accessories from all over the world. They had one of the most exquisite arrays of elegant clothing lines and sportswear for the ritzy lifestyles their clientale included all types of celebrities, entertainers, to the high profile ball players, executives and professionals. Their shop was one of the most sought after clothing specialty boutiques at the Apparel Mart. After meeting them I could tell right away that, Bernard and Jacquelyn seem to be happily married and still very much in love for well over ten years. PJ had expressed to me early on how easy they made marriage look; plus they both obviously enjoyed working together. They told me how much they loved the apparel business, and had just made it back in town from one of the hottest shows in New York that morning; they said they had to get back because they were expecting Jon Paul's arrival and were looking forward to meeting me. They were very well dressed for an early Saturday afternoon, although they were casually adorned, with such grand taste. Judging by all the sensational apparel, and the pricetags in their Boutique it was no mystery that they really had it going on. It was apparent that there were no knock offs in their store only originals with price tags to prove it. One of their esteemed customers came in and purchased several garments and a few handbags, a pair of "to die for" stellidos and the accessories to make it all happen for a formal affair; walked out spending over eight thousand dollars in less than thirty minutes. Their eye for detail was very impressive; they had impeccable taste for the finer things in a girls closet...they certainly had lots of head turners and trust me once you walked in there shop, you encountered a lot of "I've got to have this!" You know those aha moments, like the American Express slogan; you can't leave home without it or you shouldn't dare try to come waltzing into their showroom without knowing that temptation was at its highest peak; so you better bring the credit, the debit or some cold hard cash.

PJ introduced me as the woman he was going to spend the rest of his life with; he was so excited and so was I, then PJ called Bernard to the side, and whispered something in his ear. Jacquelyn and I thought they were being extremely rude. Then Bernard told Jacquelyn that he would tell her about it later. Then he kissed her on her a few times on her cheek, she blushed immediatly, and told him she didn't believe it would be necessary because she and I would have our own little secrets too. We were scheduled to have dinner with them at their home, but they told us they had made reservations on this Yacht for dinner, that sailed out into the ocean. The name of the Yacht was "The Astonishing". Which came about after the owner met his wife, she attended the first dinner party that he hosted on his yacht, which to him was one of the most astonishing things to happen to him after meeting her her. It was extraordinary because his Father told him that the moment he opened the yacht as a Dinner Cruise that he would meet her. I had never been on a Yacht before, I was ecstatic the dress attire was formal. I was honored that PJ wanted me to wear something exquisite for dinner from his cousin's boutique; I thought we had already purchased what I would wear. But, PJ had other ideas, I watched him as he strolled around the boutique as if he knew exactly what he wanted on my body. I felt like the most precious treasure my heart skipped beat after beat. He came up with two different gowns that he and Jaqueline both approved, after looking at a few of the price tags I decided I better sit down and try on a few pair of to die for shoes that kept talking to me from the show room. Because the prices that I would pay no longer existed.....folks. Jaqueline handed me PJ's choices and I tried hard not to look at the price tags, so I didn't make it obvious. I would just do it with class, you know while I was in the dressing room as I got undressed, I could barely believe my eyes I thought I was going to have a minor heart attack when I glanced down at the black tag a huge smile came across my face; as he held up both dresses I remembered that look on his face when he looked at this gorgeous black silk dress with these beautiful sparkling yellow diamond rhinestones on the straps with the most elegant black chiffon wrap and the shoes were made for nothing but a "Red Carpet Affair." Of course I had to save the best for last; so I tried on this stunning hot pink number; that had my unamious vote; it had a low V in the back and front V that stopped just where it needed to; the hot pink silletos said exactly what they needed to say to stop all traffic or conversations going on in any room. As I walked out of the dressing area; PJ just starred as if he had forgotten my name. He was speechless he told Jacqueline that he would take all of it and he defininately wanted the woman who was wearing it. He was so silly; he asked me to turn around at least three times so he could watch every curve on my body move in slow motion. "Come on now, this all belongs to you, you know! It is definitely an attention getting dress Jacqueline and the shoes are doing exactly what they need to do for me right now and it looks like its doing a number on my man over there." "Work it Angell, work it! Bernard yelled out." "Come on baby, you either have to take the dress and shoes off, or somebody may have to call 911 and arrest me tonight, baby. Because I'm about to be a moving violation." "Thank you, for the compliments, I don't think 911 will be necessary for this little number; let me change into what could really get you arrested. So I hurried back to change into the hottest black dress I had ever seen, it was a perfect fit, I decided to pull my hair up and use this gorgeous hair pin with yellow rindstones; that I found before I walked into the dressing room. When I came out of the dressing room he was standing there with his wallet in his hand; then he dropped his wallet and he knelt down at my feet and said, "Baby I've just got to have you, here's my wallet you can have my money, my credit cards, my debit card, my car, my house, my everything, just take me with you where ever you're walking or going." I was so embarrassed he could be so silly. Then he kissed me from my ankle up to my leg and then on my arm I felt like Martisha from one of the old comedy shows, called The Adams Family, as she was being overwhelmed by the kisses from her husband Gomez, it was getting very warm in the boutique. He got up and whirled me around in his arms and kissed me, we couldn't even control the passion we felt. We finally came up for air and Bernard and Jacqueline just stood there shaking their heads and clapping their hands. Bernard said, "Bravo, Bravo, Listen Jacqueline maybe you need to try on one of those black dresses over here and let me see if it has the same affect on me." Jacqueline said, "No darling, I don't need to do no such thing, we just got back to work after spending quite a bit of time together in between shows while we were in New York I think we shared quite a bit of excitement this week, don't you? We need to stay focused and take a range check a little later, I'm sure we can come up with something creative. They smiled at each other and told us what a nice couple we made and how they could see why PJ felt the way he did about me. After our intimate public performance; PJ purchased everything I tried on; I loved the fact that they had black tags with white letters instead of the traditional white tags. Her merchandise came from one of New York's finest emporiums. PJ also purchased a very classy black suit and some other items that he wouldn't disclose; he made a few remarks to Bernard and couldn't stop cheezing. We told Bernard and Jacqueline thank you and that I couldn't wait to see them later for dinner.

What an incredible day I was so excited; I felt so fortunate. I can't even describe the feeling that rested inside my soul to share moments of love that the heart longs for. While we were on our way back to the beach house all I could do was hold his hand and thank God for his grace that he would be mindful of little old me; to allow me to trust, love and be free to be me. This man seem to be too good to be true; but he had his shortcomings and so did I and we both weren't afraid to admit them to each other. I've learned so much about communication with him, we didn't always talk all the time sometimes being with someone that you could love in silence was just as golden and don't get me wrong we did have our disagreements at times, but we had the kind of chemistry that kept us in touch with each other. We spoke with our eyes many times and the vision of his love opened up the window to my soul. The feeling was something that I would treasure the rest of my life; if I never saw him again I would never forget his love, it was genuine, honest and real. My heart reflected on how much God must love us; when we truly give our heart, mind, soul and spirit to him. We are then transformed to receive exactly what he has set forward for our path to cross in our lives. You hear this all the time as you travel in life "Everything happens for a Reason" and it's true; everything does happen for a reason in its due season. Timing is very important in every aspect our our lives; being patient as we endure the many obstacles, hardships and even misfortunes in our lives gives us strength to move forward to receive the prayers and promises that await us to be answered at His will not ours. However, many times his will is revealed but we become afraid of the timing when we don't feel were ready, or we don't feel financially stable, or we find some excuse not to accept that divinely appointed time for love to come into our lives. Many people follow their heart and receive everthing that was predestined for their lives; and those who procrastinate waiting on sign, after sign, after sign; find themselves alone trying to connect the pieces; by the time they become too broken to put together, it's too late and one person or the other moves on and many times finds someone else. Carrying with them the love that was between them when they met someone else.

Good Things Come to Those Who Wait!!!

When we got back to the Beach House we had just enough time to shower and get dressed. Our reservations were at 7:00; when we arrived to the Yacht the entrance was remarkable. The dinning room was so elegant, there was a beautiful ivory grand piano playing softly at the entrance. Everyone on board were dressed for the occasion. I felt like a precious jewel out in the middle of the ocean with PJ, he treated me like I was the only woman in the room. Shimmering crystal chandeliers sparkled all over the room, the tables were dressed gorgeously set for four with beautiful crystal goblets with the finest china and silverware, wow I thought to myself now this is way over the top of elegance. The yacht was tastefully decorated throughout the corridors of the room, with nothing but sentiments in everyones eyes to remember. There were no prices listed on the menu which meant priceless if you had to ask you were boarded on the wrong side of money.

While we were sitting there PJ's phone rang Bernard and Jacqueline had been detained by one of their high end clients; they sent their love and asked if we could have a rang check. They invited us to come by their home on Sunday; after all they were exhausted from their trip from New York. PJ expressed that we understood and how we looked forward to seeing them on Sunday and told them to get some rest; we were not on any schedules so we'll just show up some time later tomorrow if that was okay; then he looked over at me and asked if that was okay and I said of course. Afterwards, he motioned our waitress and told her that our guest would not be able to join us, immediately they moved us to a table for two with the perfect scenery. "Jon, I love this table the view is so tranquil and private." "You're right it has a serene feel about it, I love you baby, you look just like the name of this yacht, Astonishing." "Thank you sweetheart, I love you too, you look just as handsome." Then a sudden sadness came over me. It wouldn't go away, I tried hard not to let it show on my face, but PJ could sense something was bothering me. Although I kept smiling at him, he said, "Baby what's the matter, I know there's something wrong, What is it?" "No, nothing really," I said. "Are you sure, baby?" "Yes, I'm sure Jon." "Well, why don't we go ahead and order something to drink and our appetizer I'm sure you're starving." "Yes, I am." Afterwards we can go ahead and order something delicious for dinner, immediately our waitress came and he ordered for us. We ordered cocktails and mushrooms stuffed with crab with grilled citrus scallops and a very delicious cold pinapple and coconut soup, served with silver dollar shaped buttered bread which was so light it melted right in your mouth. For dinner we order the flamed lobster with an incredible garlic sauce, beautifully adorned vegetables with all the drippings and fixings.

Deep down in my heart all I could think about was the fact that we would be leaving soon, in the middle of this wonderful dinner. All of a sudden a real sick feeling was in the pit of my tummy, butterflies were flying all around and having a party inside my tummy. PJ just kept starring at me, and said," Angell are you OK? " Honey, I'm fine, being here with you this weekend has been...so...I can't even describe it, I guess I'm not ready for it to end, that's all". "Baby, I understand," then he moved over closer to me and placed my hand in his, and said, "You know baby, I've been thinking the same thing." You know we really have had an amazing time together. I'm so thankful that we decided to wait until we really got to know each other before we went away together on a trip. Those first ninety days with you in my life, was so much more than I expected; I thought it would be hard, but you made them so easy for me to learn how to love and respect you. You know when we reached that one hundredth day of being faithful and committed to each other we became closer. It made me feel like a king, patiently waiting for my queen with self-satisfaction and patience. Now I understand what being equally yoked is all about. You are a part of my yoke and you've made me feel like no other woman that I've ever met, and

I want you to have something and it goes with that key I gave you when I first met you. Do you still have the key I gave you, Angell? "Yes, I do". "That's what I want you to say 6 months from now, those exact words." "With nothing but pleasure baby, I can not wait." Then he handed me this lovely black silk handkerchief with a pretty red string tied around it. As I opened the handkerchief, I noticed a delicate round crystal, the crystal was very frail all I could think of was, this is the most unique Lalique Crystal is this something to put his key in, what is this is it something else in this circle. Then tears started rolling down my face, because in that precious round crystal was an inscription on it that said, "You Hold The Key To My Heart." I looked at the circle and I said, "honey what a beautiful crystal," then he said, "Go ahead baby, it opens right there do you see it, in the middle?" "Oh I see it, right here, how cleaver." When I opened it and there was the most incredible designed yellow diamond platinum ring, it was magnificent. "Oh my God, Jon, it's gorgeous." Then the tear drops started to fall, I could not believe it; this was like a dream come true, I was in a trance because no one had ever given me a diamond ring before in my life. I had always read about stuff like this happening to people in movies, books, or magazines. I was totally overwhelmed, he got up from our dinner table and walked over to my side of the table then he removed the ring from the crystal case, got down on one knee, and very romantically ask me to marry him? I was very surprised, by his proposal he totally caught me off guard. There were people around us who actually stared in awe and yelled out congratulations. I was touched by his spontaneity, he loved to surprise me, I was totally captivated by his love.

The Astonishing Proposal of Marriage

(As he placed the ring on my finger he spoke these words to me)
Angell, I want to marry you on the first day of Spring
When all things become new,
I want my love to be pledged only to you,
You are as precious to me as the splendor of New Beginnings.
(Then he kissed me on my lips and whispered softly to me these words...)
"You are my precious flower, I promise to love and treasure each petal...
If you can love me until death parts us, I promise to share the brillance
Of sunshine and showers of blessings with you all the days of our lives,
In the hope that it would enhance the beauty of our love.
"Will you marry me, Angell DiVine Summers?
"Yes, Jon Paul Morgan, I will".

We sealed the proposal with sweet tender kisses, he kissed my hand and he got up off his knees. Our waiter brought us a complimentary bottle of champagne; the tears finally stopped, we were in such an elite atmosphere, I had to get a hold of myself and remember where we were. Deep down inside I just wanted to grab him and hold him close to me and never let him go. Jon Paul was something else, I had no idea he was going to propose to me, he has always astonished me; he had such a serious demeanor, which made it hard to tell when he would amaze me. All this time, I thought we were just having dinner on this yacht, he really built it up and made it seem like he wanted me to experience this kind of atmosphere with him; he even included Bernard and Jacqueline. I could not believe it, I was delighted and totally overwhelmed; because he was such a romantic. Deep down inside, I believe every woman loves to be romanced whether they admit it or not. Jon Paul was a man after my own heart, he was charming inside and out, attractive, intelligent, noble, honest, and trustworthy. He had integrity and walked with the spirit of authority with a very inviting spirit. When he walked into a room, his aura was very captivating. I noticed that people seem to welcomed him, where ever we went, he was very cordial to them with a sense of benevolence. I could not believe that my God thought so much of me, to send me a man like this. Finally our dessert arrived with a bottle of champagne we were told that it was complements from the owner; the yatch was famous for this incredible white chocolate brownie explosion drizzing with a beautiful strawberry sauce topped with finely chopped walnuts and fresh strawberries. It was delicious but not as delectable as PJ's lips looked to me, at one point I had to pull him over closer to me just to touch him. Then I started to caress his face I had to contain myself, and I said, "I love you, so much." "And I you, baby." I could hardly eat and look at him because I was so overwhelmed by the food, atmosphere, and don't forget the sparkles blinging from my finger had me tingling all over. We finally finished off our dinner and our waiter came over and opened the bottle of champagne. We sat at our table for a while and sipped the champagne, I couldn't really drink that much because it always makes me feel a little out of sorts, but for this ocassion I had indulge just a little.

I asked PJ if we could go outside on the deck and get some fresh air, PJ signaled our waiter and took care of the bill but to our surprise the owner and his wife were on board and sent word that our bill was taken care of. We were so grateful; PJ left our waitress a very nice tip and we went up to the deck and watched the waves in the water as the yacht sailed back across the ocean he put his arms around me and asked me if I was okay. I told him I didn't think I could get any better. Although champagne makes me a little fuzzy, I just needed him to hold me closer to him. He held me a little closer and he told me that I had made him one of the happiest men on the face of the earth. "Dinner was totally over the top Jon, thank you for making it so special tonight." "You deserved it." We both stared out at the water it was a full moon that night; and the mere radiance of the moon made it so complete. I looked down at my finger and became amazed all over again, then a feeling came over me, I wanted to give myself to him over and over again right there on the yacht. It was the most marvelous night filled with sure delight and aspiration; I had never experienced anything quite like this. Being able to relax and free to enjoy each others company was more than I ever dreamed of. The night was filled and complete with the devotion of our desire to be content and affectionate toward each other.

The fantasy was over, the proposal, the long anticipated dinner cruise, as we left the magnificent Yacht called "Astonishing" the owner walked out on deck and greeted us along with his beautiful wife which made the evening so complete. They congradulated us and we expressed our gratitude and shared how much we enjoyed such a lovely unforgettable experience. Then we drove back to the beach house, we couldn't keep our hands or our eyes off each other. When we got back to the beach house, we turned on some music and went out on the patio and danced under the moon light with our evening clothes on. We finally went back inside and I noticed there was a box on the bed, that said, "open this if you love me." I turned around and looked for him as he was going into the bathroom; I opened it and it was a stunning red silk nightgown with a gorgeous robe and matching underwear. It was a beautiful set, it was soft and elegant, I thought this looks like the lingerie I admired earlier, at the boutique, but how on earth did he have time to buy it and lay it on the bed without me noticing. He was just full of surprises tonight; I never knew what to expect from him, my emotions started stirring back inside my head and my heart. Because I had never ever met a man who had everything executed so well, he could really move me. His timing was impeccable, which made me love him even more. He was always doing something very unique to surprise me. The gown was impressive, I dropped down to my knees, to praise and thank God. Everything was happening so quickly, I wanted God to know that I would not ever forget about how much I loved him, no matter what was going on in my life. I wanted to ask his permission for what ever might transpire tonight, I knew what I wanted to do and I just wanted to acknowledge him and pray. I thanked him for such a wonderful courtship that only he could have joined together the way he did. I expressed to him, how much I loved PJ, and I prayed that he would lead us into a strong foundation of love and unity being equally yoked in our mind, heart, soul and spirit. Then I asked him to bless our union and I prayed that he would always be with us, guide us, direct us, and teach us to do what was right, just and fair for each other and others. I told him that I was so grateful that he allowed us to spend this special time alone together as we celebrated more than six months of getting to know each other, and finally just being in love, without me breaking the vow I made to him. Knowing that we both realized the importance of our relationship, finding someone special in our life that He had chosen for us was even more important. I told him that I had never met a man like Jon Paul who respected me in the manner that I always wanted to be respected and I was so thankful.

I was just about to get up off my knees, because I can really get carried away when I am intimately talking to God, and besides I was talking awfully loud, I opened my eyes and looked around and he was standing there in the doorway just listening to my every word. Then a smile came across his face which made him lean down to where I was kneeling and he kissed my hand and he lifted me up off the floor. I looked at him and I said, "thank you for being you, and for making the past three days so special." He kissed me gently on the lips, and said, "you deserved all of it," "Honey thanks for the gown, you know me so well, what I like and what I will adore, and what turns you on." Then he said, why don't you go and freshen up. "Thanks again for everything." When I got out of the shower, I dried off and I tried the gown on and I asked him to close his eyes while I came out to model it for him. I asked him to turn on some music, then I told him to open his eyes, I had on the high heel shoes he bought me and I got whistles, and a standing ovation with lots of bravo's behind the ovations. "You are so crazy," he loved the way the gown looked on me, then he came over and picked me up and layed me down gently on the bed, then he begin to draw the gown on my body, brushing his fingertips like the wind of a feather. My guards were already blown away by the grenades for his love, exploding all over the place. It wouldn't take much more for me, I knew that, he didn't need to do anything else that night my composure was about to be lost to explode all over him.

I told him I had a special surprise for him and I wanted him to give me a few minutes; immediately I decided to use a little reverse woman psychology, I went into the bathroom to pull out my bag of desire tricks just for him. I bought a bottle of scented massage oil with me from home. I went into the kitchen to heat the oil up. Then I lit some scented candles all over the bedroom. I took the handkerchief out of my purse and I scented the ends where I would tie it. Then I went over to the bed and I told him I was going to cover his eyes with a blind fold I fanned it in front of his nose first, then he began to tell me how sexy it smelled. He starting smiling and said, "Ooh I like this game," I said, "Oh I just bet you do." Baby, you sure smell good, what is that scent your wearing?" "Something hot and very sexy especially for you." Then he really got excited, and tried to reach for me with the blind fold on. "No, No, No, not just yet, turn over on your stomach PJ." "What?" you heard me, "okay baby I'm turning over, here I go." So I went quickly to the kitchen to get the massage oil, when I got back the scent of the candles had just started to permeate the air. I leaned over and told him first he would feel something wet and juicy, then he would feel something hot and sensual, then he would feel total relaxation as if he had been taken on a trip out of this world to mine. I whispered in his ear, okay baby, here goes, wet and juicy...then I kissed him straight down the spine of his back. All he could do was moan and groan, then I walked around and kissed him on his lips very softly as I began to drizzle the warm oil on his shoulders caressing and massaging them very intensely, then I leaned beside him and squeezed oil down his back, his reflexes jumped a little; but it was only the beginning of a massage guaranteed to totally relax every part of his body. Then I heard him moan just a little as his body became more and more calm, yielding to my every touch. The music was still playing in the background and I kept the motions of the massage in sync with the music. I knew it would take his mind off his hidden desires, no matter how strong he said he was. Cravings are hard to put to bed, literally speaking, they can overwhelm you, hunt you down and overtake you. I wanted to give it all up, to no one else in this world but him, but before I knew it, I heard the sound of relief as he snored I removed the blindfold very carefully then I finally laid down next to him he was sounded asleep. As I began to drift off to sleep, I placed the ring back on my finger, all I could feel were his arms reach over to hold me closer to him. As I moved closer to him I looked down at my ring again, I could not believe how beautiful it was under the candle lights. I laid there in total amazement and thankfulness then I heard him say how beautiful the ring was on my finger and that I needed to remember that he would never ask me to do anything I didn't want to do. "I know you're nervous Angell, and I know what you tried to do tonight by taking my mind off of wanting you but nothing will work until he can truly feel his love inside mine. I want to make love to you, and I promise not to ever hurt you. Nothing or no one can stop me from marrying you except you, if you decide you don't want me the hardest thing in this world for me to do; would be to move on, but I will. I don't think I would ever find another woman that makes me feel the way you do; you are a rare find which is why I wanted the diamond in your ring to be unique just like you. It's not just about sex, it never has been with me and you, but like I said a few minutes ago I want you and I want be totally satisfied until I have you. The choice is yours if you go all the way with me tonight you'll make me the happiest man on the face of this earth; and if you don't I want love you any less. Always remember that I love you baby, and I plan to share the rest of my life making you happy by showing you how much I love and care about you. Tears begin to fall down my face as I leaned over and whispered how much I loved him too, then I began to kiss him softly and very passionately on his lips. As we shared the most enchanted night captured by the essence of our love. I never thought I could feel what I felt for any man; he held me with such love and intensity. My body felt as if it were created for his hands to caress me, my lips felt as if they were meant to be kissed by his. As our love melted inside each others the sweet sensation of true pleasure entered the room. All I could do was whisper his name over and over again, as he whispered mine. The love we created was more than captivating; it was something that we would always treasure in depfhts of our soul. I didn't think my heart would ever stop racing; finally he turned me over and placed my head gently on a pillow then he rested his head on my heart. He kissed the spot where it was beating and said please don't ever leave me, keep me inside you. Tears begin to fall again from my eyes as I closed them; I asked God not to ever let us loose sight of the love we both felt in our hearts for each other. As I ran my fingers through his hair and caressed his face and we both began to drift off to sleep. It was the most amazing days that I've ever experienced my heart was overwhelmed yet totally complete. All I could dream of was that moment; seeing him knelt down before me kissing my hand as he prepared to ask me for my hand in marriage. I loved him so much, and finally being able to touch and hold him and even becoming his wife in less than a year was going to be unbelievable. All I could do was thank

God subconsciously even in my sleep, for being who he was in my life after waiting for so long but trusting that he was going to honor my request in prayer. Keeping myself for this moment felt reassuring because I believed its much easier for a woman than it is for a man. Unless he is a man of the cloth, with an established covenant to God and himself. A woman can go much longer than a man, we were equipped with the stamina to handle the endurance. But a man will do what he feels he has to do, to fill that void of emptiness when his needs are not met in time, if we're not careful it's so easy to loose everthing that you've built over your own principles. Which we must use an extreme sense of wisdom, knowledge and understanding when it comes to every aspect of sustaining the relationship. We can not leave it up to one person or the other; it takes two to make it work, after God has made it all possible. It's a whole different feeling when a man wants to obtain a license to love and honor you; the ring signifies that he is serious about the love you share and letting you know that he has a plan to take the time to set the time and date to get it done and make it legal, shows you the initiative, that he is very serious and sincere; and that you are his final decision.

When I finally woke up PJ, was watching me sleep he was looking at the ring on my finger. It felt so mystical to even wake up to see the ring still there as it glistened under the nights light. "Hey baby, I know you're probably sleep, but I woke up wanting you all over again, then I rememered that we didn't have a chance to thank God for each other. Do you mind if we say a prayer together and just thank him. We said our prayer and we both got a little emotional, he spoke to God first and then he gave me time to speak. At that moment we both became moved by the whole encounter, it was hard for us to contain ourselves while we held hands. After our prayer we held each other for a long time while we were on the floor, it was real different for both of us which made it even more special. It was Sunday morning, the day of departure we decided to leave a day early so we could get back and rest a full day before getting back to work. Our trip was filled with a week-end of enchanted love and a lifetime of memories, prayers, and dreams that came true. I was now engaged to marry my friend, a man of God, and I pray that we will live up to the vows that a husband and wife should honor. A covenant of honesty, commitment, respect, and trust need to be able to endure in our marriage, through out all the tests that times will bring. When we finally got up and got dressed, he looked at me and said, "I love God for making it possible for our paths cross. The first time I saw you, I could tell the moment I looked in your eyes. The fact that we followed our heart, without questioning why we were being guided to each other. You know Angell, you intrigued me by all the memories of when we first discovered the chemistry that we felt for each other that turned into an amazing love." "Well PJ, I love you because you always remember the little things. The fact that you are not afraid to speak to me about anything makes me even more excited to be in love you." "Angell do you know I used to think I was strange, because of my faith and the way that I believed and worshipped God, morning, noon, and night. But when I started to seek him on a regular basis, he began to show me more of him in so many ways. I really wanted him to send me someone so special to him that she would understand how much I loved him and that she would feel the same in her own way. I never dreamed how much I would be fulfilled when I found you, but I'm so grateful, and satisfied. And you know what, finally getting a chance to really spend some real quality time alone with you has made me feel something inside my soul that I've never felt; total satisfaction. Thank you. My mind has changed about how a man and woman should love each other; making love to a woman has also changed in my mind and heart. Making and creating love is more intriguing, more intimate, and more meaningful to me now. I love you so much and I pray that nothing will ever come between us, Angell." "That goes without saying, I can tolerate anything except unfaithfulness; the hardest thing for me to do is live with something like that whether it's before or after we get married. Six months is a long time and I really would like to know if you think you can handle a vow of celibacy until we cross the finish line." He turned around with this look in his eyes, then he said okay, what you don't think I can handle it?" "No I didn't say that, I would just like the intrigue and excitement to build up all over again." "I'll do it on one condition;" then he whispered some very erotic things in my ear that made my whole body tingle. That one condition was simply mind-blowing; as soon as we agreed to it; his touch seem to overwhelm me all over again, and mine seem to highten his sense of awareness with the most astonishing level of fulfillment. Oh God how I loved this man, he knew just how to touch me, which makes all the difference in the world.

Finally it was time to leave, the memories would be forever cherished. "Let's get going Angell, remember we were invited to stop by Bernard and Jacquline's; do you want to take one more stroll on the beach before we leave?" "Yes, honey I would love that!" "Tell you what let's get everything loaded up in the car first, after we finish our walk we can head out." "Sounds like a plan." We did exactly that, we walked for a while and took some more pictures, then we came back to the beach house and headed back into Houston, Bernard and Jacquline didn't live far from the airport which make it even easier. We had a late flight out all we had to do was turn in the car. We held hands all the way; you would have thought we had already gotten married. When we got to their house they both could'nt wait to see the ring; both Jacqueline and Bernard wanted to hear all the details, so I had to spill the beans and tell it like only I could tell it. They told me they already knew what PJ plans were, which was what he whispered to Bernard when we arrived at the boutique they played it off really well by telling me we were all having dinner on the yacht together. I must admit PJ planned that part to the maxx. We had a very nice time, I throughly enjoyed their company. They ooh and aaahhhed all over my ring and we let them know when we were planning to get married. Jacqueline told me she could help me find a dress as well as anything else to do with wedding attire. She gave me several of her business cards and I gave her mine. When we got ready to leave, we gave them both a hug and left for the airport.

When we arrived at the airport everyone thought we had just gotten married and were newlyweds because we both were so into each other; it felt like we were the only two people at the airport and on the plane. We looked so blissful to the airline stewardess that she kept walking by us to ask us if we had gotten married over the week end or something. We just looked at each other and smiled and told her that we had gotten engaged and we would be getting married on the first day of Spring next year, after she informed the other stewardess they all rushed over and congradulated us and immediately asked for permission to see my ring. They told us we looked so radient and so much in love, then they asked us what was our secret, and PJ told them it was our love and respect for God and each other. After the flight was over we held hands and talked a little while when we went over to claim our bags. Then we walked to the parking area to pick up PJ's car, when I got into his car we didn't talk much I took his hand and held it up close to my face and I closed my eyes, and kissed it. I told him thank you for making the week end so special for me. Then he took my hand and kissed it and said "You have been a pleasure, I enjoyed every single moment. Before I knew he was pulling up to my apartment. "Let me see you inside." He came around unlocked the trunk and opened my door and helped me to the door.

He stayed for a few minutes and then he drove home. Finally I was home it looked like I was in a strange land, then I plopped right down on my sofa. I was exhausted, yet exhilarated, yet ready to explode; I decided to turn on a little music so that I could calm down. Then my telephone rung, and the voice said, "Well Did he ask you?" "What? Who is this, the voice continued, "I said, did he ask you?" At first I did'nt recognize the voice, then my mind started to click, and come back to earth, it was PJ's mom. "Mom, you already knew he was going to ask me?" "Well did he?" "Yes, Ma'am he did," "Oh how sweet, well I know you just got in, and I don't even have to ask you what the answer was." He told me that he had been thinking about it for a while, and he wondered how I felt about it and I told him that I knew the first moment I heard his voice about you, and even more so when I met you, you just fit right into his life perfectly. It took him a long time to finally find someone who finally made him truly happy. The fact that he found someone who would love him the way he should be and needed to be loved, makes me happy. I knew that it would just be a matter of time, because you both deserve each other." "Thanks, Mom you are so sweet, now I know where PJ gets all that sweet sugar from, I love you so much." Mom, PJ wants us to get married on the first day of Spring next year. Then all of a sudden PJ's voice came into the line, and said, "Baby, she could'nt even wait until I got home, isn't she something else? I'm still in my car she just called me and made me call you right after she got me, then she told me to be quiet while she talked to you. You know she always gets her way with me, and now I guess I'll have to split it two ways between you and her." "You know, honey I thought I heard something going on in the background, that's why I didn't recognize her voice." "Well, she wanted to be the first one to know, but Angell I want to be with you when you tell your mother, I am little old fashioned and I want to ask her for your hand in marriage even though it's a little after the fact." "I'll say...Thanks, Mom, your son is so sweet I adore him. What am I going to do with the both of you? Well, I guess I'll just have to love you both, that's all." "Goodnight Angell." "Goodnight to both of you, take care Mom." "Again, congratulations to you both, Angell we'll talk later I can't wait to see that ring." "I can't wait to show it to you." "Take Care, sweetheart." "You too Mom. Honey, don't forget to ring my phone when you make it home." "I planned to do just that...until then, baby." "My God, that boy is something else."

It was good to be home again, even though it was nothing like that beach house. But it was home, I finally got everything unpacked and half way put away. I decided not to call PJ, since he had already let my phone ring three times which was his signal of letting me know he made it safely...we had already said, goodnight. I took a long shower and decided to just relax and watch a little television, and then I called my Mother to let her know that I had made it back safely. It took a lot out of me, not to tell her the most exciting part of the trip, I did assure her that PJ, was the perfect gentleman. I told her that I would come by and see her Monday since I was off work, and PJ said for me to tell her hello and that he would stop by and see her soon. She was glad I called to let her know I'd made it back safely. I did not return any other telephone calls but I did check my messages and I had quite a few. I decided to rest Monday and enjoy the day off. My mind was filled with explosions and air bubbles of love bursting inside my head like fireworks during the Fourth of July. I tried hard to calm down, so I turned on the television, so I would get sleepy, I was tired; I really wanted to go to sleep. But I was not the least bit sleepy, I tossed and turned but I could not go to sleep. Then I said to myself, look girl you are too old to count sheep.

Maybe I'll just make a nice hot cup of tea and light some candles surely that will relax me and I'll just go to sleep. Before I knew it was 12:45 a.m. I could not go to sleep I felt like I had insomnia, I kept saying to myself, What is it? What is it? Then I thought to myself, Oh my God I need him, I miss him, the warmth of his body, my physical sleeping pill. I'll just think about him, because I don't want to call him, it'll make me get up and go over there. Just then as I begin to speak the words to myself, the telephone rang, and I jumped up and answered the phone. "Baby, I couldn't sleep either, I miss you too." "Me too how did you know?" Then my eyes got a little glassy. "Baby, don't do that, you know I'm not there to kiss that tear away, but I do love you, then he asked me to give him a kiss over the phone. Then he gave me a kiss, "Honey you know me so well" "Yes I do, you need me to tell you a bedtime story?" "No I need more than that, I'm missing your touch and the warmth of your body, but I'm trying to be okay now that I heard your voice, maybe I can go to sleep now, I really miss being with you, we really got spoiled didn't we?" "I guess so baby, I guess so, I can't wait to find you in my bed every night; I want you right now." "Me too." "Hey, Baby come open the door." "What? You're at my door." "Yes, I couldn't stand it." "Honey, what time is it?" "Baby I don't care what time it is, can you open the door. I want to spend the night at your place." "Are you serious?" "Yes…I am…come on baby unlock the door." "Okay." I got up and walked to the door and there he was; at well after one in the morning; both us standing there like me some love sick puppies. We couldn't even stand to be a few hours apart; although it felt so right I knew how addictive this bond of pleasure could be. But I made a vow to grant him three encounters of uncontrolable sensations of our love at his wish and command. We agreed that one would be at my place and the other two would be his call; he would be given grace from our love as we made the vow the morning after our engagement. The pleasure of his love was never to be mistaken or taken for granted he called this first encounter his Bedtime Story; it had to be one of the most enjoyable bedtime stories I've ever read no pages can ever compare to it, as we turned the pages one by one.

After the next morning, he left nothing but his love in my bed and the joy of becoming his wife filled my head. Following that night our relationship developed even more as we reached more levels of creations of our love. The affection we felt was so real and full of true emotions, it was the kind of oneness that every woman wants to feel, but doesn't quite believe is possible. As I gazed down at my ring, I could not believe he would spend so much on a whim with such dignified spontaneity; five carats. To think I almost missed an opportunity of a lifetime; it had nothing to do with the intimacy that was uncovered; it had everything to do with timing or lack thereof. Afraid to follow my heart based on principles that could have spun out of control; by trying to control something that had already been orchestrated on the basis of timing and certainty which leads to faith and belief. But I learned a valuable lesson over that weekend, how significant it was to let go and follow my heart; it never lead me astray from that moment on.

(There really are some good men and women out there, we just have to be patient and wait on the one that God has chosen for us, once we agree to take a leap of faith and trust that feeling that He gives us, the deal is sealed the moment we get out of our own way and just let it happen. Because it's so easy to be tempted, its unfortunate that we always seem to choose the same man or woman; you know the one that looks good, got that good job or career, car and nice place. There are a lot of women who say, "they love a man who will be good to them." Love is not just giving you some money or simply having the ability to buy you with their expensive gifts. It's much more than that. All we need to do is take the time out to explore what that "It" is for each of us individually and try not to be so influenced by things a man has or what he can buy or where he can take you, or our friends who will swear by whatever they think the man may have. Learning how to seach your own heart for what you want and need is a challenge at times but you have to know. Because what "It" is to me, may not be what "It" is for you. We don't need to always worry about the finances they will be taken care of and so will we, we have to remember that everything takes time; a lot of hard work goes into each person that we invest it in. If we each give more than a 100 percent in the whole relationship we want have to worry about coming up short; especially being selfish; it is the ones who believe in the 50 / 50 are the ones that fall short together; nowdays you need a 100 percent from each other which gives you a double portion from each side, once calculated right way you're both giving 200 percent with out a doubt. Whenever something is done half way it's not complete what makes anything complete is giving it the best you got and each person should give more than half in order to make it work. If you each don't give the maximum percentage of 100 percent; selfishness can creep in and you'll find yourself not getting enough of what you need. It's so easy to not get enough attention, tlc (tender loving care), time spent together, not enough I love you's instead you get (me too), the dating stops, and the intimacy gets lost between jobs and becomes more of a chore with no pleasure, instead it becomes an obligation with no feelings just a routine checkup; the gentleness and sweetness walks out on courtship and what really comes up missing is the other half that existed when you met; you will find the other 50 percent in a state of MIA's (missing in actions). Then you get the attitude that produces bitterness, spite, (which is simply unkindness and nastiness), then hatefulness and dishonesty walks into the household which introduces self-centeredness into the walls of the heart which turns into multiple relationships outside the marrage and ultimtely you turn into the marital problem.

Have you ever really searched out what being selfish means, it means to be self centered, egotistical, self seeking, only interested in themselves. A man's role is to be the provider but he has to be willing to love, honor and respect you; the role of the woman is to support him meaning she should be there for him, to nurture him with care and affection no matter what he does. Supporting a man does not mean you pay all the bills and let him live off of you and what you provide; that's when you move the numbers around you can't give 90 percent and he only gives 10 percent just to have a man in the house. Support means the livelihood of your home being able to uphold, endure, maintain, make provisions, maintaining you and your home in order for both of you to live. Sustenance plays an important role as well, which is making sure that you add nutrition to the marriage, preparing the food with provides nourishment, and subsistence which is part of it. Support in a marriage comes from both parties, we as women must provide the help just as it was intended in The Word Of God. Which describes the woman as being created to be the help meet, we as women help meet the needs in the marriage, that instills beliefs in the man, that gives him the endurance, the strength, the assurance and the motivation to be a good provider and husband to the woman. How the woman nurtures and supports the man will build a strong foundation for the marriage and gives birth to him to become the best man he can be and sooner or later he will become a good father simply because of the encouragment and support. After the man shows the woman security by being a good provider and partner, it aids in helping her become a good mother. When the man and woman knows they have a good partner in marriage backing them, having each other's back, and being the back bone to each other, there is so much that they can achieve. Let's face it, it takes a lot for a man to care for us, we as women have more needs than they do, we have a lot more intricate things that we have to worry about, than they would ever dream of. Especially when children are included in the midst of the foundation. It takes strength, endurance, trust, patience, and a sustaining love to build a strong foundation. When the woman or the man is not loved and cared for the foundation will be shaky no matter what happens, it will not stand. It will be blown down by the first tornado of life that comes their way. The emotions must be nurtured by woman to the man, support must be given to each other, communication must continue to flow together no matter whats going on.

Love is not selfish it is freely given, most of the times by many and any means necessary. But true love comes to those who believe it will come for them, and most people who believe that, trust what they believe in, and through it they discover and create the opportunity for them to love and be loved. And that means with out a condition, that's what unconditional love is. God's love for us is unconditionally he knows our hearts and it is through him and our belief that we will be given the desires of our hearts, but we must trust and believe in his will for our lives. His grace is amazing, he accepts us just the way we are imperfect beings. But he and his love is perfect, he never makes a mistake; even if it appears to be to us...he always know whats best for us because he knows exactly what we need. We we need to be corrected in our ways or our thinking it all works together for our good. When we allow God to teach us his way, we must understand that his ways are not our ways and his thoughts are not our thoughts. His patience with us will truly last forever, he won't ever give up on us, we are the ones who give up on ourselves and him. Giving up stops you from trusting him, then you will seek advice from others who you believe can help you much quicker. God gives all of us a chance to have a life and he wants us to love, share love and be loved. If you've ever heard of the serenity prayer, its so much wisdom and truth in it...that we rarely see the entire prayer written...it such wonderful prayer.

The Serenity Prayer...

God, Grant Me the Serenity to Accept the Things I Can Not Change...
The Courage to Change the Things I Can
And The Wisdom to Know the Difference...

Were all familiar with the first three verses...but the later of the prayer we rarely ever see the entire prayer in its original form...

God, give us grace to accept with serenity
the things that cannot be changed,
Courage to change the things
which should be changed,
and the Wisdom to distinguish
the one from the other.
Living one day at a time,
Enjoying one moment at a time,
Accepting hardship as a pathway to peace,
Taking, as Jesus did,
This sinful world as it is,
Not as I would have it,
Trusting that You will make all things right,
If I surrender to Your will,
So that I may be reasonably happy in this life,
And supremely happy with You forever in the next.
Amen.

That was the orginal version was written by Reinhold Niebuhr, who graced the world with his presence from (1892 - 1971) the verses have been used to touch people lives around the world, from giving strength to our soldiers at war to rendering peace of mind to those who face many challenges or trials in life, through overcoming addictions. When you see it in its original form you can certainly see why it almost gives us an innate power for the strength to go on. Understanding that we need the grace of God to get us to that level of serenity when its not easy to accept things that we can not change. But knowing that we can look forward to God to give us the courage that we need in order to change those things that can be changed. We desperately need wisdom so we can tell the difference between the two of them. Once we undestand that serenity gives us the peace and tranquility to calm us down so we can accept things that we can't change. Knowledge blesses us with the information or the facts, that allow us to learn exactly what we need to know in order to change the things that we can. Finally, wisdom is simply our own common sense, reveals to us the understanding to know the difference. God is who gives us, the serenity, knowledge, wisdom and the understanding, we simply have to seek him and ask for it. Just as freely as he gives it to us, he can take it away in our disobedience to trust and believe in the truth. However, through our obedience, is where we receive more of what he has intended for us.

We are responsible for yielding to our destiny, we have to be able to recognize what his will is for us. We have to submit to his will and seek him, in order for us to find out what our destiny really is. He assures us and will teach us all we need to know about what our purpose on this earth really is. All we have to do is trust him, nothing in this world is promised to us, we have to take each day at a time through obedience and earn the blessings he has in store for us. "What ever thinketh thou, thou art," in others words we are what we think we are. If you think you're low you are, if you think you're nothing you are, if you think you can't you probably never will. You have to know, that you know, that you know, that you know God, and recognize and acknowledge his leadership in and for your life. And give him a chance, to reveal himself to you. The best thing we can do is, get up and do something with our lives for our own sake and those that may be depending on us. Showing ourselves approved to him daily is very important. By not just sitting around and letting life happen to us, understand how wonderful and rewarding it is to be about something in our lives. Afterwards, we will find that there is someone inside us who has something worthwhile inside to offer. Each of us were given some type of purpose in life even before we were born no matter how big or small. If you don't know what it is yet its no need to worry there is always a chance to find out. Seeking God in prayer, is the one true way to find out what our purpose is. Many are called but few are chosen. God does all the choosing he will lead you all the way to him to reaveal what your purpose is. If you run away from what is destined for you, it may and can be given to someone else. Afterward, we may not be given any thing to do for him of the same magnitude because we ignored what we were called to do. Our disobedience allows us to understand why many are called; because the called usually let it slip right through their hands and their mind because of fear of the unknown when they don't have a connection to God. Getting spiritually connected will help us find the way to living a Godly Life. We all need to try our best to give an account to much more than our bank account. God is our keeper and the real book keeper of the book of life. He knows all who belong to him, even those that are chosen, who stray away from the path of purpose and return back to him with a few bumps and bruises from lifes experiences. He is all that, all knowing of those true believers who stay on the path and are truly living a Godly Life. We are classified as his sheep, and has many advantages, with Jesus being the Good Shepherd and always keeping track of his ninety and nine or what ever the amount is, knowing that there may be that one that has been left behind who has strayed away. He will still go out and look for the one that's lost no matter how many mistakes they've made, forgiving and praying for our heart to change and come back to him and receive forgiveness and a new start. If we could look at the book of life, and see the pages that belong to us individually may surprise us. Knowing how much is written would probably put more fear in us and help us to live a better quality of life. Prayer really does changes things, and I am a true believer of it being true for me. Each one of us will be held accountable for every thing that is written on our pages in the book of life.

Being taught right from wrong early in our lives should give us basic principles to live by, with an understanding of how important it is to do what's right. Learning that you will suffer the consequences when you do something wrong; it may not be right away but at some point in your life it will catch up with you. If your conscious bothers you when you do something wrong, then there is a chance that you have a Godly conscious instilled inside; which will eventually help you to mature with the kind of values, morals, and integrity that makes you keenly aware of your actions. When you do something good for someone, you receive a good feeling inside, those feelings give birth to becoming a good hearted person with a caring spirit; just by taking time out of your life to care. Caring is loving tenderly, with affection and devotion. Really caring about our lives and recognizing how much God cares for us is a blessing of acknowlegement. After we put more care and faith into our lives; it allows us to pick up the pieces of what may have been a broken life, and allow us to move on and try to live a more productive fulfilled life by doing something worth while. God can restore us and give us a new start and a new life that will be full of hope, tender loving care, joy, forgiveness and peace.

Life Goes On... As Time Waits for No One...

The day was finally here, Oh boy was it a Tuesday, lots of work to catch up on and questions and curosity was at it's highest peak. I thought I would never get through my day, rumors started generating all over the office. Everyone wondered where I had been, and why I had such a glow. People that didn't usually talk to me at work were suddenly speaking and telling me how much they missed my presence. All kinds of people were coming by my office to see and speak, everyone wanted to see if I was really glowing and to take a look at what was really blinging in my office. My assistant, Destiny was the first person to notice my ring with her magnifying eye glasses, but wanted to brief and update me on the project we had just completed and the new ones that were coming up. She filled me in on what had gone on while I was out of the office. Although she couldn't stop starring at my hand, immediately she began to comment about the radiance that I had, and commented that everyone was wondering if I had gone off and eloped. I told her that I had a wonderful week-end get away and the highlight was getting engaged to PJ. Of course, she wanted all the details, afterwards, she gave me a big hug and was full of compliments afterwards she went on and on to inquire about how many carats it was. After I revealed to her the number she continued to stream about how gorgeous my ring was. PJ called me about half an hour later, I was so relieved to hear his voice. I felt like I was stuck in a time zone, and it was taking forever for the time to change. People just kept walking by my office looking and whispering about my ring, and wondering who my man was who. Although there were a few guys, Jeremy and David who thought they would be the one; how I have no idea but believe me they both showed up in my office and brought me coffee and asked why

I wouldn't give the more than the time of day. All I could say if you have to ask there is your reason. PJ marveled at the attention I must have been getting and told me to tell Jeremy and David it was too late; if they didn't have what it took by now...it was over. He said he was sure they would be talking about that glow in my office before and after our wedding day. I loved him for being who he was; he made me so dreamy I couldn't hardly think straight.

My day was finally coming to a close, and I was scheduled to meet PJ, at my Mother's house. While I was on my way to my car, I saw my boss, Mr. Jones in the parking lot. He was fumbling with his keys and kind of staring at me at the same time. "Mr. Jones, are you okay, is something wrong?" "No, not really, I was just thinking about the wife and wondering if a week end could make you look so vivacious, and well rested, that maybe I should step up and put everything behind us and just take her away on a needed vacation for about a week so we can soak up a little sun and see what else might transpire." "You know what sir, that's the best suggestion I heard you say this year." We both laughed and I told him. "Thanks for the compliment, you and your wife deserve a week of vacation in the sun to rekindle a little romance back in picture. Why don't you just take the time off and take advantage an opportunity to relax and have fun with her again you both rediscover each other." "Angell, I believe I will do just that, thank you. You know we both need a week off, maybe I'll take her on a cruise or something." "That's sounds great, Mr. Jones, I'm sure she'll love that sir, you have a nice evening and get to planning." "Hey Angell, that really must be some fellow; looks like he has the same taste in jewerly as he has in women; I don't think I've ever seen you so happy. You better hold on to this one." "Thanks again Mr. Jones, I intend to do just that." "So have you guys set a date yet?" "Yes, The first day of spring next year, God willing." "Oh that sounds like a plan, Congradulations Angell you deserve that and more. Many blessing to the both of you. Tell me what's his name." "Jon Paul, but everyone calls him PJ." "Tell Jon, he did good." "Thanks, Mr. Jones, I will." Wow I had never had a personal conversation with Mr. Jones other than good morning, afternoon or evening you got that report done yet; Angell what are you working on now. He was always very short, very approachable when it came to any subject matter to do with due dates or deadlines our office. I didn't even know he was still married; he stopped wearing his ring a while back. We thought they must have gotten divorced because he never talked about her. Wonders never ceased to amaze me about people; I had been praying for Mr. Jones and whatever he was going through in his life; and it looks like God answered my prayers unawares. To listen to how open he was in his conversation with me he ended up giving me an PJ his blessings. The power of our prayers is really something especially when you not even aware of what some one is going through.

I drove off and got through the evening traffic and finally made it to Mother's. When I got there, my brother was outside washing his car. Then I heard his voice, "Hey Sis, you really got it going on, where you been? Girl you looking good." "Hey brother, you doing okay?" "Fine Sis, but not as fine as you must be doing." "Boy you are something else!" "I know, that's what all the ladies keep telling me." Then I walked into my mom's house and as always I smelled something wonderful coming from the kitchen. I walked into the kitchen, then I remembered my ring then I stuck my left hand in my pocket. Oh my God, that what's my brother was talking about, I hope he doesn't come in asking any questions before we tell Mother, Jesus. Hey Mother." "Well now don't you look all rested up...you guys must have had a real good time?" "Yes maham, we had the best time. What you in here cooking up for dinner Mother?" The smell just came and grabbed me from out side. When I saw "Slim" standing outside washing his car close by the house, I knew you must have been cooking up something in the kitchen for him to still be hanging around. "Well I'm fixing a Roast, with some fresh carrots, roasted red potatoes, green beans with garlic butter and some homemade mac and cheese. Oh my God, Mother what's the occasion...I smell something else in the oven. Oh I almost forgot, I got some fresh garlic bread in the oven." "Oooh that's already making my stomach hurt...that sounds delicious, Mother." "After I told your brother what was for dinner, he asked me if he could eat the leftovers. I told him that you were coming over and where ever you are... PJ couldn't be too far away." "Mother, what makes you say that?" "Just as

I said that PJ walked in the kitchen and said because my Mother knows me and my appetite." Then he reached over and kissed my Mother on the cheek and she shouted, see, I told you he wasn't too far behind you. "Well don't you both look like you been bathing in the sun, I can tell that both of you had a good time; it written all over your face. Just look at the two of you; you both can't seem to stop smiling." Yes, Ma'am we did! Your daughter is defintely the one I love, and guess what? I think she loves me too, you know she could keep her hands off me." "Is that right?" Then he reached over and kissed me on my lips and said, "Hey baby, did you have a good day?" "I did honey, what about you?" "My day is getting better and better the closer I get to you." "All right now, you little love birds after all that sugar you both won't need any dessert." "I love you too Mother, we always got room for dessert." "By the way, mother you didn't say we had dessert, what did you fix?" "Bannana Pudding." "Oh my God, be still my heart, that's exactly why I love this woman and her mother; I came with a hearty appetite when will everything be ready?" "In about 10 minutes." "Great Mom, we both brought you something back from our trip. Then he stepped about two steps over into the hall way and picked up two bags and placed them on the dining room table. She hurriedly walked over to the dining room and if she could open them. "Abosolutely, Mom." As she opened each gift she was elated with each one, then she took all the bags into her bedroom. When she got back, she told us how much she loved her gifts; then the telephone rang. Immediately, she went back to the back to answer it. When she walked out PJ quickly reached over for me and grabbed my hand and led me to the laundry room; immediately he began to hug and kiss me softly, as he whispered in my ear how much he missed me. Then he asked me if he could come over later, and I told him I didn't know because I would have to get permission from my Mother. Then my Mother walked backed in the kitchen as she passed the laundry, and said permission for what? "What are yall doing in there, whispering like no body's business." Immediately we came waltzing out of the laundry room a little embarrassed like a couple of kids. "My God, I told you it's PJ who can't keep his hands off me. So, Mother what do you have extraterrestrial radar hearing or something?" "Must be that something you know; wait till you have kids, my dear, its something that all mother's develop over the years. So what do you need my permission for." Which set up an excellent opportunity for PJ to ask her the big question. "Well Mother, I asked Angell if I could come over to her house later and she told me I had to ask you, Mother, can I please, go over to Angell's house, please, pretty please?" Boy you are so silly, you know Angell will let you come over to house anytime you get ready. She's a grown woman and I can't tell her what to do?" Well if that the case PJ said, then he got down on one knee and said, Mother will you please do me the honor by allowing me to ask you for your daughter's hand in marriage? Could you please give us your blessing and make me the happiest man on earth?" All of a sudden, Mother started to blush, and turned so red I know she was so embarrassed because he caught both of us off guard. I had no idea he was going to get down on one knee and ask her like that. He was so silly, when he wanted to be. She looked at him and said, "PJ are you being serious?" "Yes ma'am, I am, I love your daughter and I want to marry her." Then I took my hand out of my pocket and gave it to him; he placed the ring back on my finger. And tears of joy began to flow from her eyes, and she said, "Oh baby, how beautiful, what kind of ring is that, I've never seen anything like it. Come on son, get up off the floor and hug my neck, of course you can marry my baby with my blessing." Then PJ got up off his knee and hugged her, then she came over and hugged me. "Did this happen over the week end you too, "Yes Maham." "Oh, my God no wonder you both are glowing like the lights on a christmas tree." We both laughed. "Thank you Mother, for giving us your blessing." "You're welcome baby." You both deserve the best things in life that God has to offer you, the both of you are a sweet little couple, and I pray that God will bless you both and keep you, just keep on loving each other no matter what." Me and PJ both gave her a big hug together. Then PJ pulled away, just like a man and asked her what was for dinner and if he could eat now, because he was starving. We both laughed, and Mother told him everything was ready now, that he could wash up and bless the food so we could all dig in.

Dinner was wonderful, it's nothing like your Mother's cooking; I don't care where you go or what you do, you always have room for that good old fashioned meal that I call Mother's lovin from her oven. Afterwards we cleaned up the kitchen for my mom, then we got ready to leave. When we got ready to go, we both kissed my Mother goodnight, then PJ followed me home and we both parked our cars and went upstairs. PJ sat down on the sofa picked up the remote control, and turned the volume on my stereo to low, then he hit the button for the TV to watch the 9:00 news then he stretched out on the sofa and took a nap. I couldn't believe he had gone to sleep so fast. "PJ?" I called out to him but he didn't answer me. I went ahead and fixed us both a glass of cold water with some crushed ice and a wedge of lemon. Then I went over to the sofa and I put his water right next to him, took off his shoes and threw a throw blanket over him. I went into my bedroom and took off my work clothes and I got into the shower and I put on something very comfortable. Then I went back into the living room and checked on PJ to see if he was still asleep and he was. I decided I would lay down and rest my body too, because I realized that we were both up late last night. There was no telling what time we finally drifted off to sleep. It was well after one o'clock in the morning when he got here this morning. Poor baby, he's tired, well I'll just lay down and rest too, and wake him up around eleven o'clock. The alarm clock came on and it went off around eleven I hit the snooze button and fell back asleep. When I woke up again it was three o'clock in the morning, PJ had gotten up and gotten in the bed with me. I looked over at him, he was lying next to me on top of my comforter. "PJ, honey wake up, its a little after three in the morning," "What? Baby are you sure?" "Yes honey it really is, we both sort of overslept. You better get going so you won't be late for work in the morning." "Baby you're right, listen thanks for waking me up, I'll call you when I make it home. Baby I'm thirsty, I need to get some water," look in the refrigerator its a glass already ready for you and take a bottle with you out of the frig. I walked him to the door and kissed him goodnight. When he got home he called me to let me know he had made then we both went to sleep.

The next morning, I had to call my best friend Daphine. I had sheduled to meet her for breakfast on our way to work, I hadn't seen her and knew she needed a little TLC. So I stopped and got her some flowers on the way to surprise her. The momen I arrived we were both excited to see each other;

seems like it had been so long. Although she looked a little pale, she told me she almost overslept because I had her waking up so early she could'nt hardly get her makeup on because her routine was sleeping during the day because she worked at night. Even though she complained, I knew she loved the attention. As soon as she saw me she knew something had happened between me and PJ. Then I showed her my ring; she almost passed out. I told her I had the same reation. She wanted all the details and I asked her if she would be my Maid of Honor and she got all teary eyed; we could barley eat our food. Although she smiled, I felt like something was wrong. Which made me a little worried about her, she didn't seem to be herself. I told her I hoped it wasn't Maurice and she assured me that it wasn't him then I asked her if she was pregnant and she told me I was about as sick as the patients that are in the hospital. We laughed, then she told me she loved the flowers and asked if we could have lunch soon because I needed her help planning the wedding. We both agreed and I went to work. I knew my best friend, it was something she wasn't telling me. But in due time she would tell me. I'm sure she didn't want to say anything after all the news and details that I dropped on her she would tell me at some point. As soon as time would permit we would get a chance to talk about Maurice, William or whoever. I loved her just like my own sister; and I sensed that something was wrong.

'Tis the Season to be Jolly...

The season for falling in love; went by so fast, the fall ended with lots of planning and plenty details set into motion for the wedding. Before I knew it, it was time for Thanksgiving we spent the holiday with PJ's family, because a lot of his relatives were coming up to meet me and my Mother. We were both invited for dinner, PJ and I were four months away from our wedding. Our mothers were both such perfectionist, they wanted everything planned to the letter. Dinner was prepared by his Mom, and my Mother brought her famous to die for German Chocolate Cake and some delicious Sweet Potato Pies. They were always so delicious, I don't know what she put in them but everyone just raved about them. PJ had a nice family, they were very generous they offered us cashiers checks, gift certificates and early wedding gifts of promissory notes. I couldn't believe it, we weren't even married yet and they were asking me what we needed it was happening so quickly. They all told me that the gifts would be delivered the week of the wedding. After getting to know them, they were prominent people with strong values; they kept their family traditions. My Mother was very pleased and so was his, PJ and I were the center of attraction. Although PJ's brother, Pierce didn't get a chance to make it he sent his love and a voice mail letting us know that he was in Germany on business and couldn't make it in for the holidays but would be there a few days before the wedding. I had never met Pierce, because he was always on the go; he lived abroad and lead a very mysterious and it seem to me exciting lifestyle. He was home for Labor Day, but PJ and I had just left to go out of town for the holiday. I noticed that when he was in town, he was in town, when he was gone; he was gone for long periods of time which is why I'm sure PJ had such a close relationship with his mom and his sisters. I often wondered if he worked for the government or the CIA or something because of his level of comfort and extensive levels of travel.

After such a delicious meal we decided to steal a few moments away from the dinner table; so we excused ourselves and went upstairs to the study. Pj asked to sat on his lap and we just held each other and gave thanks in private and took avantage of those stolen moments of time. As soon as we approached the stairwell PJ decided to to kiss me before made it near the end of the steps and standing at the end of the stairs was his Uncle Pete of all people. His voice was like roaring waters, you could swear he was DJ on late nights playing music on what they call the quiet storm. He yelled loud enough for everyone to hear, "Stealing a little time away were you? Looks like some hanky panky might have been going on up there to me." We were so embarrased. Then he reached out and said, "Uncle Pete I just couldn't resist." "I don't blame you boy, if your Aunt Jasmine and I was as young as you and this little Angell you got here; I remember back in the day when we did all kinds of things. But I wouldn't have stolen a few moments, we would have been gone for at least an hour, if you know what I mean. "Uncle Pete, my goodness, you better go on now, what would Aunt Jasmine say if she knew you were telling secrets?" "She wouldn't deny it because I was a bad boy back in my day." "Uncle Pete! I said with surprise at his candor immediately PJ's Aunt Jasmine walked in. "Pete, I could hear you all the way down the hall, leave Jon and Angell alone they don't need you going on and on about the kind of stuff you use to do." "Come on Jazzy baby, you know you couldn't resist all those hot stolen moments we use to have together, I couldn't never get enough." PJ and I looked at each other then we looked at Aunt Jasmine "Oooh Uncle Pete." Aunt Jasmine was so embarrassed. "Pete come on before I have to hurt you." He laughed, then he yell out. "Hurt me baby!" "If you don't get out of this hallway making a scene, I'll hurt you alright." "You right son, it's that irrestible charm the men in our family have...running right through our blood line, she know she wants me, keep them home fires burning son...if you do she'll be just like your Aunt Jazzy here, she won't be able to keep her hands off you." We all laughed histercally. He was a very funny man, who kept the family filled with fun, laughter and lots of stories, he really had a great sense of humor. I fell in love with him the moment I met him. Thanksgiving Dinner was coming to a close, everyone started to leave one by one. Finally, everything had been cleaned up and put away. I was exausted, PJ and I decided to spend the night at his Mom's. We wanted her to know how much we appreciated her because she had gone through a lot to make sure everything was so nice for Thanksgiving as well as our private engagement dinner for their family. She had one of the most beautiful homes on about five acres in the northern sector of Dallas. She had five bedrooms and three bathrooms, she turned one bedroom into a wonderful office/study. PJ's Mom had a very successful business, she catered to some of the finest homes and businesses, she designed menus and contracted as a marketing consult for the upper echelon. PJ's Mom was one of the most detailed cooks I'd ever met; who could come up with some of the most elaborate food displays with delicacies. I was intrigued by her in the kitchen, she was a delightful host, she wanted everything to be mouth-watering, and delicious. I adored her love for details, she was fascinating. With an exquisite taste for the finer things in life and didn't mind telling you. Her boldness made her one of most sought after caters in the business; she developed a superb clientele that made her very comfortable finantially. PJ's father was deceased just as mine was; both my Mother and his had never remarried; they were both widows. We both had a lot to be thankful for this year.

As I began to think back in time, I couldn't believe that just a year ago I was alone, and now for the first time in my life I was engaged to my love of a lifetime during the holidays. I couldn't wait for Christmas. If PJ never got me another gift, he was the present I always wanted and I would cherish the gift of out love in my heart for ever. Love is so special, but when you have someone in your life who really loves you and you know it makes all the difference in the world. It's the kind of assurance that gives your heart a feeling of security and sets your mind at ease that you will only know it by experience. Being able to really experience true love of the heart is a miracle within itself, and that is ever lasting. Hearing that persons voice, seeing that person's image even when they're not there with you, you find yourself feeling their presence as you lay awake late at night, that feeling will make your heart ache for them and long for their return. That kind of love can be enriched and enhanced as the foundation is being nurtured, created and built to withstand the tests and expanse of time.

We spent the Christmas Holiday with my Mother's, the whole family came up for the holiday and it turned out really nice. New Years Eve rolled into our lives with a special covenant that we made together that no matter what the storms of life brought us, we declared that our love would withstand more than a countdown to a New Year of resolutions. We were expecting Bernard and Jacqueline to come down from Houston they invited us to a New Year's Eve Dinner Party with them and what a nice party it was. Jacqueline and I made plans for me to come down to Houston three weeks from then to look at a new line of gowns she thought I might enjoy seeing. After dinner, PJ and I decided to slip out and go back to his place; about an hour before the New Year came in. He and I both wanted to be alone to bring in the New Year, we were partied out from all the Holiday parties we attended during the month. So we left about a half after ten before the traffic would catch us, I always heard that the way you bring in the new year patterns the way you will spend the rest of your year. We had an incredible time together when we were alone on the lake, he was going to be leaving to close out a business deal in Italy for two weeks then he would be in France for three to four weeks. I only had five days before he would be leaving and I wanted to spend each day with him. This was the first time that he would be gone back to back like this for a long period of time. But it was going to be such a great opportunity for him. The company he worked for would be giving him a sensational promotion based on him being able to close both contracts. Being able to travel and do business in both places was a extraordinary opportunity for him; because he was also working on some things to start his own company. Our New Years eve alone together was just as incredible as the weekend of our engagement which was his second request. It was like touching him for the first time; we created memories that we both would never forget. Bringing in the New Year with him was one of the most unforgettable nights that I will cherish in my heart forever.

We spent the next five days together, stuck to each other like glue. I wanted him to hurry up and get the trip over with already. When I met him I knew that he traveled all over the world and I was willing to take a deep breath and love him and just live with it. Our departure was not easy, but we both knew that he had to go, so I swallowed my silently selfish pride and got over it. I took him to the airport and you would have thought he was going off to the armed forces or something. Holding each other, exchanging kisses, I was saying stupid stuff like I was'nt going to see him again, "Jon, honey take care of your self, please have a safe trip, I love you so much and I'm praying for both of us." Then he'd say, "I love you too, baby, you take care of you for me, don't worry so much, I'll be home at the end of next month, we'll pray for each other...come on baby, kiss me again...until then." Then we kissed all over again, we just couldn't get enough. I wanted him to hurry back to me, I knew that this trip would be different, because he wouldn't be back until the end of February. Then before I knew it he was gone.

I had a week end trip planned near the last week end in January to go to Houston to look at the new wedding line and do my fitting for some gowns that Jaqueline wanted me to see. Before my trip I wrapped myself up in planning for the wedding, I couldn't believe that I had gotten all the details signed, sealed and waiting to be delivered. I missed Jon, but I had to keep my composure and finish up what he requested for his part of the wedding and the honeymoon. Finally I was only a few final details away; I didn't want to have any problems at the last moment. The trip to Houston was well worth it, my best friend Daphine, Linda and my sister, JK went down with me. PJ's cousin, Jacqueline had become such a dear friend to me, she actually provided me with a private bridal show in her home. I couldn't believe it, she had three models who wore seven different gowns that she had chosen for me. I felt so special, the show was fabulous and the gowns were incredible. I chose the last gown, which was the seventh one...seems like she saved the best for last...it was simple, but oh so elegant. She also had gowns set up in the show for my brides maids, they were exacatly what we wanted. The show was so grand and personal the models wore samples of the gowns that were in her showcase. The gowns that we purchased were in the front on her display rack in the studio part of her home. I walked over to the gown and I asked Jacqueline if I could try the gown on?" You better believe it Angell, that was the whole point of all of you guys coming down, Daphine why don't you Linda and JK go ahead and try on the bridesmaids gowns you guys agreed on, lets see how well they work together?" They were breathtaking, the perfect compliment to the other; they were both designed in Paris France. When I looked at the designers information on the gown, I thought about PJ, on his way to Paris and I wondered what he was doing at that moment, I missed him and could't wait for him to make it back home. I thought to my self, he had four weeks to go; I can't wait for him to see me walking down the aisle. The gown fit me perfectly, I didn't even have to have any alterations done.

Jacqueline had really done her homework, she had all our sizes set up, my measurements were covered when she came down for New Years Eve, from top to bottom. After we made our decision she told me she would have our gowns shipped by the following week. For our convenience, PJ's mother asked if I would have everything shipped to her house so her son wouldn't be poking his noise around looking for my dress. Jacqueline agreed to take care odf all the details, she was very professional and really knew the clothing business. Jacqueline was able to coordinate everything from the veil to the hosiery, to the shoes, to the accessories. I really enjoyed experiencing her level of expertise it made everything run smoother than I ever imagined. She was a natural for details and had some impressive suggestions for the whole wedding. Through all the working on and planning of the wedding, four and a half weeks had zoomed by. I was sitting in my office on a Wednesday morning, feeling a little empty, and in a deep trance when someone knocked on my door. When I looked up a courier was standing in the doorway of my office with a small box. He told me he had a package for me and I needed to sign it, so I signed for it as usual, then I thanked the courier and I opened up the package when he left. It was from some company that I had never heard of; it was a magnificent picture of a scene in Paris France in a very aesthetic frame. It was incredible, I wondered if PJ sent it. Sure he did, I looked inside the box to see if there was an invoice or something, but I didn't see an invoice or anything else in the box, but the picture was breathtaking. Immediately after looking at the picture and the details of the small frame I knew PJ must have sent it to me!. Suddenly the courier came back and knocked outside my door and said, "Excuse me ma'am, I'm sorry to bother you, but I forgot to give you this envelope that should had been delivered with the box. It says it right here two items, one box and one envelope, I'm sorry about that I almost missed that one, could you please sign your initials right here?" "Well, I was wondering why there was no note or invoice." "Thanks, and have a good afternoon ma'am." Immediately, I opened the envelope and there was a letter inside which said...

> I'm just sitting her all alone, in great anticipation of when I'll be home.
> All I seem to think about these days, Is how much for you my love, I crave.
> It is so beautiful in this part of the land;
> just take a look at that picture and you'll understand
> While I'm wishing you were here with me, my heart is aching for you
> Even though Valentines Day Comes once a year
> You mean much more to me every time you come near
> It's your sweet voice that I long to hear; Now I realize how much I miss it in my ear
> The love that appears in your presence, makes my love for you be such a true essence.
> Happy Valentines, Angell,
>
> > With all my love
> > Your Soon to Be Husband Jon Paul...

(God, he knows how to make me blush and melt, now I really missed him. Now I want be able to concentrate for the rest of the day.)

I was about to put the letter back in the envelope when another envelope fell on the floor, I looked down and picked up the envelope and there were some words written on the second envelope and which said...

"Missing you with all heart."
Happy Valentine's Day Baby...

I opened the envelope and there were two airline tickets in it, I looked at the destination and they were to Paris France. I almost fell out of my chair, I pulled the tickets out of the envelope and there was a little post it note on the back of it which said,

> If you don't hurry up and get to me, I am going to go crazy
> I'm missing you with all my heart,
> I'm about to fall apart.
> Find any way you can, to show me you love me again.
>
> Jon Paul

God, I couldn't believe it, two tickets to Paris France, Oh my God, this man is all mine. I love him so much that it's making me sick to my stomach. I've got to get out of here and go to him right now, my palms were sweating and I was extremely nervous all of a sudden. I could hardly think straight I never expected him to send for me. I dropped the envelope on my desk, and I went straight in to Mr. Jones's Office and asked him if I could be off on an emergency leave for the rest of the day through next Tuesday. I told him that all the projects I was working on were completely finished and if he needed anything Destiny could assist him. Mr. Jones asked me if I was okay and told me to go ahead and fill out a leave request and take it up to the personnel office. I finished up for the day and went straight home then I called the airport; checked the flight information and the weather on my computer. By now, I learned a lot from PJ, he always checked or had me verify the weather where ever he was going. Aftering checking I learned that the weather was pretty cold to me high in the upper 40's and the lows were in the upper 30's, immediately I figured out the type of clothing I should pack, then I packed my bags, my flight was scheduled to leave at 7:30 p.m. Wednesday arriving in Paris France at about 4:20 a.m. our time and swinging ahead seven hours into France's Time Zone. I would arrive at 11:20 a.m. on Thursday morning, exactly seven hours into the future. I had never been on a trip out of the country before, but thank God that I already had my passport on standby for any upcoming opportunities even before I met him. PJ was proud to know that. Over this entire time that I've known him he taught me to always be prepared for just about everything because of how he was and how he lived his life. He wanted me to know that if I ever had to go out of the country with him or on my own he had given me all the rules on "what to do and what not to do in his lecture series volume I & II." Although I could hear his speech going on in my head; I was still just a little nervous, but I had to prove to him and myself that I was an adult and would boldly take a trip anywhere in the world as long as I would find him there waiting for me. I was very confident that I could do it. Paris France was like a dream to me, I never thought I would actually get a chance to go until I met and became engaged to him, it really taught me to believe that anything is possible. When I called my mother and told her where I was going, she was ecstatic gave me the be careful of strangers speech and all her other motherly concerns; she wanted me to call her as soon as I arrived at the hotel. I was in awe all the way to the airport, I could not believe it. I had to call my best friend and tell her what was going on. "Hey girl, you would not guess what I'm doing right now?" "What, are you doing right now girl?" "Well are you sitting down." "Yea I'm sitting down, talking to you, what is up?" "Girl I'm at the airport…" "Girl I will kill you if you tell me you're on your way to Paris?" "Well I can't tell you if you gone kill me!" "Girl shut up! Details, I want Details…What did do? and How did he it?" "Well girl, he sent me a box and a note by courier, and the courier forgot to give me the note then stupid brought it back…and oh my God there was a round trip ticket to Paris inside the envelope. Thank God the stupid courier brought me back the envelope…but who cares…I'm at the airport right now about to board my plane." "What, girl this is like a dream…Angell, babe, you deserve this. I can't stand you…or PJ…yall both make me sick. You guys are too much. I'm so happy for you both, girl do everything that I would do. You mayhave to take your panties off for this one." We both just cracked up and I felt so much better after talking to her. "I love you so much girl." "Me too Angell, girl…take care and don't talk to strangers and if you do make sure he's cute and French so you can get you a little French Mack on before you see the man with the plans for the rest of your lives. Call me when you land…you both make me sick. I can't wait to hear all the details when you get back especially what happen with your panties and everything." We both laughed again and say our goodbyes and I boarded the plane. After getting off the phone with her, I realized how much I loved my best friend. No matter what the weather, she always knew just the right things to say to me and vice versa. Before my plane took off, I decided to call and order her some roses and have them delivered for Valentines Day just thanking her for being my best friend and for loving her through thick and thin. Trust there had been a whole lot of thick and thin. Immediately, I thought to my self of how blessed we both had been to have each other in our lives. Then a feeling came over me, that if anything ever happen to her I don't know what I would do and what was weird is that I knew she felt the same way about me. It's a great feeling to have a best friend that you know you can share anything with and it stays right there between the two of you. It's a rare fine when you find a friend closer than a sister or a brother whether it's a male or a female it's really is a connection in the soul that's a blessing. As I checked back into the space where I was sitting on the plane, another feeling came over me in the form of a loving thoughts and a prayer. I'm not even on my honeymoon, what a way to celebrate Valentines Day. No one could have told me in a thousand years that I would be on my way to Paris France for five days. Life just keeps getting better and better, God I love you so much, you are just too amazing. This man I'm in love with, totally sets my soul on fire with excitement and charm God I can't wait to see him.

When I made it to the check in at the airport, I went through all the necessary travel procedures, verification of identification, checking in my baggage, tickets, boarding passes, etc, etc. Finally I got through everything, I was about to board the plane when I saw this little old lady rushing on her way to board the plane behind me. Out of respect I let her in to board the plane ahead of me, she had such a sweet smile, she was very attractive with the most beautiful French accent. When I boarded the plane I noticed my seat was right next to hers in first class, she was so pleasant and had such a remarkable demeanor. We befriended each other the moment I sat down next to her, she shared some endearing and personal things with me.

I shared some things with her and she told me how special she thought I was and that I was my husband's destiny and that our love would give birth to real love that would be restored back into the world but to remember that true love always comes with sacrifice. Goose bumps went up and down my arms and legs, I took her hand and squeezed it, and I told her, "I Bless God, for sending you on this flight to keep me company, because I was a little nervous to take such a long trip alone. What a sweet angel you are to say such a thing, but I do know that that we are never alone." "I believe that God always sends his special guardian angels to watch over and protect you; because you are a very special girl." I gave her a big hug and told her,"thank you for making your acquaintance." She told me some very exciting things about Paris, the amazing places to go and some breath taking things to see. She gave me a personal little history lesson and some key words to remember in French. We practiced and I couldn't believe I was becoming a natural for the simple words in life; she told me exactly what I needed to say to PJ when we met at the airport. I was so thankful that God would send me such pleasant company; a lovely native woman born in France who had lived there most of her life. I loved it, God was so special, he sent someone to comfort me so I wouldn't be afraid to travel such a long distance alone. Someone to talk to that would help me become a little more mature and the fact that he blessed me with the presence of someone who had loved and obeyed him for fiftty five years of her life. Ms. Ruth was her name, she told me that she was 70 years old I couldn't believe it, she looked to be no more than fifty five at the most, she was very refreshing and full of wisdom, her hair was very long and white; she had such a radiant glow about her. She told me she believed strongly in her love for God and Jesus Christ. She marveled at my age, and told me how delighted she was that I was there with her, then she told me she would send me a special gift for my wedding and would pray that it would be my most beautiful and delightful days. I thanked her and told her we both should try to rest up a couple of hours before we landed and she agreed. When I woke up, we were just about fifteen minutes to arrival in Paris, my heart beating outside my chest. I was excited, on a heavenly cloud of splendor and glory in my mind. When we departed from the plane, I hugged Ms. Ruth and I thanked her for her companionship. Immediately I texted PJ to find out where he was...he texted that he would be in baggage claim...as I was walking with Ms. Ruth to baggage claim area, I saw Jon standing there I almost didn't recognize him he had grown a nice clean cut beard and he had on a hat, I took a deep breath and he walked over to me and just held me real close, then he kissed me like never before. We stood there for a while glued together in each other's arms. He told me how glad he was to see me, and how proud he was of me for coming by myself. I told him nothing would stop me from getting to him. Then I begin to tell him about Ms. Ruth, I turned around to look for her so I could introduce her to Jon but I didn't see her anywhere, there were so many people in the airport she could have easily gotten caught up in the crowd. "Oh honey, I missed you so much, you are the most romantic man I have ever met, I am so in love with you." "Baby you think you're in love with me look what I just went through to get you to me! You deserved it; you've been working so hard on the wedding plans and I feel terrible not being able to be there with you because of my job. Angell, you know that I would have been there if I could have, it really made my heart ache not to be there for all the little details you had to handle alone. Decisions you had to make with out me, being there, but I have confidence in you and I trust your judgment. I appreciate you for being so understanding about my job, and I want you to know that I would never leave you alone on purpose. Business is business and pleasure is pleasure, and now it's my pleasure to let you know that my business is over here. Fortunately, I was extremely blessed on this trip to get both parties to sign the contract agreement with us, so my boss gave me a round trip ticket to Paris as a gift plus my additional signing bonus and I got the promotion. And I sent you the ticket and the bonus will go toward our honeymoon vacation. I will be going back home with you Tuesday. Oh Jon, that's great news honey, congratulations. I love you too baby, and I'm going to show you how much every day that you're here. Come on Baby, lets hurry up and get your bags and get out of this busy airport. I know you need to get some rest after being in that seat for so long. I want to take you to the hotel and let you rest and let your body catch up to this time zone. Then we can have dinner by the time you get rested, I just want to hold you in my arms again, Angell and just sleep." Then I whispered in his ear some sweet French nothings in his ear; he could hardly contain his self. Immediately he spoke these words to me, "ooh bebe, ne dites pas des choses comme ca pour moi en public…je peux te ramener chez moi (which meant ooh baby, don't say things like that to me in public…can I take you home with me then I spoke back with an understanding "Oui, monsieur peut-on aller en ce moment…(which meant, "Yes, sir can we go right now.") He marveled and said, "Qui etait bebe si sexy." (which meant, that was so sexy baby.") Speaking us sexy, I love your little shadow beard, I think its making me want to do something to you before we get to the car. "Girl you better stop this…before you drive me crazy at this airport." We picked up my luggage and drove on to the hotel he could'nt keep his eyes off me so I just curled up next to him and he put his arms around me.

When we got to where we would be staying he told me that the Company had put us up in a suite at a private villa. Talk about historic, I was overwhelmed it looked like the picture that he sent me. "Baby does your company always put you up like this?" "Well Angell, I guess they do treat me very well and I appreciate it, because I really bust my butt for them and then some. I put my life on hold just to take care of major business negotiations for this company." "Honey I am so proud of you and I know they are too, I love you and I just want to take off my clothes and lay down and let you hold me in your arms. "Will you do that for me, baby?" "Yes I will, baby you don't have to ask me but once." So we did just that, it felt so good to be held in his arms again." "Baby, thank you, for trusting me and coming all the way to France without hesitation." "Honey, I would travel across the world just to be with you." I let him know how much I appreciated him always preparing me, for all kinds of things. By exposing me to some of the finer things in life, I learned to really trust his instincts and mine too, and the faith he had in us. We just held each other in silence for a while then we both drifted off to sleep, when we woke up it was about seven o'clock in the evening we had slept for almost eight hours straight. When we got up we took a shower, got dressed and took a short tour of Paris at night, it was unbelievable and much more breathtaking than the pictures I'd seen on TV or in the movies. PJ told me we would take more pictures during the day and make some wonderful memories while we were there. Afterwards, we had a delightful late dinner while I teased him and whispering sweet nothings in his ear in French, he admired the fact that we were able to hold the sweetest conversations but I had learned a lot more French while he was away also how God had blessed me on the plane with Ms. Ruth to control my tongue and speak with assurance and ease. He was impressed and very turned on and so was I to hear the excitement in his voice every time he spoke to me. We ate at some of the finest restaurants for lunch and dinner. People in France are light on breakfast but they loved and were big on their afternoon lunch and tea. The Mediterranean Shore was breath taking it was a like a magnificent dream that you never wanted to wake up from. I asked PJ to pinch me to let me know that I'm not dreaming then he put his lips on my neck and before I knew it he bit me slightly on my neck. "Ouch what have you turned into a vampire since I've been away from you? then he replied "Yes and I want to taste your blood," then he chased be around this big huge monument downtown. He was so silly, I can't believe him sometimes. But he always made me laugh which is the key to a lifetime of good love; we had a wonderful time that day, I was romanced in a boat that floated down the Riviera. A very talented artist painted a portrait of us in a place known as Le Artist Square, where local artist gathered around to paint. Each day was filled with little pieces of joy of our love, which was like a puzzle of amazement of anticipation of long awaited love and passion toward the man I would be married to next month. I so much wanted him more now than I ever did before, I couldn't wait to let him encounter the depths of my love for him. This was a Valentine's Day that I would always cherish, I thought to my self, could our wedding day and our honeymoon be more precious than this.

Splendid has to be described the way our love was unfolding for the both of us. I never dreamed that I would get such a pleasurable trip before we got married. PJ spoils me, he purchased some wonderful souvenirs that he scheduled for delivery to our home. (Wow our home, I can't believe the words "we" and "our" were now a natural part of both of our conversations.) Before I could catch my breath, he was always exposing me to something else, he took me to a place where they specialized in creating personal oils, scents and perfumes. He wanted me to have something special to wear that was created just for me. When we walked in this beautiful shop that looked like it was made out of crystal there were beautifully cut perfume bottles everywhere. There were quite a few people that worked in this very uniquely designed perfume shop, scents everywhere, from all types of florals, fruity, to fresh and natural, to designers select choices they were absolutely fantastic. They tested a few on my skin and came up with a very unique scent then they asked me what I'd like to name it, I said "Le Vrai Amour". Immediately, the lady behind the counter responded, "ce qu'est un beau choix, le vrai amour, belle ma dame." (which meant what a beautiful choice, Real Love! Beautiful my lady). Immediatley, I remembered what Ms. Ruth told me on the plane that PJ and I would give birth to real love into the world but true love always comes with sacrifice. She was such a remarkable woman, I was honored to be in her presence; then I began to think of how easy our love had been for each other and wondered what is there to sacrifice, when you know how much you love someone and how you would be willing to do almost anything for that kind of real love. This had been the birth of a love experience that I never thought I would experience but in my heart and soul, I always knew this kind of love existed and I wanted it. Prayer covered things that were always possible once you attached your belief to it and you trust what you believe in, you never know how far your faith will take you and just how much God will love and take care of you by showing you things that you've never seen before or thought possible for yourself. Until you fall deeply in love with loving him with all your heart, soul, mind and strength he immediately unveils the love in his heart for you then you feel how real that faith really is.

After I chose the perfect bottle, they allowed me to put some on then they put a label on my new scent "Le Vrai Amour" and wrapped it up for me. PJ just kept sniffing me and telling me how delicious the scent was smelling on me; he told me he couldn't hardly concentrate on the tour that he was giving me. Then he whispered these words in my ear, "votre parfum rend veulent faire l'amour de vous dans les rues de Paris. Je ne peux pas attendre pour vous retour a l'hotel." (which meant, that my scent was making him want to make love to me on the streets of Paris; he couldn't wait to get me back to the hotel.") Then I said to him, "Le parfum est un cadeau de mon finance...qui doit penser qu'il a plus qu'une seule demande et necessaries pour utiliser a bon escient...(which meant that the perfume was a gift from my fiance...who must remember he has only one more request and needed to use it wisely...) Immediately he says,"Qu'est-ce... non quickies mon amour?" (which meant, What? No quickies my love...)" I responded, Pas d'amour...pas mon quickies jusqu'a ce que nous nous marier alors vous pouvez tout avoir wuickies, longies...quand et quel que soit...vous voulez que votre souhait sera ma command...) (which meant No my love...no quickies until we get married then you can have it all, quickies, longies...whenever and whatever you want your wish will be my command.) His eyes got so big...he could believe I said that and he was even more impressed that I knew how to say it. ("Now, you know you are really driving me crazy, baby...you got me thinking all kinds of things that I want to do to you." "No, No, No my sweet, lets concentrate on our walk and the drive you promised me or you might make me start something right here and right now." "I wouldn't object, baby!" "You think I don't know that, just keep walking and we'll get through this without any traffic jams!" "I love you baby" "I love you, too honey." Whilel we were walking we met some extraordinary people in Paris. When we got back to the hotel to our surprise, some of his business associates found out I was there, and sent us several wedding gifts to the Villa, wrapped in beautiful gift boxes. They didn't even know me, but they were some very lovely people that didn't mind showing us how much they appreciated me for coming to Paris and marrying one of their colleagues. It was amazing, that we just wanted to be with each other and feel that level of security from the joy of our love which gave us strength. We had come a long way from nine months ago, and were very comfortable with our levels of intimacy. It was so much to see in Paris, France it was simply the most beautiful countryside filled with delicious food, and vintage wines. It was a host to a history full of art, monuments, architecture and some of the most friendliest and inviting people that I'd ever met it's was no wonder that PJ wanted me to experience this, it was an opportunity of a lifetime. Just overwhelmingly beautiful, water surrounded France which made it so impressive so many famous museums, entertaining venues, sights, and so many inspiring places to venture to it just left you in awe. After a day filled with gaze and amazement I couldn't take it anymore I had to go rest my mind we had so many pictures I was running out of mega pixtels in my camera. We decided to have a nice quiet dinner at the Villa; we spent the entire night speechless soaking the experience all in, it was unbelievable. The next morning was Sunday which brought about a very ethereal spirit in France. We were invited to attend Mass service at one of the most historic cathedrals in Paris, The Cathedrale Notre Dame De Paris; it was breathtaking to see such ecclesiastical architecture we were moved emotionally by such a divine experience. PJ's colleague had already briefed us on the length and details of the service, so we knew exactly how we needed to proceed with honor and respect as we were welcomed to participate in the Mass. After we left the service we decided to sit outside and cuddle up and take it all in…the spectacular view of the Eiffel Tower was like the center of a dream come true. We were told about the light display and planned to see it later that night and while we took on the unforgettable view of the city from the tower. As the chill of the air set into our body we decided to venture out a little farther from the city; we found one of the most charming and romantic spots that seem to be hidden from the outside world. It was filled with the warmth of love with the scent of rich delicious cuisine, because it was the eve of Valentines Day the city had the most extradinary feel of care, love and compassion everywhere we ventured to. What a feeling, you will have to explore it for yourself, trust me there is nothing like it that I had experienced on this side of heaven. The people at the small quaint eatery encouraged us to try everything, of course we had to oblige them; we were overstuffed by their loving hospitality and each delicious selection. Thank God we hadn't eaten anything all day, the warmth of atmosphere; the fireplace, candlelight and décor was filled with loving memories that we would cherish for a lifetime. When we left we realized that we were exhausted and too tired to catch the spectacular light display at the Eiffel Tower, so PJ promised that we would go on Valentines Day. When we got back we decided to cuddle up and rest from the entire experience from the day we had gotten up so early we were beat, we couldn't do another thing. After I laid down on the bed, I don't remember anything else. When I woke up it was about 2:45 in the moring, PJ was laying at the end of the bed baby sitting the remote control while the TV was watching him.

"Honey wake up and come to bed, we were beat down by the entire day." "Ooh Baby we were beat down..you have worn me out...I've been more place with you than I had, before you got here." "To think of you enjoying all this alone just couldn't of happen with out me." "Oh is that right." "Je t'aime pour l'attente sur mon amour..." "Oh..vous ne vous ne.." "Oui, je ne..." "Promets-moi..." "I Promise..." "Je t'aime bebe.." "Je t'aime toujours.." (Which meant, I loved him for waiting on my love, he responded with (Oh you do...do you) and I responded with Yes, I do...then he asked me to Promise Him...and I assured him with I Promise...he ended with (I love you, baby)...I ended with I loved him, always.

When we finally got to sleep sweet splendor entered the room as we slept until morning greeting us with an array of sunshine outside the window. The weather was promised to move into the upper 50's which made us feel like we were home. Before I could wake up we had a delivery of a small bouquet of miniture white chocolate roses surrounded by strawberries and one single long stem rose with a card that said "Angell, you are the one that I've longed to share my heart with on Valentine Day will you accept this rose and be my Valentine from this day forward every day of the year. Of course I accepted his inviting proposal...then I gave him a card filled with sentiments of my love for him and then he handed me his card that he had for me. He was such a romantic I loved him for having the ability to take my breath away each day. I only hoped and prayed that it would last us a lifetime filled with what had been an awesome love affair. We stayed in most of the day and enjoyed the comfort of the villa; they had some remarkable celebrations going on. Afterwards, we had an early dinner at an historic French Restaurant across from the Eiffel Tower which allowed us to end our night witnessing the beautiful visual of lights that ended with the most romantic interlude of irrestible touch of love that fulfilled his final request which he called a "Une nuit a cherir Valentines" which meant A Valentines Night to Cherish." Tonight had to be the most treasured time that we had ever spent together...it wasn't just because it was Valentines Day...it was more or less the place, the time, the scenery, the feel in the air...it was almost magical watching the Lights of the Eiffel Tower slowly sparkle like the diamonds in my engagement ring...the light just seem to twinkle like the stars in the sky it was almost indescribable. How God could allow us to experience moments of pleasure beyond anything we could have ever imagined before we were married; was unbelievable we could do nothing but cherish each moment. The next day we rested after one of the most unbelievable nights that we had ever had. Before we left for the airport, we took a long drive around the French Quarters and shared our love of the french culture by having afternoon tea. Later we left to catch our flight home, we arrived at the airport it was way past three o'clock in the evening, our flight was scheduled to leave at four-thirty. Our scheduled arrival time was around nine-thirty in the morning which was great, it would give us time to swing back to our time zone and rest all day. When we boarded the plane I was pleasantly surprised when I saw Ms. Ruth. She was delighted to meet PJ she asked us to come near to her and gave us a beautiful blessing in French. As she held both our hands, she kissed the both and whispered the prayer to our hearts…"Que l'amour que vous avez trouve…Que Dieu vos benisse a travers toutes les epreuves a venir…Que votre coeur a trouver leur chemin du retour a votre ame… Real Love est une benediction de Dieu…Librement il donne…Librement he Loves…" She had such a strong dilect I could hardly understand her; but when I looked at PJ's eyes and they were sort of glassy it was as if she had spoken directly to his heart. I understood some of the words but couldn't wait until we got on the plane to ask what the true meaning was. We were so honored as I had told PJ so much about her…she smiled at both of us and sent us away with a kiss on our cheeks as if she were our Grandmother sending us off to another country in the hopes that we would be careful for nothing especially strangers. Immediately I gave her my business card and told her how much of a joy it was meeting her and if she ever needed anything not to hesitate to call me. PJ gave her his card and thanked her for the prayer and sent his blessings with her and asked her to keep us in his prayers in french. "Merci, pour vos paroles de sagesse, s'il vous plait nous garder dans vos prieres." Which meant "Thank you, for your words of wisdom, please keep us in your prayers."

After we boarded the plane we could barely keep our eyes open…we held hands and drifted off to sleep before the airlne stewardess rolled her cart by. We were worn out, it felt like we had been on a honeymoon before our honemooon...but having that feeling of being on our way back home with PJ right next to me meant so much. It's amazing how time changes and how certain events can change a person's life forever; its certainly true and a statement that I live my life by...If you can change your mind... you can change your life. Life is a wonderful teacher to us of lifetime of experiences, as it moves you to new heights; it's a blessing to reach those pivotal moments especially when you've grown from each lesson. After our trip we felt as we had been transformed by the memories that dwelt in our hearts and mind. Everything we experienced and encountered were filled with something that not many would experience in their lifetime.

The Closer I get to You

The closer we got to each other, the more our love seem to open up as we discovered the importance of giving it all we had, in order to make it what we wanted and needed it to be. Although our level of intimacy had reach a whole new level, my love, respect and honor for God was much richer and deeper than I had ever experienced; it had also reached another elevation of intensity and truth. My trust was placed in a consciousness inside my total being that kept me focused; it never abandoned me, even when my body was feeling weak I had to abandon what our flesh wanted and focus on the desire of our hearts. Although trials and tests approach us everyday of our lives to find out if we're really free from entrapments that can make us weak and hinder us from believing in or receiving real love.

As I sat on my sofa, I began to recapture the essence of our relationship in my journal and private thoughts that were surfacing across my mind. I went over every thing in my mind, the anticipation of awaiting, expectations, foresight, my fore thoughts, intuition, what I was looking forward to most in life and the inner strength that every marriage needs when its tried and tested in order to make our union stronger. What stood out to me was what I felt in the core of my being, which would have to be the day I would be married to my soul mate, the man who had quenched my thirst for love, the one who would finally satisfy my intimate appetite, the one who would set my desires on fire and let them burn for him until the early morning sunrise. Then I thought of how much I wanted to become one with this man who had touched my soul, who together with him I felt whole, complete, and equal too. Immediately I began to write poetry of the love we had experience with one another.

It's Friday, the week before our wedding, as we got through all the details and planning, I couldn't believe that we were this close to the first day of Spring; about to spring forward into a new life chosen just for us. The flowers are all coming into bloom, because the newness of life is near. The birds are chirping and everything is turning green, oh I love the very essence of Spring, if you close your eyes you will be able to see. The flowers, the trees, the grass, the plants are being sprayed by the showers of blessings as they become new. Oooh mother nature is so incredibly beautiful too; the power of creation is being adorned by the sunlight and the spring rain. Every day nature takes on the array of sunshine, there's a lovely flower where a bud was the day before. Leaves on trees, were they weren't are now there, as the rain falls down with its purified love, don't forget the brilliant light of hope beaming straight from above. What can compare to this glorified sight, the phenomenal power of rays of sunlight, strengthening each part of nature bright in our sight as we watch it unfold. Nothing on earth compares to the renewing of life being re-born all over again. The seasons are adorned in all its splendor to show us love in the distinction of his glory.

Just as I was caught up in the essence of new birth, in anticipation of his magnificent splendor; the phone rang...it was PJ...he was at the airport in Chicago, on his way home which was his last trip before our wedding. His trip was a sensation, he wanted to reassure me that he was OK, and couldn't wait to get home. He told me that he loved me and would see me as soon as his flight got in; but he wanted me to know that his flight had been delayed for an hour in Chicago and good thing he was only four hours from home. PJ had been gone for well over three weeks it seemed like forever. He left a few days after we got back from Paris, he was upset about it but they promised him a very generous bonus; to take care of all the last minute details that had to be taken care of under the original contract agreement. They requested that he be there immediately to see the project to completion. I really started to get the "missing him blues," he knew with all the planning that I had to do without him there had began to make me feel kind of lonely by now and he was right. I had not heard his voice in twenty one days we had made this stupid vow that we tested...by an old wives tale...to find out if absence makes the heart grow fonder. This was the first time he had been gone that we didn't talk by phone or correspond by letters or postcards. By him being gone for three weeks my heart was aching for him. We both couldn't believe that we would be seeing each other in 4 hours. "Baby, I can't wait to see you, I been craving you like an addiction" "Me too, God it's been hard not the pick up the phone and call you…I guess it's true." "Yea baby that old saying is true alright, I can't wait to see you and just hold you in my arms." "Me too, I love you…I'll be at the airport waiting for you, honey I missed your voice." "Not as much as I missed your voice precious, I can't wait to see you and touch you." At that instance, I heard the sound in the background announcing his flight, my heart was beating so fast. "I've got to go baby, they just announced my flight, Oooh baby, I can't believe how cold it is down here, it has been freezing all day. It was snowing earlier but I understand it stopped a couple of hours before we landed." "Oh no, honey I know how cold it gets down there." " Don't worry about anything baby, it looks like everything is clearing up, but they are expecting and cold front in a little later with some more snowfall, thank God we'll be long gone by them." "I can't wait to warm you up, honey." "Me too baby, I've got to go so you can do all of that, I love you. Until then."

After his call I got down on my knees and prayed, thanking God that he was able to finally call me before he left, then I prayed again for his flight and safe return, although he sounded like he may have been coming down with a slight cold. I better make him some cough medicine; and yes I am one of those all natural women who makes my own cough syrup; with three natural ingredients. Fresh lemons, pure unfiltered honey, and some all natural herbs and spices. I made him a care package with the homemade cough syrup, a few cold tablets, some fresh herbal tea and a bottle of orange juice from my refrigerator. I wanted him to get a good night's sleep then I packed it up and put it in a bag to give it to him as soon as I got him home. Every since he'd been in Chicago, I had been having an awfully hard time sleeping. I understood his job was very time consuming and since he got the promotion it might get worse, for the three weeks he told me he would be tied up in meetings after meetings after meetings trying to get the companies to agree on every single detail that was in the best interest of all parties. He had an impeccable memory for details and was always able to pull up everything out of his mental computer. Because he recorded all of his meeting and kept excellent records on his laptop computer that he carried with him everywhere. The President of the company trusted him because of his expertise and his professionalism. They said he had a exceptional way with people, and they really respected him because he was a man of integrity, who was dedicated and very versatile. He was able to speak several foreign languages fluently, French, Italian, Spanish, and he knew the dilect in Japan and China. They valued him and allowed him to have a lot of flexibility with their clients and they never once questioned his ability or his reliability. He had worked for this company for several years, he was one of the top candidates before he graduated from college then he immediately climbed up the corporate ladder after being highly recommended by the Vice President of the company. He proved himself to be very reliable, and was always willing to travel where ever they needed him to. They were extremely proud of him and the associate team that traveled with him. I really appreciated the way he handled his self in all of his business negotiations. He taught me to be stronger in my career as well simply by his own ability to handle his business, he was so intelligent and sharp. His wisdom and knowledge is what encouraged me to apply for and receive a promotion in my career.

It had been a long week although I felt a sense of relief, but I had been able to really sleep well at all. For the whole entire week I had been up for long hours on end, just fatigued I didn't really know why, I decided to lay down and rest my eyes for little while, before PJ's flight arrived. I was exhausted, I had been running all week long. The people at my office had given me a very nice wedding shower at work earlier today. I had been excited all day, I didn't get any work done at all, after the wedding shower Mr. Jones gave me the rest of the day off so that I could get everthing home. He turned out to be so sweet expecially after he got back from his vacation with his wife which they decided to renew their vows in their marriage he was like a new man. She asked him to thank me for insiting that they go. He knew I had been a nervous wreck all week with the bridal jitters because of the weather. I was due three weeks of vacation for the year and I was taking two weeks of paid vacation for our honey moon, and one week off without pay for the wedding we had received so many gifts, cashiers checks and cash, which paid for my salary for more than a month and then. I knew I was not going to be back into the office again, until around the end of April; I was ready to be off…my nerves were working overtime. I was already nervous because PJ had been gone for three weeks which seemed like an eternity. Talk about love being tested, there were no phone calls, no letters, no post cards, the endurance level was weathered and finally would be conquered. Thank God, he was on his way home, the delay was over. I can't wait to see him, hold his hand and hold him in my arms and squeeze him real tight…..I finally closed my eyes and rested, for about two hours straight, the alarm went off, and I woke up and I looked outside; it had just started to get dark and I noticed it had been raining. Then a chill came over me, because I thought about how cold it was in the Spring in Chicago. I better start getting ready now, since its wet out, and get an early start because the traffic is going to be horrible getting to the airport on a Friday Night. The rain started again before I left home, it got a little heavier, the wind was high. I started getting chills over and over again and a strange feeling kept coming over me. So I got ready and packed up everything, grabbed my all weather coat, my umbrella and left my apartment two hours ahead of the scheduled flight arrival. I felt nervous as my mind started wondering what the weather must have been like in Chicago. He would never tell me if the weather was real bad, because he didn't want me to worry. What if it started snowing again, Oh no, now I'm really going crazy; not knowing what to think, my mind starting playing the "What If" game. You know how it works, What if…he gets snowed in, or What if the plane slides on the runway…you know all that crazy stuff…stop it you stupid brain and watch these crazy people driving on this freeway. Stop thinking negative thoughts, just be careful and take your time and every thing will be fine. Then the notion to pray until I got to the airport came to my mind, so I prayed and prayed. Before I knew it I was there, at the airport arriving at my exit for flight arrival parking. I looked at my watch and one hour and 15 minutes had already gone by, thank goodness I left early, by the time I park and get into the airport, I'll only have to wait 30 minutes, he'll be here.

I parked and got out of the car, and I noticed the air in my front tire was a little low, PJ had taught me to keep some fix it flat in my car just in case of an emergency late at night, and to always make sure I could lean on my AAA membership as a backup for my car insurance. But after I examined the tire; it didn't look too bad. I thought to myself I'll worry about that later, because it was getting late, it was rainy and dark and I didn't want to be in the airport's parking tunnel by myself. So I grabbed my purse and headed for the arrival gate, I left my umbrella in the car because the parking lot elevator allowed you to get off inside the airport to avoid bad weather, which was an excellent idea. When I got inside I checked the over head chart of arrival flights with his flight number against what I had written on my note pad. And my heart skipped a beat as I walked toward the baggage claim area, the chart read, (flight delayed due to inclement weather). My heart sank deep into my chest, I couldn't believe it, so I went straight to the desk to ask the reservationist but, the line was too long. I started to get irritated, so I got out of line and went up to the information desk to ask them about the flight. All they could tell me was the reservationist had to confirm the posting and they could let me know about the flight being rescheduled from the computer but I had to get to the back of the line. "Oh brother, do you see how long that line is, I have to go all the way through that line before someone answers my question?" "I'm sorry Ms. but the only way you'll find out is to stand in that line, I only direct people to the gates, baggage claim area and I report lost items." Calm down Angell, calm down, I said to my self. Once you get through the line you will find out the answer." I stood in line for almost an hour, when I finally got to the desk, I asked about the flight and she confirmed that it had been delayed sure enough, but it was due to a snow storm. My heart started beating real fast, "has the flight left the airport or was the flight cancelled?" "Right now, Ms. we don't know yet, we are still waiting on confirmations of the location of that plane right now. I understand that the flight took off and ran into a some turbulence while it was in the air but we are trying to find out if the flight was able to land safely after it turned around." "Oh my God," The whole computer system has shut down in Chicago and we can't tell you or anyone else what happened until we receive word from O'hare International Airport. "What do you mean you don't know what has happen?" "Ma'am please I don't want to alert you or any others here until we receive final word, we are working as fast as we can to get the information posted. As soon as we know something, we will post it up on the screen, why don't you have a seat ma'am and try to calm down. Come back and check with us within the next half hour or so; we should know something by then." My heart just stopped beating for a moment, then I looked at the woman and said, "I'm sorry ma'am, I'm just kind of nervous right now, I didn't mean to sound so rude, thank you for letting me know what you could. I'll just come back in half an hour as you suggested; do you really think you'll know something by then? "Yes ma'am I'm almost positive we will, as we speak right now, they are connecting the problem with our back up system; trust me I've worked here for seven years and this is not uncommon. The emergency backup takes about thirty minutes to an hour to reboot the entire system." Oh my God, I can't believe this, why is this happening? I said to myself in a mere whisper. "Well ma'am, you can't argue with mother nature we have been under a severe storm most of the day and we do have to look after the safety of all our passengers." "I'm sure you're right, ma'am I'll just go and get a cup of coffee and come back in about 30 minutes to an hour." "Yes ma'am like I said if there are any changes we will post it on the monitor. I walked away thinking to myself, from personal experience of how cold it gets in Chicago even during the Spring. I better check my cellphone to see if Jon left me a message, Oh my God I saw where I had missed five calls from Jon, I never heard my phone ring. Then I noticed it was on vibrate, I was devastaed. So I tried calling him back but I could'nt get him. So immediately, I called my voicemail to listen to my messages, but they were all hang up calls. The last call had a long pause of about 3 minutes of silence with a lot of background noise I couldn't make out anything that he was saying, before he hung up. Oh my God, all of a sudden my heart started beating extremely fast and skipping beat after beat, then a tear fell out of my left eye, I felt like a little girl who was lost at the airport. My world had been shaken up by the fear of the unknown, immediately I hung up the phone and sat down at one of the coffee shops near by. I ordered a cup of black cofee, I didn't want any flavor, sugar, cream; I felt like this black dark empty space that reflected my emotions in my coffee cup, void and unknowing. As I wondered back over near the reservationist a few cups later, all I could do was hope someone might soon be able to give me some updated news on his flight. Right away I began to think about all the other passengers on that flight, the husbands, wifes, children, parents, aunts, uncles, neices, nephews or somebody girlfriend, boyfriend, friend or coworker. Immediately out of compassion I began to pray inside my soul for everyone on board as I looked around, I started listening to the hearts of others that were waiting and concerned just as I was. You could feel the emotions in the air; I know longer felt alone, as my heart reached out to them in prayer, I began to embrace a prayer of intercession for everyone who was just as afraid as I was. So I prayed without ceasing not just for Jon but for everyone on that plane and those who were waiting on those due to make it home or arrive into the City. As I waited with a very heavy heart of compassion, thirty minutes passed then an hour and fifteen minutes more had passed. Still there was no update on the flight. The overhead chart of flights read the same for two hours, I thought I was going to go out of my mind. I continued to call Jon but could not reach him; his phone kept going into voice mail. Then finally I looked up at the schedule and I saw cancelled beside the flight number. So I got up slowly to ask if they knew the status of the plane or the passengers. Immediately the little woman at the counter confirmed that the flight had been cancelled due to a severe snow storm and that the passengers had to experience an overnight layover in Chicago the entire airport had been shut down and was snowed in. "Ma'am, they say it just starting snowing very heavily which caused the computer and radar problems, and none of the flights in Chicago were able to get off the ground, the roadway became too slippery due to the ice. They experienced several delays tonight and most of those flights were canceled until late tomorrow afternoon due to the snow storm." "What happens in these circumstances? Should I just go home and come back in the morning?" "Yes ma'am that will be a good idea, the best thing I can advise you, is to go home and get some rest and wait until this snow storm passes over tonight keep in tuned with the weather and use the number that you have to check the flights. I'm sure the airport will send us a schedule of updates with new flight arrival times for all the flights that were delayed tonight." "Will the people who are on those flights have to stay at the airport all night long?" "Usually they do, however, there are some people who elect to go to hotels near the airport because of the inconvenience." "Can you please tell me what the temperature is currently in Chicago?" "It's about 17 degrees, with a wind chill factor of -10 below zero; but they are expecting lots of sunshine tomorrow, I hear let's just keep praying for the snow to melt." "Oh my God, I had no idea that it had gotten was that cold." "Yes Ma'am I understand the temperture dropped earlier this afternoon. If you know the windy city the Winters in Chicago always seem to linger on for a while late into the spring, which is usually colder much longer than it is in Texas." Just then I got a chill of the memories of what that hawk was always like for me when I was in Chicago. Then I thought about how tired PJ must have been, I'm sure he's more worried about me than he is about his self. I better get home before it starts back raining or we'll both be caught up in a mess of storms; I'm sure he'll call me on my cell whenever the weather breaks. I'm sure it's affecting the phones and everything. So I hurried to the parking lots elevator and rushed to my car, as I approached my car I noticed the tire was lower than it was when I arrived at the airport. Then I thought I better get that fix-it-flat out of my trunk and put some of it in this stupid tire before I'm stuck on side of the road somewhere in the rain. I opened the trunk and there was no fix-it-flat. Oh no, what did I do with it, I looked inside the car in the back seat, the front seat, and then again in the trunk. I know I put it in the trunk of the car where is it? I looked and looked, and looked, I couldn't find it anywhere. My goodness, I said to my self, "where on earth did I put that stupid can." I went over it and over it in my mind, about what I could have done with the bag I got from the auto store last week; Okay when I stopped and got my oil changed I picked up a new flashlight and the stupid can of fix it flat. Think, Angell, think, so I got back into my car and sat down so that I could think, I had been off in the brain all this month with so many things happening, that my mind was blank. I had really been doing entirely too much that I couldn't remember what I had done with the bag because I didn't see the flashlight either. All of a sudden it came to me, after I purchased the flashlight, I went over and picked up some air fresher; after I paid for it I put it in the bag with the can of fix it flat in my purse. After I got home my cell phone rang and I acidentally took the bag upstairs with me. When

I got home, I realized that it was in my purse so I put it in the hall closet. Then I experienced that feeling of being unprepared, forgetful, and now being alone with a stupid flat tire. What a nightmare this whole night is trying to be, I better go back inside and ask for help. I felt a need to call my Mom and let her know where I was, and what was going on. I wanted my Mommy, isn't it funny that when things are going wrong in your life, you think about calling your Mom. You don't quite know what to do, because of the things happening in your life, no matter how old you are, you will still think of being comforted by someone you love and are very close to, who's always there when you need them.

When I got back inside the airport I decided to check my phone again, because I could'nt get service in the parking lot. "Oh my God, I had three missed calls; it must been when I put my purse in the front seat while I was frantically looked in the trunk for the stupid flashlight and fix it flat. Two were from PJ cell again and the third was from a number I didn't recognize. When I checked my messages there was still a lot of static on the phone, I could barely hear him, but thank God I heard him say that he was OK, the he went on to say by now, I probably knew what was going on. He asked me not to worry about him; he wanted me to get home and he would try to call me later by that time he would be settled. He told me that he had no idea what time or when they would be able to leave Chicago, and for me not to be nervous about the weather. Then he asked me to be careful driving home, because he heard it was raining. Then he told me to get some rest; he said the phone signals were all screwed up and that I may not be able to reach him. The third message was from my mom, asking me to call her when I got back home. I called her to let her know what was going on, and she told me that she felt like something was wrong, "a mother's intuition is always right on target," then she asked me to tell the people at the information desk and see if they could send someone out to help me with my tire, and they did, because I didn't not want to call triple AAA or anyone else; I would have been waiting forever since it was raining. I was so thankful, my mother knew exactly what I should do, I'm certain I would have thought of the same thing, that was an easy thought which made perfect sense; but I was and had been a nervous wreck all week. I hadn't been thinking clearly since I heard the news about PJ's flight. Immediately, airport security sent someone to walk me out and they fixed my tire and sent me on my way with a smile. They apologized for the inconvenience and told me that they would have someone call me when a new schedule of flight times had been posted.

When I finally got home it was almost two o'clock in the morning due to a severe thunder storm that passed over the metroplex. After I finally made it home, I was wet and exhausted, after I got out of those clothes and I took a long hot shower and got in the bed and tried calling PJ but still couldn't reach him. I felt like I had been lost in space and time. Although I placed my phone in the bathroom I never rang. Finally, I checked my voice mail and realized PJ had called, it was sort of a weird call; he never told me what hotel he was staying at but he mentioned that he was okay and wanted to just lay down and go to sleep. Chicago was on the same time that we were, I knew he was tired although it seemed a little strange for him to leave that message on my phone. I was exhausted my self but nothing would keep me from calling him. So I tried to dismiss, what I was feeling and tried to call anyway but all circuits were busy. Maybe, that's why he left that message, he was probably just as frustrated as I was. I trusted that everything would be okay, after I finished praying and just prayed I would see him the next day. Immediately I got down on my knees and prayed through it all, that this nightmare would soon be over and that God would send as many warm rays of sunshine to melt as much snow as possible at O'hare International Airport. Then I thanked him in advance answering and hearing my prayer. Just as I got off my knees the phoned rang. It was PJ, "Angell baby are you okay, I have been calling you all night long?" "Honey, I'm fine, I been trying to call you too, are you okay?" "Yea, I'm okay I was just worried about you. This has been one of the longest days of my life, I can't believe it; a snow storm, but you can never predict what Mother Nature will do in the windy city." "Honey, I'm just thankful that they didn't try to fly that plane in that snow storm, aren't you." "Yea, me too, I'm sorry that I'm stuck here in Chicago until this snow melts down. The weather is reporting that it should be sunny but still it's going to be very cold tomorrow, we may be getting out of here in the next day or so depending on the snow melting. Baby, I miss you, I can't wait to get home. The company put us up at a Hotel near the airport, we'll stay here until they clear the run way. By the way what took you so long to get home? I was worried, is your car okay?" "Honey is there anything you don't know?" "I felt like something was wrong because it took you too long to get home from the airport." "Well to tell you the truth, I had a flat tire at the airport, but the people at the airport were able to help me; they took care of it for me." Just then I was saying to myself, please don't ask me about that stupid can of fix-it-flat. Because I did not want him to know how stupid I was, putting it in my hall closet instead of my car. Then he said, "that's great, that was the least they could have done." "You know, we were just about to take off on the run way when the snow storm hit, I kept thinking to myself, surely I'm not going to go out like this, and leave you to be an engaged widow, before we even get a chance to start our life together. My mind was playing all kinds of tricks on me." "I know, honey mine too, but I feel much better now that I've talked to you." "So do I baby, hey they are calling me up to the front desk. I'll talk to you some time tomorrow, get some rest would you." "I will, if you will." "Sweet dreams okay I'll see you soon, until then." "Before I could even say goodnight or I love you, he was gone." God that was strange why were they calling him up to the front desk? What was he talking about? I didn't know what to think about how anything. I was thought out...my brain was on overload... I was just too tired for any other irregular thought patterns.

I finally laid down in my bed and I drifted off to sleep; then I entered into the nightmares from hell, they were all terrible - from crashed flights; to being snowed in by 15 feet of snow; to PJ not getting back home for weeks; to our wedding being canceled due to snow on the first day of spring which would not be unusual. When I woke up I was awaken in a cold sweat, after that I could not go back to sleep at all. The clock read 3:45 a.m. then 5:15, then 7:50, when I finally went back to sleep I don't even remember what time it was, I was so tired and exhausted from everything that Freddy Crugar had dished out in my sleep, that I slept until 4:30 p.m. in the evening. I turned the ringer off on my phone by accident, I don't even remember when I pushed the button, at some point during all the nightmares from hell I must have knocked the phone off the hook or something. After I fell asleep the whole world was shut off, I never heard the phone, or the alarm go off or anything else. I checked the clock again, I could not believe that I had slept that long, I picked up the phone to check my messages and I had missed PJ's call he was at the airport. He had called me several times and figured I was still asleep, he left me a message and told me that his flight had been rescheduled and he would be arriving at the airport at 6:15 p.m. I jumped straight up and got into the shower, I got ready and then I left again for the airport. My heart was beating at 70 mph almost as fast as I was driving, I was driving about 80 to 85 mph, I said to myself, you better slow down girl before your heart goes faster than your car. You certainly don't need an unforeseen unexpected heart attack. Then I started to do some breathing techniques to calm me down. I noticed that the weather was a whole lot nicer today than it was yesterday. The sun was shinning it looked to have been a very nice day, I was glad I'd slept late I felt refreshed and a whole lot better. Here's the exit for the airport, I pulled into the parking lot and a feeling came over me, I don't believe it but, there was one park left it was the exact same one I parked in last night. "Speaking of dajavou, let's try this again. So I pulled back into the park and went inside, when I got there the flight had already arrived, it was right on schedule. My heart started skipping beats until I got to the gate; I noticed that everyone had already started getting off the plane as I was walking up. I stood there for a while, but I didn't see PJ anywhere, which was strange, then I looked around the airport since it looked like everyone had already left the plane. I didn't see him anywhere then I saw the airline stewards get off the plane, then the pilots; so I walked over and asked them if all the passengers had gotten off the plane and they told me they were sure they had because they are always the last to get off. I went over to the baggage claim area where most of the people had already picked up their bags and were walking away, only a few people were left waiting on their bags to surface. PJ was no where within my sight, then I thought maybe I'm just going crazy could I have misunderstood his message. So I pulled myself together and dialed my voice mail to recheck the number of the flight and I wasn't crazy he really did give me the same flight that had just arrived. Just as I begin to hang up the phone, he walked up behind me and scared the daylights out me, he grabbed me from behind and pulled me real close to him. I thought I was going to jump out of my skin; I almost fell down, then he started kissing me on my neck. "Hey baby, were you looking for me?" His voice went right through me, "Boy you know I was looking for you, don't you ever scare me like that again." He turned me around in front of him and we held each other, and then he kissed me right there in the baggage claim area right next to the payphones; we must have kissed for about ten or fifteen minutes. We got so caught up that we totally forgot we were in the airport, I felt like I was on an island of paradise somewhere. I had longed for him and when his lips touched mine, we couldn't even part from one another. There was a little old man on his flight, he walked over to use the payphone. "He said excuse me sonny, this little number must be the reason you were not able to sleep last night, give her a little air would you so I could call up mine we might not be able to kiss like that. But I'm sure we can try until we get something working for us." We were so embarrassed. "This must be your bride-to-be, son. Congratulations. She's sure looks like a good catch sonny, you both make a swell looking couple; I'm sure that airline stewardess over there staring at you both wishes she was you. I can always tell." "Who? What stewardess is she talking about?" "Just some one I knew from a long time ago, I often see here on a flight or two every now and then. I was telling the old man about you when I realized that she overheard us and seem a little disappointed to hear the news." "What? Are you saying there something going on in the past or what." "Something like that." As soon as he said that, the last of his luggage came up and he very quickly loaded it on his dolly. Then he began to tell me why I didn't see him when he got off the plane. Then went on to say that he was the first one to get off the plane because he was looking for me, and had quite a bit of luggage. I asked him what did he have in all those bags?" " I have a few surprises for you, it maybe a little something old, something new, something borrowed or something blue, plus I purchased a few things for himself. "Let's get out of this airport now, I don't want to be here another minute. By the way how are you doing today, you look so beautiful and refreshed! You must have slept like a log?" "Well, at first, I had nothing but nightmares from hell, when I finally got to sleep which was sometime this morning. I'm sure

I'll sleep better, now that you're home". "Angell, I'm so glad to finally be home, I felt like that was the longest trip I have ever taken in my whole entire life." As we walked out of the airport, I could feel the eyes watching us as we walked out the door. When you are a woman, it's that woman's intuition...that intuitive radar that we were equipped and born with. After I informed PJ where I was parked I realized time was getting away from me, so I quickly told him,"Honey, I need to run back inside to thank the lady at the reservation desk that I was so rude to last night. She asked me to let her know when you got back safely; I told her about our wedding scheduled for next weekend and I promised to let her know you made it back to me safely." Not only did I need to do that, but I had broken radar that needed to be fixed. I had already clocked the "Something like that" which was what he referred to airline stewardess as. When I walked back in she and several others were standing at the same counter I was making my way back to, which was to my advantage. When I walked up to the counter, the reservationist recognized me immediately, I thanked her and told her that my fiance finally made it back to me safely. Then I looked over at her, and said hello, PJ told me about you, I don't think she was expecting me to be so blunt. I looked at the name on her badge and it read Cheri, pleased to meet you. She congratulated me, as she looked at my ring, then she said a little more than she should have. I could tell by the look in her eyes that she was surprised by the news, and I could sense that it had been a little more than just a chance meeting on a flight every now and then. But at the same time I thanked God that he never keeps us, meaning his children ignorant. Instantly by looking her straight in her eyes, I knew it was much more than they both were letting on, by the tone in her voice that she was somewhat embarrassed by the mention of his name. Of course I had to make sure she knew our wedding was this time next Saturday; I know it was a little boastful of me, but I couldn't help myself. You know how we women are; oh well that's the way cookies crumble. Crumble, Crumble...

When I got back to the car, PJ had already loaded all his bags in the car, and he told me he wanted to drive, which I would'nt have it any other way. We went straight to his house unloaded every thing and then he took a long hot shower. I decided to lay down on the sofa while he was in the shower to rest my eyes with a slice of peace on my mind. I hit the remote and turned on some music because I did'nt want to see anything on TV. Then I noticed that his cell phone was ringing; I don't usually look at his phone but something told me to look. The name Cheri, popped up and left him a message. Then out of curiosity I checked his phone and her name and number was all the way through his phone more than twenty times; incoming and outgoing all hours of the day and night. My heart began to sink I didn't know what to think, first I began to think about any woman that would be in her shoes who may be loosing a man like him. Then as a woman you always need to know that there is always someone from our past that wishes it could be them. Especially when we finally meet that person that we want to spend the rest of our lives with; its always sombody lurking around in the backstreets of our desires that we hold on to; called the "Just in Case" men and women from our past. Which is how the enemy works, the moment he sees an opportunity to slide through the crack of the door or window; his job is to creep through and get in any way he can. I began to sense more than I really wanted to know; I decided to observe him and pray for wisdom and discernment. Immediately, I began to seek God; because I had this feeling that he had been with her as recent as last night. Only time, his actions and reactions would tell me the truth. When he got out of the shower, I told him that his phone was ringing earlier; I put it back in the exact location that he left it upside down. I didn't mean to pry but at the same time I didn't want anybody to make a fool out of me, not even him. No matter what was going on whether it was a day, the day of or days before the day of our wedding, something as frivioulous as this could change the course of our lives. As I laided there, I observed his eyes and his reaction to what must have been on his voice mail. Then he looked over at me and began to walk out of the room, I didn't say anything he was at home he go where ever he wanted to go in his house. I just watched him. For the first time in our relationship he appeared to be a little uncomfortable while he was in the room with me. Then I heard him call his Mom to let her know that he had made home safely from all the snow and freezing temperatures. After their conversation he passed me the phone so I could say hello to his Mom. We said our hello's and she asked me if we would be at church on Sunday, because they were scheduled to announce our wedding, I told her we would be there. When I hung up, PJ knelt down beside the sofa and begin to do a few unusal things while I laid there. "Jon, what are you doing?" "Come on baby it's been way too long." "Too long, for what? What are you talking about? Are you really taking my panties off." "Yes, I am. Come on, baby I need to feel you inside me, it doesn't have to be long, just let me get inside." "Get inside, You are kidding right? Come on PJ we promised each other that we would wait, it just seven more days, come on we are not going to go there." Then he started to get an attitude, which was something that I had never seen before. "Okay, Okay, this is stupid I almost lost my life last night and all I could think about was being with you that's the least you could do." "What do mean its the least I could do? What's going on PJ? I realize how you must have felt; I feel the same way, but we discussed this and we both said we would wait. Is it something you need to tell me, you are acting like an animal whose been locked up in a cave or something. It's something different about you I can feel it?" "What do you mean different? I just need to make love to you tonight." "I could PJ, but I sense its something else, its in your touch; it seems rough and almost demanding like if I don't do it, you will. It's all in your tone towards me, and the way you're holding me right now. Maybe I shoud go home and meet you at church tomorrow." "Come on Angell, I'm on fire, baby." Then he took off his towel. "What? On fire. Where is this coming from, why are you standing there like that? I've never seen you act like this." "I want you right now, can't you understand that! I've been gone for three weeks. I need to have you right now." Immediately I got up because he was definitely not the man I knew. He was beginning to scare me, then I said something that I shouldn't of said. Before I knew it we were experiencing our first argument, which was nothing I expected to happen a week before our wedding. Then I said what was on my mind out of anger. "Who the hell do you think I am, You must think I'm Cheri, you act like you're lost in a time capsule or something and maybe you got me mixed up with her. The name is Angell, and whatever happen between you and Cheri is not happening between us right now. My intuition is telling me that more happened between you and her in Chicago than just Something like that. Remember those are the words you used to describe her. So I tell you what, why don't you call her back and maybe she can stop blowing up your phone. I might be young but I'm not stupid. I can tell the way your standing there you want more than what you're asking for in more ways than one." By the way I had a conversation with your girl Cheri and she said a little more than I cared to hear about between the two of you. She told me she lived in Chicago and had ran into you on several occasions and that you guys dated before I met you and it was pretty hot up there in the windy city. She express how happy she was for both of us, but from the look on her face she wished you had chosen her instead me. "Come on baby, it's not like that. I love you I don't want her she didn't mean nothing to me and I just want you right now." "No, Jon I'm not going there with you. Did you sleep with her Jon?" "Baby, why would you think that." "It's just a feeling I got in the pit of my stomach." "It wasn't like that, Angell." "Oh really what was it like then." When he didn't answer, I got so upset, before I knew it I yell out. "I tell you what why don't you take this ring and shove it. (Then I took off my ring and threw it at him.) Why don't you call Cheri, maybe she can blow off that fire that burning in front of you. Especially since you and her both have been blowing up each other's cell phones all hours of the day and night." "Angell, it's not like that." "Oh really then what has it been like?" "I't not what you think baby, I'm sorry I'm just a little crazy right now." "Yea you're crazy alright." Before I knew it I had grabbed my purse, my overnight bag and walked out the door. Tears were flowing down my eyes as fast as I could walk, I couldn't hardly think straight. As soon as I got to my car I heard him walking out the door behind me, trying to stop me from driving off telling me he was sorry. Asking me to forgive him; I thought I was going to run over him. I was so angry and hurt and more than that disappointed.

As I drove home, I noticed his car was behind me, then my phone started ringing. It just kept ringin but I still wouldn't answer it; so I began to think should I go home and have him banging on my door all night, then I thought Oh Jesus, I forgot he has a key. Oh God what do I need to do? So I decided to go by my best friends house. I picked up my cell phone and called her, thank God she was home. She could hear it in my voice that something was wrong. She thought it was PJ's flight, then I explained that he was okay, but I was so upset with him. I began to ramble and asked her if I could come by her place right now. She told me to come on. So I speeded up and drove like a mad woman until I lost PJ; then as soon as I pulled up to Daphine's house I was a wreck. When I knocked on her door, she let me in immediately. All I could do was fall into her arms and boo hoo...like only you can on your best friend's shoulder. I could'nt stop crying. She asked me to sit down on the sofa while she got me some kleenix, a couple of pillows and a blanket. My phone just kept ringing; then finally Daphine's phone rang PJ was on her phone telling her he knew I was there because he was outside. She looked at me and I just shook my head "No," I told her that I didn't want to see him right now. She told him that she was sorry but she couldn't let him in.

Immediately I began to think to myself, PJ had been half way around the world, I would be a fool not to believe that he hadn't been tempted with plenty of women all the time, I'm sure he saw and even entertained many different kinds of women that could show him one hell of a time. And I was certain that he would'nt be far behind them keeping up. When another woman tries to tempt your man and possibly succeed it can put him into a state of craving all kinds of lustful desires, if his needs are not being taken care of on the regular. And here I am refusing his attempts of making love, am I crazy. No I'm not crazy, I love him and I don't want to lose him, but more than that I don't want to lose where I stand with God. So I had a choice, I had to stand on what I believed in, and keep the promise that I made to myself and to God which meant a lot more to me. As I sat there on the sofa, I cried until I couldn't cry any more, Daphine being the kind of friend she was, never asked me one question, she just let me cry on the shoulder of her sofa. She fixed me a cup of hot tea and brought me some PM tablets and I finally fell asleep. When I woke up the next morning, I didn't feel like doing anything especially going to church. I felt empty, and alone, my ring was no longer on my finger. I begin to weep again; Daphine came in and asked me if I wanted a cup of coffee or wanted to talk about it, she was there. I didn't know what to say, because all this time I had been engaged to the greatest guy in the world. I had counseled her through so many bad relationships I didn't even know where to began, not that I didn't really know what to say, I just didn't know how to say it. Then I told her that PJ and I had our first real heated argument and that I said some terrible things and he said and did some things. Then before I knew it he started taking off my panties like a mad man, girl I think I left them there. " Then we both laughed. "Okay we can look at this like! Now, we know your panties are still there which tells me at least you left something behind. Well, where they pretty panties? Or some you can let go." "Girl you are crazy, oh course they were pretty, you know me, they were definitely Victoria's Best kept secrets." "Well there you go, that's was the problem, you always did wear pretty panties. Maybe if you didn't have all those pretty panties you wouldn't have tempted the man. Next time, you don't want your panties taken off just wear some granny panties, I guarantee he won't think twice about taking those off." Then we both laughed again. Look Angell, this man is practically your husband, why didn't you want to just give up a little bit. Look at everything you both had been through in the past 6 months not to mention this last trip to Paris. Come on don't be so dramatic. You guys have got to work this out, you have to apologize to each other and forgive each other. Isn't that what you always tell me." "Yes it is, but it's not the same. It's not that simple." "Look Angell, I don't know any two people that love each other more than you and PJ; you guys are soul mates, you both were made for each other." As the tears began to form in my eyes, I didn't know what else to say, I didn't want her to know anything else. So I asked her if she could go and get my purse and bag out of the car. When she left, I got up and went to the bathroom, then I fell down on my knees and prayed and all God kept bringing to my mind was everyone makes mistakes, he loves you and he loves me. Then I started talking about the vow I had made to him and the vow PJ and I made with each other. Then God reminded my heart of how different men and women are. He began to whisper to my heart that men are not built like women; many times women can go much longer than men when it comes to establishing a covenant of celibacy. His words echoed to me that he had been committed to me and really wanted to spend the rest of his life with me. He whispered to me that the choice was mine. As the sweetness of his voice whispered to the ear of my heart, he reminded in such a gentle voice, "Forgiveness is what I give each of you every day, brand new mercy each morning of your lives, which is what I expect you to give to each other. Just then, Daphine knocked on the door and told me my bag was outside the door, I opened it up and decided to go ahead and take hot shower to cleanse my mind of all the thoughts that were rushing through it.

When I came out, Daphine had made me another cup of tea, I never got a chance to drink the first cup. "Hey, are you okay, you look much better than you did when you got here. You scared me girl. I just want to say this before you go to sleep; I don't know what happened between the two of you tonight; but you can't erase every single thing that you both have experienced and the feelings you felt for each other. She grabbed my hands and said, I tell you what if you don't marry him, just give me the ring and I'll marry him. Then she looked down at my hand and the ring was not there. "Angell, Girl, what did you do? Don't you dare tell me that you gave him back his ring; what happened over there tonight?" I tried to open my mouth, but I couldn't say anything. "Look Angell whatever happened I'm sure he going out of his mind." "Daphine, I love you for being my best friend, but I don't want to think anymore right now; I'm so tired from everything can we talk about it in the morning." She embraced me, "I love you too girl, listen I know how you can just shut down and not talk to anybody." Tears began to come to my eyes again, because she knew me so well. So I shook my head then she asked me to try to rest. As I laid there, the phone rang again I knew it was PJ. I heard Daphine say that I was laying down; and it was best if he gave me some time then I heard her hang up the phone. I didn't want to think anymore, I just wanted to go to sleep; the pm tablets started to make my whole body feel heavy, my head was pounding at first then it finally stopped. As I tried to search my mind to find the answers, I could'nt think about anything other than what God had spoke to my heart. Forgiveness is what he gives us every day, brand new mercy that he gives us each morning of our lives. Although deep down inside my soul I felt an emptiness in my heart I was still comforted by the echos of God's love in my ear. My eyes became heavy then I fell asleep.

Forgiveness Restores the Yoke of Unfaithfulness

When I woke up it was almost 9:00 am; I just laid there trying to collect my thoughts, Daphine had a very comfortable sofa once you sat on it you were immediately pursuaded to relax and take a nap. When she heard me stiring around on the sofa; she walked in. "Good morning, did you sleep okay?" "Yes I think so, although my eyes feel a little puffy but I think I'll be okay." "Well, I hate to mention his name as soon as you wake up, but PJ has already called a couple of times and he came by to see you early this morning; but when he got here you were still alseep; so he asked me if he could just watch you sleep. I thought it was a little strange but he told me he couldn't sleep at all last night, and how sorry he was about what happen and that he loved you too much he couldn't stand it if he couldn't wake up every morning and see you. He told me he didn't have a chance to give you the gifts he brought for you from his trip. He asked me if he could leave that one for you over there sitting on the dining table. I'm sorry Angell, but I let him in and he placed it on the table then he walked over by the sofa and stared at you for about 30 minutes it may have been longer. I just sat over there in that chair, and watched him; I have never saw so much love in a man's eyes than what I saw in his eyes this morning." I was motionless. "Daphine, you let him come in without asking me?" "Yea, I sort of did. I'm sorry Angell, I didn't want to startled you and wake you up either with him sitting here or being at the door." "Look I'm not upset with you, I'm just not ready to talk about anything." "Trust me I know how you are and I respect that. Well will you at least look in the box, I am dying to know what's inside." Immediately she rushed over to get the box off her dining room table and placed it next to me on the sofa. Daphine was acting like a kid at Christmas. I really didn't care. But for her sake I told her I was going to open it just for her. When I opened it there was this gorgeous mustard yellow dupioni silk fishtail dress. It was so soft and silky, the way it was packed it was wrinkle free. I didn't know what to say, Daphine did all the ooh's an aah's for me. My heart fluttered when I saw the note on top of the box. The words expressed everything that he felt; he knew how much my heart was hurting. His note ended in his own words with how much he loved me and never ever wanted to lose me. He asked me if I could find it in my heart to forgive him and meet him at church this morning and that he would not ever stop loving me no matter what happened. The tears begin to flow again and I didn't know what to say. Daphine came over and embraced me and told me that everything was going to be okay. "Thank you for being my best friend and always being there. We have shared more than a few tears together over the years and I would'nt know what to do without her. Can you give me a few minutes? "Sure I can, I don't know what I would do without you, Angell." Then we embraced. "Let me hang this up for you, take your time. She told me for some reason she was exhausted herself and needed to lay down for a few minutes while I took my shower. I asked her if she was okay, she told me she hadn't been feeling too good for the last couple of weeks but she had a doctor's appointment at 9:00 Monday morning; then she smiled with that beautiful smile of hers and I knew everything would be okay. I told her I was sorry, that I had been so absorbed with all of the wedding details that I had neglected to ask her how she was doing throughout the whole planning process. "Do you need me to go with you in the morning?" "I just might need you to be there, Angell." "Remember I'm off work, I can definitely go with you." "I hate to drag you with me to the doctor the week of your wedding." "Daphine, you mean the world to me you've been my best friend since Jr. High School, it's nothing I wouldn't do for you." "Thanks, Angell. So tell me are we going to church or what?" "You go lay down and get some rest until about 10:30 or so, I'll let you know when I wake you up; I'm sorry me and PJ kept you up most of the night and the morning." "No worries God knows I've kept you up since you became my best friend. I love you both of you guys, it was no problem. Wake me up when you decide okay?" "I will, Daphine." "Angell, you know I'll love you through everything girl." "Me too, always through everything." Which is what we always told each other; sort of like through thick and thin.

When I got to the bathroom, I sat down to collect my thoughts as I begin to think of my best friend, so I immediately began to focus on her then I prayed for her. Aferwards I reflected over PJ's note then I decided to try to make some sense of all of it, and think things through; so I prayed and asked God what should I do? The memoirs of everything that PJ and I had ever done began to overwhelm me; almost every event, the conversations, and so many memories that we had accumulated surfaced through my mind like a rushing wind. I could'nt shake him from my thoughts and what we'd meant to each other over the past nine months. It was difficult to pray about it anymore, my heart was so heavy as tears filled my eyes the thought of unfaithfulness seemed frail. As the soft spoken words continued to flow to my heart from God..."Forgiveness is freely given each day to all who ask for it, repentance is equally expressed by those that truly mean it. Your covenenant of celibacy is with me; the vow you made stands in the dephts of your soul which you gave to me as I allowed you to share your heart with the man I sent you to love. The choice is yours to love him in return. Love never fails, you'll need now more than ever." My heart quicken as I felt the overwhelming essence of love for me, it surrounded me with a level of inner peace and comfort that makes it hard to describe. I thanked him so much then I praised him with every tear that flowed down my face.

When I got out of the shower, I felt a new sense of direction and compassion for who I was and especially the genuine relationship that I had with God. It was a reawakening of what he was and always had meant to me. To love me as much as he did, to allow me to listen to his sweet still voice in the mist of heartache in my soul was more than I could ever ask for. I decided to go on to church; so I began to pull my self together. I put on my makeup and combed my hair. Finally I went to wake up my best friend and thank her for being who she was. While I was walking into her bedroom, I noticed she was'nt in bed her dresser drawer was opened and there were several bottles of pills in there. Then I heard her in a very nauseated state as if she had just finished vomiting in her bathroom. I ran in and asked her if she was okay, she told me she was fine and had eaten something that didn't agree with her earlier. She told me that she had just gotten up and was about to get into the shower because she knew I would probably go ahead and go to church. "I just felt a little light headed and sick to my stomach but I'm okay now." "Daphine are you sure you're okay, maybe you should lay back down?" "No I'm okay, I just need to get whatever that was out of my stomach." "I noticed that you left your top drawer open, what's the deal on all those different bottles of pills?" "What pills?" "The ones over there in your drawer. Some of those are pretty old, I got them a long time ago, I never did finish taking most of them. Some are pain pills, and some other stuff." "Like what?" "Come on Angell, do we have to talk about this right now?" "Well yes, we do?" "Angell, listen I have always tried to keep you in the loop about everything; just like last night I don't want to pry about what happen between you and PJ. I sort of feel the same way you do about this, I want to make sure I know for sure before I say anything to anybody. It may not be necessary to go into anything before then, I hope you understand. I had some tests run and I'll find out tomorrow what the results are? If you can be there with me, I would really appreciate it. If not I understand." "You had test run! For What? Are you pregnant?" "Angell, come on I don't think so, at least I hope not. I'm a little bit too careful for that; look I love you and I want this week to be about you not me. Let's get ready okay. You go put on that beautiful dress and I'll see if I have anything that can even compare to being seen out with you in public. Because that my sister, is a badd AAA dress; that man you will be marrying Jon Paul has excellent taste in clothes and in you." "Thank you, you are so sweet I love you girl, I pray that everything is okay with your test in the morning. If you are having a little bambito, I can't think of anyone that would be a better mother. You know you own a piece of my heart, you can have it anytime you get ready for it, I love you so much." "I know me too, my heart is going to fall into pieces right now, if we don't hurry up and get out of here. Come on you know it takes me forever to put on my makeup, I'll see you in a few minutes. If you want you can help me find somethng to wear." "Okay, okay." So I did exactly that, I gave her the dress I was orginally going to wear from my bag. She loved it; it went perfectly with those beautiful hazel eyes of hers. I would do anything for her. When we arrived at church, it felt so good to walk into the balcony as I begin to think about everything that God had done for me and all that he had allowed me to experience in the past year I was so moved by his love for me. PJ and I had always sat near the end of the aisle and the seats were avaiable but my heart missed a beat when I saw that he was not sitting there. My heart skipped a beat in wonderment as my soul began to ache for his presence next to me. As the music seem to bring a sense of inner peace, the announcements were about to be read there was no sign of him in the santuary as my eyes scanned the whole entire church. I searched my soul wondering what I would do when our names were announced. While my heart tried to come to a level of understanding my best friend reached over and grabbed my hand and whispered, "Don't worry,God's love is surrounding us and his angels are watching over you, he'll be here. As soon as the announcements started, Sister Anderson asked if we would stand, my legs begin to tremble as I stood up. Immediately everyone looked upstairs I stood alone, then PJ came into the balcony from a total different direction and knelt down beside my shaking legs. He grabbed my left hand and asked me to forgive him…then he paused…for being late. Then he asked me to marry him in front of the entire congregation at church, then he placed my ring back on my finger and sealed it with a kiss. As he raised up, yes was in my eyes, and forgiveness rested in my soul. When we embraced me the beat in our hearts were in unison one with the other. I closed my eyes and he whispered in my ear that he loved me so much. All I could say in a soft whisper was, "I love you too. I forgive you." Then I heard Sister Jones say now that's what I call love. I did love him more that day than I ever did. At that instance, when I forgave him I had to forgive myself and what could have come between us. Although we ask for forgiveness it never stops us from reaping what we sown from any sin that we have committed. When we walked out of church everyone was giving up their congratulations and giving us their blessings. PJ asked me if Daphine and I would join him for lunch and Daphine answered for me by accepting his invitation. She told him that we could meet him there or follow him it was up to Angell. I appreciated her for protecting me, so I told him that we would follow him. He leaned over and embraced me and kissed me on my cheek and told me that I was rocking that dress. Then I told him the man I loved brought it for me, I heard he had good taste in clothes and his choice in choosing me. His face lit up, and he began to blush then he leaned over and kissed me soflty on my lips.

Before we got to the restaurant my phone rang, "Hey I just wanted to hear your voice, I love you baby." "I love you, too I'll see you in a few." "Okay, baby until then." When we turned into the restaurant, Daphine and I both realized how hungry we were. Before we went in, she asked me if I was okay and I told her that I was. She asked me if I was okay again, I told her that I said I was okay. Then she told me she had my back and if I asked her to put her car in reverse it was nothing but a word it would be a done deal. As we sat there our mouth was watering for every culinary delight we saw. We all really were starving; as we begin to order, William walked in; we were all full of smiles, laughter and cheers. William always knew how to add some good laughter to any conversation. As we sat there, with my Maid of Honor and his Best Man, PJ began to grab my left hand and caress it with unspoken words. My heart raced to feel what he must have been thinking and feeling. Then he pulled my chair over very close to his and kissed me, I couldn't refuse his spontaneity as forgiveness restored the yoke of unfaithfullness in my soul. After we finished our lunch, PJ offered to drive me to my car. As soon as we got in his car, he grabbed my hand and said, "I didn't mean to hurt you Angell, I realize what a stupid mistake I made, I wish I could take it back but I can't. I only wish I was as strong as you are, I admire you for sticking to the promise we made to each other. It showed me the kind of woman you are, you have some strong values that are very difficult to contend with. I'm proud of you for not giving into all that pressure I must have put on you." "You know PJ, I was totally shocked by the way you acted and all I could think about was losing you to some one else who could give it to you any time you wanted it, especially right now. I know its hard to stay true to a promise, but I made that promise to God first and then to you after we met, because you were the one who suggested that we should wait until we got married; you asked me to share three special occassions of our love and I did that for you because I knew we loved each other and were engaged to get married. We talked and agreed that afterwards no matter what or when that we would honor our vow. I really admired you for that, it made me fall deeper in love with you. When I realized that you could really stick to that promise for me and for God; I adored being in love with you and being loved by you. Because it wasn't about the sex; it was about us and the love we felt for each other. PJ it was hard for me to resist you everytime we were together, I don't ever want to put myself in that position again." "Angell you don't know how difficult it is to resist you, many days and nights I have broke out in a cold sweat after just being with you, rubbing up against you, holding you, touching your skin, and especially kissing you. You remember when we saw each other yesterday at the airport how we both couldn't even stop touching and kissing each other at the airport. Chills ran up and down my spine while I held you in my arms at the airport. When I didn't see you after my flight arrived, all I could think about was getting to you. I ran around that airport rushing to get my bags so that I would see you when you finally walked into the baggage claim area looking for me. But I had so much luggage to check in that I didn't see you when you got there. I was so nervous, and on edge until I saw you standing there on your cellphone. Deep down inside I wanted to just totally undress you right there at the airport and just love you until I couldn't take it anymore. But I knew I couldn't, but I'm telling you the truth, I wanted you real bad, after not talking to you for three weeks and when I finally talked to you I couldn't even see you. My mind was playing tricks on me, and my inner desire for you shot up to the highest peak." "After I talked to you that morning, I realized when my flight was delayed by the snow storm it was probably because of what I was thinking about; when I was leaving Chicago that Friday night, God didn't want me to see you. Because if I had seen you I would have had two days to make you feel the need to be with me before our wedding and I probably would have accomplished it. I am so glad you asked me to stop, because I almost messed up the best thing that has ever happened to me in my life. I couldn't imagine my life without you. And I'm not going to apologize for wanting you, but I am sorry for the way I went about it, that was wrong and I'm sorry. Cherri meant nothing to me, she always wanted it to be us, but I didn't feel the same way she did; I did yield to temptation many times before we met and while I was in Chicago which is where she lives, she ended up trying to get me to spend some time with her she just kept blowing up my phone, but I was so busy, but when I finally met up with her and it was on several ocassions; and she tried her best to get whatever she could out of me sexually. On Friday night she thought we just take up from where we left off, she came to my room after we checked in to see if I was okay but that wasn't all she wanted. I reminded her about you and she still didn't want to accept that it was over between us. The whole relationship before you and I met was always an evening of sexual convenience. She wanted to have one of those for old times sake flings that night, but I never loved her or wanted a long term or long distance relationship with her; we were always off and on and on and off. I had been drinking a lot of brandy in my coffee all night long; it was colder than any weather I had ever experienced since I'd been traveling to Chicago. The weather had been trecherous for two weeks. I must admit Cherri called me everyday, she told me that she had broken up with some guy that she had been with pretty consistently for the past couple of years. I would talk to her and try to console her but she wanted to see me. I told her I didn't have time and I immediately told her I was engaged to be married as soon as I got back home. She asked me where I was staying then she came by the first week I was in Chicago. I told her that it would never be anything between us anymore, but if she wanted to be friends that was all we could be. She was devasted, she started professing how much she loved me, how she had tried to get over me over the years and never had. When she came at me, the first time I asked her to leave and she did all kinds of stuff to make me change my mind. But that night we were all snowed in at the airport several guys on my team were down drinking shot after shot in celebration of a prebachelor party they promised to give me when I got back home. She must have called me at least ten times that night, then she came by my room and before I knew it I had yeilded, we never made love; when I realized what she elected to do I felt like such a fool who had sacrificed and betrayed you, the people I loved and cared about most of all God and myself. I fell for the oldest trick in the book then I stopped her before everthing got compeltely out of control. I don't expect you to understand, but I fell for the oldest trick in the book, to take away one of the most priceless gifts; the covenant that we promised to God and each other. I pray that you can really forgive me and that you'll let me spend the rest of my life proving to you how much I love you. I hope you believe me and can find it in your heart to trust me again." "As hard as all of this has been I know I love you and I forgave you in my heart and soul; every memory and emotion tied to us meant to much to me to let you go. Because I felt the same way; I wanted you too every single night that you were away which is what happens when that door is opened and we opened it royally while we were in Paris. I couldn't bare the thought of anything happening to you or you being with anyone else. Thank you for being honest with me, I had gone through my own nightmares of hell Friday night. I'm glad we were able to keep believing in what we had together. We discovered a lot about love, and I know how rare it is to find somebody to share your whole life with; but I'm grateful that God gave us back to each other."

Then he reached over and held me closer to him and kissed me on my lips then on my hand and said, "I love you and I thank you. I think it will be a good idea if we stayed away from each other for the rest of this week. I know we have a lot of things that we both need to take care of every day this week. I need you to let me know all the details of what we need to do together. What time we need to be here and there and when and what time the rehearsal, and dinners and whatever else, okay. Believe me, baby it will be safer for me this way, not you." "PJ, it will be safer for both of us." "Until then okay, lets just keep our hands off each other". "That sounds like a real good idea honey, we both need to go home and get some rest. Call me later PJ, I'll see you later tomorrow right. I'm sure we have a lot of little things to take care of together but we can do it anytime." "The afternoon would be better for me baby, I've got to go to the office in the morning and turn in some final paper work and get everything cleaned up in my office before the wedding and our honeymoon; I have a month off and I am going to take full advantage of it, I be in the office first thing around nine in the morning, it will only take about an hour or so. I want to go back home and try to get some sleep. Would two or three o'clock be too late? "No honey that'll be fine." Then I'll come by and pick you up and you can run down everything to me. Baby, I'm exhausted." "I know you're tired, me too." "Baby, I haven't slept seems like in weeks. I need to nurse whatever this is I'm coming down with." "Honey, I forgot look in the door of the refrigerator you'll see a bag in there with some cough medicine I made you some tea and some cold tablets...get all that in you and you'll feel better in the morning." "Angell, how did you know." "Well I heard it in your voicemail last night before you made it back before everything went stupid crazy." "Thank you baby for taking care of me." "Come on let me see you to your car, do you need to go back to Daphine's place for anything, no I don't; I loaded everthing in my car this before we left this morning." "Baby thanks again for the dress; I love it and I love you." "You are welcome, I love you too. Baby, drive safe okay...Until then. Then he walked away and got back in his car.

Love turns the pages in our lives as we weep and wonder over heart aches and pain, and even the tears of joy can flip the script on us. As the sudden presence of the unknown is unveiled and leave us pondering how we got to a certain place or how it played out a certain way. Circumstances can change overnight and put us in a state where all we can do is wait, trust, pray and believe in what we sometime can fear the most, the unknown. When I got home the strangest feeling came over me, I thought about, Ms. Ruth and what she uttered to us in prayer. I had thought about it many times as the words of her prayer started to surface into my heart like a flash and bean of light. "Que l'amour que vous avez trouve. Que Dieu vos benisse a travers toutes les epreuves a venir. Que votre coeur a trouver leur chemin du retour a votre ame. Real Love est une benediction de Dieu. Librement il donne. Librement he Loves." "May the love you found bless you through all the trials to come. May your hearts find their way back home to your soul...Real love is a blessing from God, freely He Gives, freely He Loves. My God...now I see...

The Morning News Brought Unforgettable Knowledge

The next morning I escorted my best friend to the doctor, we were expecting rain that day which was not surprising for upcoming debut of the beginning of spring. As we sat there waiting on the results from Daphine's test, she shared with me how long she had been undergoing the series of tests. I couldn't believe that she had been going through this alone. I knew she had quite a few doctor appointments but that was not unusual for her. All I could see in my mind were all the different bottles of pills in her drawer. After the doctor came into his office he began to reopen the envelope that had obviously been opened previously. I looked at his eyes and the horrifying feeling came over me. As his lips moved, my heart went into a pandemonium of disbelief of what I hearing. He asked if I was a close relative and she told him I was. Then he began to read the results. "The test shows that you are in a increased stage of breast cancer; that has been rapidly moving quickly; it is at a very advanced stage. The treatments that we have been administering to you for the past year have not been as successful as we had hoped. I don't know how long you have, but the best advice I could give you is to get your affairs in order as the last stages may progress very suddenly." I couldn't believe what I was hearing. "What did you just say, Daphine why didn't you tell me? I can't believe you kept this from me for a year." As I watched tears from the eyes of someone that I loved more than anything, tears began to fall from my eyes as well. I thought to myself, God this is my friend here, my best friend, she meant more to me than anybody, even my own sister, someone that I didn't even want to accept happiness for myself until she found it first. Tears flowed down from both of our eyes like the rain falling outside, she meant so much to so many people; who loved her and depended on her smile and her personality to light up their life. My soul ached at the mere thought of losing her, I begin to ask her again, why she didn't tell me. Then I turned to the doctor and asked him what was going on, if there was anything that could be done if we cget a second opinion, go see a specialist or something. He asked me if I was her sister, then she told him I was, then he said just make her comfortable. I can give her more pain medicine but as the cancer progresses she may experience a lot of discomfort, pain and nausea. She will eventually loose her hair and her sense of taste of food. She's going to need all the support she can get from her friends and family right now. Is your mother still living?" "Yes she is." "Your sister asked me to promise her the doctor patient confidentiality which is what I've done; she didn't want anyone else to know right now until we ran the final test; I gave her my word. But since you are family we could try another test drug if she would like; chemotherapy has always been the most significant option, however we have to move very quickly as soon as this morning; but from my experience at this stage surgery is always too risky but the therapy may give her a little more time. But it's clearly up to her." "Doctor I heard you say that it could give her more time, do you strongly recommend the chemo as the better option Doctor?" "Like I said it would give her a little more time, but the results will depend on so many factors, however if she is willing we have to start right away. Would you like to try it Daphine?" "I still don't know, what are the statistics, I've read and heard so much over the past year, that I need to know if you really think it will help. We've tried so many experimental drugs and nothing has come close to really working for you. If I don't have that long to live, I want to enjoy every single day; I don't want to spend every single day throwing up, loosing my hair and just letting my life slip away. I just want to live until it's my time to go." As she said those words my eyes filled up with tears for the fighter that I knew was in her, but she wanted to fight differently from what I thought she would choose. When someone you love is going through something so severe, you don't know how you will react, all you can do is be there for what ever their wishes are. As I held her close in my arms this morning the words flowed out like the showers of the rain in response to her. "Whatever you decide I'll be right here by your side if there is anything I can do, just let me know and I'll do it." "What if I do this chemo and loose all my hair." "Honey, you've always worn very short hair, if you loose some I'm sure you'll still be a heartbreaker sporting an incredibly sexy bauld head, if anybody can pull it off it would definitely be you." We both laughed inside the pain of our tears, my love for her became inseperable. She agreed to undergo the chemotherapy and it did have it's side affects the week was filled with rain. PJ did'nt know what to say or do after I broke the news to him, I never seen him in such a helpless state of mind. We both decided to postpone our wedding; it rained so severly all week as we came up to 72 hours before our wedding day; I didn't even know how those three days passed so quickly we used wisdom got as much of our deposits back as we were allowed. The treatments were extremely long and draining the radiation began to change her skin a little darker shade and she did suffer severe hair loss before we knew it she lost it all. Daphine didn't know that we postponed our wedding, neither did she recall what day it was from day to day; as time progressed so did her illness. I couldn't imagine standing at the alter of grace; receivng such an honor while in a state of bliss and even on our honeymoon as I envisioned my best friend's life was slipping away from our mist. PJ came to the hospital everyday and before we knew it three weeks had past and so had many options for her. One day she began to get better, she sounded like her old self then she began remembering things that kept the flame in our friendship burning. It seem that she had never been happier than the last moments of her life; joy filled her eyes as it began to leave my heart. We were about to enter into the fall season when I got word that the cancer had gone into remission, which was great suddenly they couldn't find no trace of it but had taken a toll on her whole personhood. Prayers were flowing in; her Mom who I loved so much, even as my own; was so precious to me watched her get from worse to surprisingly better to living again. As her spirit stood inside the shadow of my original fear almost loosing someone that meant the world to me. Daphine lost her battle within the next couple of years to come, she fought as long and as hard as she could and for the first time in my life a piece of my soul had been taken on a flight to heaven on the wings of love. With her went so many prayers.

Everyday I miss her presence in my life and one of the most beautiful smiles that could light up the life of anyone in her midst. With all the love in my heart she will always live in the heart of my memories until eternity. Not long after that Jon's mother became ill, and was diagnosed with what many of us fear today, lung cancer. We were both hit with two devastations all at once. Jon had to rearrange his whole life to center it around the tender loving care that he gave to his mother. He moved in with her and gave her twenty four seven of the best love and care that a man could give to his mother. We never once thought about what we had; time was more precious than our love could ever compare. Everytime I would see him I took a piece of his love with me, as I watched him loose the most meaniful gift he was given. I knew how important their relationship was to him, it was not my place to demand anything from him. We were both mature enough to know and understand the true meaning of love. I was always told that if you really love someone and you have to let them go from your heart, soul, mind and spirit; if they come back to you then you were meant to be. Several years went by, as it takes time to heal our hearts from the afflictions that wounds us in life. As difficult as it was, we went our separate ways occasionlly keeping in touch, for birthdays, holidays and at times not so pleasant events. He was the type of man that poured his focus on what was most important to him that affected his life. He always kept his property, and maintained what belonged to his family. One of the most difficult things that I experienced throughout this untimely and unfortunate period was not being able to be there with him to love and care for him during those final hours of loosing the woman I had grown to love. Truly I knew how fortunate my life had been it was truly one of the most beatiful experiences of real love I would ever encounter I blessed God for loving me so much. It made me appreciate my love for God just as much, I loved him endlessly into the dephts of my heart and soul. For allowing me to experience the love from two people that touched the very essence of my soul. My best friend, Daphine Brooks…and the man I would always love Jon Paul…I would not ever forget either one as long as my heart beats and live; so will it beat for both of them in the corridors of my soul.

Being Shaken by The Holy Spirit

At that instant, the music became extremely loud, where I was seated, When I came to my self, I looked around and there was a man standing right in front of me. "Can I get you something to drink?" "What?" "I said, could I get you something to drink?" "No thank you sir, where is my husband?" "I don't know ma'am, are you okay?" "Merry Christmas." "Merry Christmas what are you talking about Merry Christmas," Then I looked up and I almost fell out of my chair when my sister walked up to me and said, "There you are girl, I been wondering all night where you were, then I remembered you were back here. What's wrong? Are you okay? I saw you earlier talking to somebody that needs to be a friend of my mine or yours. God he sure was fine, where did he go? Has he been back here keeping you company all this time, you guys must have really hit it off, he looks like a new prospect." "I don't know about that but I think I've had a few too many glasses of champagne." "Looks that way to me too, little sis, and you were worried about me." I looked at her as if I had seen a ghost. Then I asked her, "What time is it? And where are we?" "Girl what's wrong with you? What do you mean where are we? I knew I shouldn't have left you alone with him, girl I knew he might of been out of your league. You weren't back here doing something that you had no business doing, were you little sis? Just look at you, see you were worried about me, I hope he didn't slip something in your drink." I looked down at my watch and it read 1:03, I couldn't believe it. I asked my sister again, "what time do you have?" She looked down at her watch and said it's a little after one, in the morning. Girl you're acting very strange. Are you sure you're okay, you look like you've seen a ghost or something." "Are you ready to go home Cinderella, or are you afraid you might not get a chance to loose your glass slipper for that handsome Prince to find it." Prince I thought to myself why is she talking about, Cinderella? She really has had a little too much to drink. What had just happened to me? Maybe you need to go to ladies room and splash some water on your face or something. I'm serious, you look like you have been touched by and angel or something, your face is flushed and you look weird." "Weird, sis." "Well I mean different." "Okay, you're right I do need to go to the rest room, let me go now, I need to use it really bad." "Okay, Okay, I'll be up front when you come out, or do you need me to go with you?" "No that's okay, Ill be all right." "Listen, this club closes at 2:30 on the dot, I don't want to be here any where near that time, so meet me at the dart board when you come out."

So I hurried to the rest room to wash my face my bladder was about to explode, I felt like I was a stranger to myself. As I walked to the restroom I thought to myself, everything looked so strange, it looked different. People were staring at me, and I really felt strange. I could not believe that I was at this place; the Jazz Club where people were so cool it was like they had popsicles on their toes, now I can see why the name of it was Popsicle Toes. All of a sudden, I was freezing cold. When I got to the restroom a feeling came over me, I could hear and inner voice telling me how much I was loved. The inner voice spoke to me and explained to me that I had been taken up in the spirit and that I had been given something that many people are allowed to receive. You must be worthy to receive the gift, that comes only from the holy spirit, the comforter, which is only given and revealed to the just and deserving in all honesty and truth. The vision came back to me, it was so real; God had removed me from time and allowed me to recapture every meaniful moment hidden in the dephts of my soul. He told me that my heart gave me thoughts that were true and pure that are in balance with my spirit. And those thoughts of truth were very real; then chills rippled up and down my arms and legs, and I felt my heart beat extremely fast then I could hear my heart beat in my ear. The sound vibrated down to the pit of my stomach and wrapped around it and squeezed it. Gradually I was freezing all over again, the chill brought cold tears as they started to web up in my eyes. The tears were warm and the warmth started to heat up my whole body. All of a sudden, I wasn't cold anymore. That annoying headache was leaving my brain, I felt much better. I could not believe that I lost two hours of time talking to a stranger. Because when I went to the back of that club to listen to the music alone, it was around 11:00 o'clock I remember talking to somebody, the next thing I knew I had moved to a table alone. It was beyond belief, there was a still voice that told me that I had been taken up in the spirit and that my mind and my soul was given it's heart's desire. Then I thought to myself, Thank you God, for loving me and being so good to me even in my thoughts, my dreams, my sleep, and in the visions that only you would take the time to reveal something like that to me. Then unexpectedly I heard that inner voice again, say"it's because I know you love me, in your inner thoughts, dreams, sleep, and even through the visions that I have showed you. I knew you would remain true to me, and that's why I chose to prove your love for me; I knew you would continue to love me no matter what. Like a rushing wind that voice in my ear was gone. I was scared to death, as I stood there shaking, my nerves and my inner being had been shaken up by the Holy Spirit, I saw the manifestation of my life flash before my eyes. I will not ever forget the sound of that voice in my ear. With trembling hands I finished putting on my lipstick I couldn't wait to get home; I brushed my hair, then I put on a little scented lotion on to refreshen myself up and to calm my nerves down. I was scared to death. As I looked in the mirror, all I could do in my soul was thank God in silence; right there in this strange public restroom for loving me so much. The disbelief was understanding that his loving heart will meet you anywhere that you are. If he desires to come where you are, he will, no matter where you are, he will find you and reveal his truth and love to you. Which is why we have to believe with trust and expectancy of what we ask him for from our heart and he will give us the desires of our heart.

"I need to get out of here and go home; I was nervous and still shaken. I better find my sister and let her know I'm okay. I was still in awe, and felt like I needed to drink a gallon of water, I was so thirsty. I went over to the bar, and I saw her back at the dart board where she probably had been most of the night, then I asked the bartender for a glass of water. "You mean no more champagne?" "I beg your pardon?" Well that's what you've been drinking all night?" "Have I really?" "Are you okay, beautiful?" "I think so, I'm just thirsty that's all, I don't want anything else to drink tonight". Then he filled up my glass with ice and chased it with water an added a lime and one cherry. Then a voice came from behind me that said, "Can I get you those strawberries dipped in chocolate to go with that or would you prefer some extra lime and cherries." I turned around and I recognized that it was the same guy that I had talked to earlier about the strawberries and champagne. Our conversation was coming back to me. I waited on what he would say next, I couldn't remember anything we talked about except the strawberries and chocolate. I felt terrible because I couldn't remember his name. Then finally I said, "I'm sorry but I have been a little out of it, I don't believe I remember your name." "I'm crushed, you told me earlier that you wanted a drink with my name on it, then he laughed. His laugh was so familiar; he had the type of voice that I should have never forgotten. I felt awful not to remember, then he smiled and said, "The name is Morgan. Now I remember your name I don't think I could ever forget it or you; Angell, right?" "Yes that's right, but I don't remember telling you what my name was." "Well I can understand why, you had a bit too much champagne and you told me that you had an awful headache." "I did." "Yes you did, so I went to get you some asprin for your headache while you were out back. You told me you needed a few minues to regroup and I respected that; so I gave you some time to rest off some of that combo of sparkling wine and champagne. "Are you better?" "Yes I think so, thanks for asking." "You know you look like your name Angell, I think I told you that earlier." You may have, but I don't remember, when I was born; my mother told me that she was visited by an angel who told her to name me Angell, and spell it with two L's. That's ANGELL, she was told I was a special gift from God, I came directly from his angel of love and I was given to her on Mother's Day the 1st L meant a Mother's love and the 2nd L symbolized the Angel of God's Love.

He said, "Sweet, what a beautiful gift your Mother was given, you are a very attractive young woman, and I'm very pleased to make your acquaintance." Then he reached over grabbed my hand and kissed it. My heart started beating so fast. I couldn't hardly remember what he said his name was. Then he said, "Are you okay?" "Yes I'm okay." I almost fell right out of my chair while he was talking to me. "Excuse me, I was just had a Dajavou moment or something. Do you ever get a feeling that you've done something before or been somewhere before you actually experience it. Kind of like going through channels in your life that you feel have happened before and they sort of feel familiar. Do you know what I mean or does that sound strange to you?" "No not really, kind of like you've been here in a certain space of time before. That's not strange to me it's a little deep but I can handle it if you can. Listen this place is about to close; I'm glad I got a chance to see you again before I left, I wanted to wish you a Merry Christmas and Happy New Year. I wanted to know if you were going to keep your word to me." "What word?" "I asked you to save the last dance for me. Will you do me the honor before I leave tonight." "I don't know how I could refuse such an offer." The music is a little upbeat but I can handle it can you?" "Oh it's nothing to it, but to do it." "Morgan, let me finish my water first." "Take your time." So, I finished my water then we went straight out to the dance floor. I almost forgot how to move trying to shake off some of that bubbly mixed with sparkling legs. Then I said, "Morgan, I want you to know, that I'm not the world's greatest dancer, I have not been out dancing in months. Then he reached over and grabbed my hands and twirled me around; we started having so much fun on the dance floor, we were talking about his moves, laughing and joking around about several people dancing around us. Some of them were a whole lot worse than I would ever be. Then all of a sudden the beat of the music changed and the beat got slower, then the female vocalist announced this was the last track for the night it was a special request, a song dedication for Angell. I thought my heart would leap out of my chest. He looked at me and asked me to close my eyes while he got ready to make a move on me. As he embraced me he whispered for me to keep my eyes closed then he said, "This song is from me to you, because I believe you are that special Angel, that was sent for such a special occasion tonight. Then they started to play the song, the song was entitled, "Angel," originally by the songtress herself Anita Baker.

He asked me to opened my eyes because he wanted me to look at him, I couldn't believe my eyes it was the love of my life standing right there holding my hand. "Jon. My God, where did you come from? "Merry Christmas Angell, I just made it in from New York." "What's going on I was standing here with a guy named Morgan, What happened to him?" Then he walked back on the dance floor. "Angell I'm sorry to do that to you, but I'm PJ's brother Pierce Morgan everyone calls me Morgan. "Pierce, oh my God, we've never did get a chance to meet in person did we?" "No we didn't, thank God I didn't run into you over cofee or anything else because you are a real turn on. I never usually get to make it home for the holidays, but PJ and I promised each other that we would spend more holidays together especially at Christmas." "That's sweet, I can relate to that, me and my sister always make it a point to do that." "Speaking of your sister, I ran into her a few days ago, I asked about you, and she told me she was going to get you here on Christmas Eve; she wanted me to look for you at the bar near the dart board and I could move on from there. I figured we could pull if off since we had never physically met in person. As soon as I saw you, I knew exactly who you were. I had seen your pictures displayed all over PJ's place. After talking to you most of the night, I realized how much you really loved my brother, so I called him and told him to get on the first plane back here, because I had a 911 Christmas Present Delivery." "How did you know I would be here?" "Look we are talking about your sister JK, she's always had that reputation of pulling something off." "You know you are right about that, no one could have convinced me that I would be here tonight. I can't believe I didn't know who you were, you told me your name was Morgan earlier I didn't even think about it being a last name. I did have a champagne buzz going earlier, thank's for not letting me over do it too much? Wow, now that I think about it I never connected it, by the way I love the mixure of silver streaks in your hair it makes you look so distinguished. I can not believe this, when I think back to when you called Jon or if I talked to you on the phone you always sounded and were so far a way, but in person you do sound a lot like your brother in conversation with a striking resemblance." "So I'm told, but I am the oldest; it started with me first. Again I'm sorry but I had to do this tonight, I couldn't resist playing Santa you know. I must admit I would have loved for you to sat down on Santa's lap a little later and whisper anything in my ear, but I'll leave that to my little brother here."

"Alright, Pierce that's enough I can handle it from here." "I just bet you can little brother, I don't blame you, if you didn't handle it, I may have to give you a run for your money with this one. You were right she is something else." "That right but that's for me to know and you to wonder about later, now and in the future." "Ooh I feel so special two charmers in the family; trying to brush up some sweetness on me." "No, let's make that one charmer that can and has all the rights to brush up and catch up; remember we have a marriage license which makes mine legal; the only thing that didn't work in our favor was timing. But I believe in miracles and to me that's what Christmas is all about, so thanks for the 911 Christmas call. Because this is the woman I plan to spend the rest of my life with making up for all the lost time we missed; I thank God that he just happen to send you to the same mall that your sister, JK was shopping at. Only God could do something like that and I feel so blessed that he did. All I had to do was see you and everthing that I ever felt for you filled my heart all over again." "Man just call me the match maker from heaven, I'll take the title, I knew all you both needed was to see each other, Bamm, Santa has done his magic and so has the big Guy in the sky, who makes all the magic happen at Chrismas. Merry Christmas to both of you." Then PJ looked at me and his brother and said, "Thanks man it's time for me to take over from here. By the way I'd like to introduce myself again, my name is Jon Paul Morgan, and I presume you are Angell." "Your presumtions are correct. Merry Christmas Jon Paul Morgan is it." "That's right, I believe my Christmas is going to be a lot more than just Merry. Look up." So I looked up and there we were standing under a misletoe. "May I." "I understand you still have the papers, and that makes it legal." Then he kissed me, I had longed for his lips and the smell of his skin against mine. As we released our lips yielded for each other. Then he whispered in my ear, "Baby I have missed you so much." "I've missed you even more." Then he smiled at me and we danced, and he held me closer to him for the first time in years; I could feel his heartbeat again rapidly inside mine. We had always fit perfectly in each others arms, as I closed my eyes I felt as if we had moved into another expanse of time. When the song ended we were so involved that we almost forgot where we were; our lips met again, we could'nt help the passion that was released between us, My palms started sweating. "Angell I don't want to spend another Christmas without you. Let's get out of here, can I take you home." Well my sister has been drinking quite a bit tonight; but looks like I was in worst shape than she was. Thank God your brother was here tonight; I hadn't planned on going anywhere until my sister talked me into it." "I know. I'll forever be grateful for what she did for us not once but twice." "Me too, who would have thought that God would find the way to us through our brother and sister, I am amazed at his timing." "I promised Pierce to be on that last flight from New York, I almost missed it shopping at the last minute." "Christmas Shopping were you?" "Yes I was, this Santa has lots of toys in his stockings just for you." "Oh, Santa, are you going to put them under my tree?" "Have you been a good, naughty, or nice?" "Well I can say I've been good, then I can say that I'd like to be naughty but I could promise that I would always be nice when it comes to spreading a little Christmas Cheer to you." "Hmm looks like I'm going to have to look over my list and check it twice especially if you could be all three just for me." "Well, I don't know Santa, what about Mrs. Claus, I hope she'll say yes. Then he got down on one knee and opened a box that displayed the most incredibly designed diamond ring that I have ever seen, much more esquisite than the first ring he had given me. Tears began to fall from my eyes as everyone around us on the dance floor started clapping and cheering. All I could say was, "Yes, all over again and again." As he placed the ring on my finger he moved both of his hands straight up the sides of my body and told me how much he loved me. Pierce had found my sister and they both yelled out seperately, "You Go Boy," from my sister." Then Pierce yelled out "Now that's the way its done, bother I have to hand it to you when I settle down I need to get some pointers from you." All we could do was look at each other, then he took his hankerchief and wiped the tears from my eyes. I smiled immediately and we both remembered that was how we orginally met. I love you Angell and I want to spend the rest of my life making you happy." "Oh Jon I've missed you so much, baby I love you so much. I still love you too, I don't think I ever stopped. Letting you go was the hardest thing I've ever done. If Pierce can see to it that my sister gets home safely, I would love for you to take me home. A couple of years ago I purchased a condo; now I live in the Inner City now." "That sounds real good Angell, seems like I've been away from you for ever." "You have. It's been a long time." "There was no way I would let you go again." It was perfect timing, both my sister and Pierce were walking toward us to congratulate us. "Do I need a magnifying glass or sunglasses to look at that ring? I see your prince arrived after Midnight after all Cinderella, instead of a glass slipper he came sporting something much more than a slipper. I'm scared of you." replied my sister JK. She immediately, embraced me and Jon, "Long time no see." "Did you miss me, brother in law?" "Of course I did, but looks like you caught up with what's been missing in your life." "JK thanks for helping a brother out by getting her here tonight; this meant a lot to me. I almost missed my plane a couple of hours ago, waiting on the final touches on her ring; but I had to wait it was too important to me; missing my plane would have ruined this whole plan but you know me I would have charted a private plane if I had to, to get to her." "Let's just say brother-in law that you owe me." "Tell you what do you mind if Pierce follows you home, and trust me I'll see to it that Angell gets home safely." "Well when you put it like that, I don't mind that at all; as long as Picrce promises not to try to get into my Christmas Stockings while I'm a little tipsy." "Listen, I am Santa you know, I have access to everybody stockings, I can come down each and every chimney that I choose. Don't be trying to act like you don't want me to make a special trip down that chimney." "Ah sukie sukie now, I love being turned on by Santa, cause I been a naughty girl all year." "Pierce take care of my sister, and make sure she get's in the house, because you guys are talking just plain nasty. Merry Christmas sis, and be careful driving, I'll give you a call some time tomorrow." As I walked outside to PJ's car I noticed he had upgarded to a nice black benz. He opened my door and I got in. "Where to?" I gave him directions and we drove in silence, he held my hand occasionally placing my hand with my new ring up to lips. "Merry Christmas sweetheart it looks beautiful on your hand." "Merry Christmas to you again, I love my ring and you too." "You know, while I was in New York for the past two weeks, all I could think about while I was there was you. You know I still have all those notes that you sent me right after we started dating." "That's sweet; I kept yours too." "What do you say to us setting a date to do it all over again on the first day of Spring; this time let's plan to have everything inside; something small with about

50 to 100 people. I would love that; you know what I forgot to tell you, I went back to school and I'll be graduating in May receiving my Masters Degree, thank you very much. I'm a paralegal now, I worked with some amazing Attorneys Downtown, I've been at the firm for three years now." "I'm proud of you Angell, so when is the magic date." "Friday, May 25th" "So will the first day of Spring work for you, actually it's the perfect day because I'll be on Spring Break which means we will only have a week for the honeymoon. But after my graduation I'll be able to take more time off." "Looks like you are in for a very exciting upcoming year. Speaking of the new year, Jacqueline and Bernard are having a New Years Eve Bash at their place, they would both love to see you again. "I can't think of anywhere else I'd rather be." "Excellent, I'll make reservations in a few days. After that I'll be on location in Japan for about six weeks." "Japan, that sounds really exciting, looks like the firm is still treating you well." "Not really, Pierce and I went into business together we decided to open up our own Architectural Engineering Firm. We both had established a huge clientale over the years; so we decided to use it to our advantage. The past four years have been phenomenal. In fact we just celebrated an expansion the first of this month by opening up one of our new offices in New York." "Wow, I am so happy for you guys; I'm sure your Mom would have been so proud to see you both working together. How is your family." "Everybody is okay; we are suppose to be having a small get together a few days after Christmas. Pierce and I turned Mother's house into our home office here; I kept the place up after she passed; it was paid for after my Dad died. It was just enough space for us to enjoy a full staff; while keeping her memories alive. I pretty much run my own schedule; I just need your assitance keeping me on track. I may have to steal you away from that law firm and get some of that legal expertise on our team." "Hmm, sounds like an intriguing job offer, will it matter if I'm sweet on the boss." "That depends how much sugar you got." "Oh I got enough sugar to keep you going all night." "Can I have some at the next light." "Only if it turns red before we get there; by the way you need to turn left coming up at the next stop sign; the condo's will be on the right hand side." "Before we get there looks like my lucky night the light is turning red." Immediately he kissed me so attentively on my lips, God I had missed him so much. I was so

thankful that God would give me such an incredible gift on Christmas. As I touched the side of his face with my hand a tear fell from my eyes. I was so grateful at God's amazing grace and mercy.

Even though we say as believers in God that we believe in miracles, visions and even our own dreams; when they actually happen to us they can still overwhelm us. When God magnifies his love to us, it's not easy to contain ourselves. As soon as he chooses to expose us to the true revelations of his love, it's mind blowing and surreal when those visions are manifested. I loved God more now than I ever did, he was so precise, personal, and detailed when he revealed his love. What I admired most was his impeccable timing, what he can do in an expanse of time, instaneously he changed the course of our lives, then he allowed us to renew our love all over again. After reading and searching and wondering most of my life, about finally meeting and being with my soul mate for the rest of my life. Nothing could compare to the way that I came to know, love and respect God, he had truly given me the desires of my heart. Although I thought, my soul mate was a man, God showed me that after I searched my heart, and found him in it, he was the answer to conquering love. His love taught me that "it" was the mate to my soul, after I learned to search for, honor, and respect his love first; all the things that I desired followed. Once I found and came to know him and developed a true relationship with him; that was all I needed. I realized that he was the only one who has the power to give you the desires of you heart, and when we are obedient and loyal to him we earn the right to be given it, freely he gives it, and "it" is the power of his love. Loving him totally, gives you power, over life and victorious over the broad way of temptation, above all else we must get an understanding of what's significant and what's not.

If You Really Love Someone... Let Them Go... If They Come Back...

You've heard that, if you really love someone, let them go, if they come back to you you were meant to be. I always wondered if that would come true for me; and it looks like it had. As PJ turned into my private parking space. When we got out of his car and he opened his trunk and he was certainly bearing lots of gifts. He took out what he had for me and we went on into my place. I was so glad that I decided to put up a big Christmas Tree this year with all my really nice decorations. I decided to light some candles and the fireplace and make us some hot chocolate. Immediately he found himself at home, after I gave him a tour. "Angell this is really nice, I love the open space. Whoever designed this; really did an excellent job on the structure. What a nice view of downtown from here. Oh baby you deserve this I love what you've done to it, it feels so good, it's feels like home; like I'm finally home." "Thank you, you are home; PJ I'm curious, what would you have done if I had of been with someone else by now." "I never wanted to think about you being with anybody else but me. Were you seeing somebody else?" "There was an attorney that's been interested in me for a while now, he asked me to go to a New Years Eve party with him; his best friend plays for the Dallas Cowboys." "We'll, looks like he's gonna to be a little dissapointed this Christmas, and on New Years Eve, now isn't he?" "That's too bad, he sure was cute." "Oh he was cute huh?" "Mmmn huh." "You think I can make you forget all about him?" "I don't know." "What?" "I know you can, I love you Jon Paul Morgan, it's nobody in this world that I would like to spend my life with but you." "I'm glad to hear that, Angell DiVine Summers, because I'm sure I'll be breaking a few hearts myself. Come on over here and sit down on Santa's lap and bring me some milk and cookies so I can make my rounds tonight." "I'm all out of milk Santa, can I give you some hot chocolate instead." "Mmmn hot chocolate sounds even better." Of course I brought him a little bit more than our cups of hot chocolate as we rekindled the raw essence of our love. It was one of the best Christmas presents that I had ever received, Real Love. Getting to know each other again was something that we both treasured. As we brought in the New Year's with Jacqueline and Bernard it was one of the best parties that I had ever gone to. They made it a Red Carpet New Year's Eve Party. We all felt like celebrities which is the way it was set up; the decorations were sensational and the guests list included several superstars. Being engaged this time around felt different we were more mature, experienced and comfortable with each other. Jacqueline still had my wedding dress put up for safe keeping; she said she always knew that we would end up back together. Then she mentioned that old familiar saying. "I was always told that when you love some one, and you let them go, if they come back to you, you both were meant to be together." I told her I believed the same thing and it looks like it came true for me.

Springing forward into New Beginnings...

After PJ closed that final deal in Japan, we were scheduled to get married again on the first day of Spring it was remarkable how awesome GOD is. However one of the most grateful things that he gave me that week, was hearing from my best friend sister who told me that she had a little girl right after Daphne passed away; she told me she named her baby Daphine. She was beautiful, three years old, with the same gorgeous hazel eyes and graced with that beautiful smile that brought tears to my eyes. I asked Daphine's sister if her daughter could be the flower angel in our wedding, and if she could stand in as my maid of honor for her sister; she told me she would be honored.

The week went by so fast, we had quite a few things to do everyday. Before I knew it, it was finally Thursday, the day of our wedding rehearsal and dinner at one his Mother's home which was now his office. This was where we orginally planned to have it, so we thought we would honor her by hosting it there; we transfomed the place by creating comfort and elegance which is what he Mother wanted. Everything went according to plan. We finished up our dinner early and then we all went home. I would not see PJ anymore until Friday afternoon. We decided not to call each other or see each other until then. PJ was having his bachelor party on Thursday night this time around at one of his favorite Hotels downtown and I would be hanging out with the girls for my bachelorette party at my condo. We had a blast at the party, there was lingerie everywhere in too many boxes, and some wonderful gifts my friends were so sweet. They had ordered two male strippers which was of course my sorority sisters idea about twenty girls showed up for the party. Jackie told me they invited all the sisters, so

I would get a lot of gifts, she had no idea that they all would show up on a Thursday. I also had this singing telegram by a lady who sang this song that PJ dedicated to me on Christmas Eve. "Angell does PJ always have to have the last word?" One of my girlfriends shouted out. Afterwards the lady gave me a rose and a message from him; she told me the rose was suppose to be a sign to me, for us to celebrate the fragrance of our love and life together. Linda came over and took the rose from me and said, "Girl he is just too romantic. He's just trying to get you ready for, you know the big show down. Sister Girl, tell me please does he have any brothers we could fight over." You know those girls could be hilarious, I cracked up laughing. "He only has one brother who travels extensively, but I'm taking the one that I want. The brother does have plenty of good looking friends." Then Jackie yelled out, "you know we could always go and crash his bachelor party at the Hotel for interrupting ours, but I tell you what…every woman will be fencing for her self. Come on let's go, we can all go in the limousine, so we called up the driver and he told us he would be right there in about fifteen minutes. My maid of honor Linda, had rented a limousine for us for the whole entire day Thursday and we had another one for Friday she was very friendly with the owner. We all decided to load up in the limousine and go downtown to crash PJ's bachelor party, but I had already decided I was going to stay in the car until they finished, because I didn't want PJ to see me. When we got to the hotel where the party was, the girls got out, all they had on their mind was crashing the party, they went upstairs to the Hotel Suite and did exactly that, I sat in the limo on my cell phone listening to the whole event; for about forty-five minutes to an hour. Then the driver asked me if I wanted to go up, and I told him no because we were playing a joke on my fiancee; he knew we were getting married the next day he thought that was an interesting combo, to crash the bachelor party with the bridal party. And he couldn't wait to see the outcome of what the crash would be. The driver asks me if I didn't mind him getting out and stretching his legs he wanted to smoke a cigarette? No I said, take your time; you can definetly take a break as long as you like, just leave the music playing and I want feel so guilty. I just sat there in the car by myself, then all of a sudden the driver got back in the car and started driving off, I shouted out, "Wait just a minute my friends are still in the Hotel you need to wait on them." "Stop the car Richard, at that moment I looked at my watch, it was almost eleven o'clock the driver was driving pretty fast; then all of a sudden he came to a screeching halt in the middle of nowhere. Then I heard a siren, Oh my God, I turned around and looked behind us and I saw some bright lights behind the limousine; it was the police lights shinning on us. Oh my God, I knew he was driving too fast. That was pretty stupid of him why did he do that, then I tried to open my door to see if I needed to get out of the car, but my door would'nt open. Then all of a sudden my door opened and a policeman was at my door asking me to get out of the car. I thought, oh my God, what is the deal with this guy, Richard must have gone inside the hotel and had a few drinks too many or something because he was driving way too fast. I got out of the car and the policeman told me that the driver had some outstanding tickets and that he would not be able to drive me anywhere. He told me he was going to have to take me downtown to the police station, he asked me a few questions because he found something in the back of the car. "What, I don't even know what you're talking about?" "Sure, that's what they all say," then the policeman put some hand cuffs on me. "Sir you have got to be kidding, I didn't do anything! I had no idea he had something in this car. I work for some attorneys and you are not taking me anywhere; I'm getting married tomorrow and you are not taking me to jail the night before my wedding.

Then a deep voice from the back of the limousine said, "Oh yes you did do something!" I turned around and tried to look through the bright headlights of the policeman car. "What? I did something to who?" Immediately, a man's silouette walked in front of the headlights. "She crashed my bachelor party that's what she did." "PJ are you stupid, I can not believe you Are you crazy? If you don't hurry up and get these handcups off me?" "Baby I just couldn't resist." "I just bet you couldn't." Then PJ walked around to my side of the car and kissed me on my lips; while I had those stupid hand cuffs on. I was steaming by now, then he said, "Remember we said, we needed to keep our hands off each other. I didn't touch her officer, honestly I didn't. Did you see me touch her?" "No sir I did not." "I can argue with that, your lips just touched me." Then he said, baby "I'm sorry baby but I just had to get you back, tell the truth, I got you didn't I!" "Oh yea, you got me big time, you better believe I will get back for this one. "I want you to get me too, this time tomorrow night I will be waiting for it. Anticipation with a capital A." "Boy, you are so crazy, you're sick you need to see a doctor I think I'll make you an appointment first thing tomorrow morning before we get married. Angell, you know after you become my wife tomorrow, I want need a doctor. Because you are exactly what the doctor order my (Doctor Feel Good) and you know you got all the surgical instruments that I'll ever need, and you know exactly how to take care of me and make me feel real good." "Oh I do, do I?" "Yes baby you do, I'm sorry I had you hand cuffed, but it was the only way I could get you to keep your hands off me, you know you get so carried away; the hand cuffs were my idea, you know how sick I am doctor." "True, True, as long as you know how sick you are and since I got that love potion to cure you...I guess I can live with being your doctor for the rest of our lives." Then he got the key to the cuffs and unlocked them. "Thank you, I will document all this in your charts." "Make sure you document this." Then he pick me up and sat me on the trunk of the limo and kissed me like nothing ever happen. "PJ quit trying to start my motor running." "Baby I'm just trying to get your car all warmed up for me tomorrow." "Honey trust me it's not going to take that much warming...this car is always ready for you before you stick your keys into the ignition...this engine belongs to you." "Baby don't talk like that...now you're making me want to pay you to be my mechanic." "But I am your mechanic too...I have to keep your engine running don't I?" "Baby when you put it that way, yes you do...are you always this sexy when you fix cars." "I only specialize in one car...I plan to kept it running for a long time." "Ooh, baby my motor is running hott right now." "Come here, I got just the right tools to cool it down." "Ooh baby, I just bet you do." Then I kissed him all over again tenderly on his lips and told him...we better stop because we have an audience watching us. "Oh baby I'm sorry...Vince sorry man, you can see why I love this girl...we get carried away no matter where we are...this girl sets me on fire. Angell, this is a good friend of mine, Vince who really is a police officer, thanks man for going along with this. Sorry for the side show but as you can Angell can't seem to keep her hands off me, I told you that earlier." Then he gave Vince the keys to his handcuffs. "Looks like the feelings are mutual man, congradulations to you both, its good to see two people who really love each other. I wish you both nothing but the best, Jon P you got yourself some kind of woman here. Both of you take care of your self and me and a few of the guys will see you tomorrow at the wedding. Nice meeting you Angell, take care of my man Jon P." "Nice meeting you too, Vince...although I didn't appreciate the handcuffs...the man who unlocked them holds the key to my heart...so I ain't mad at you. Be careful." "No you two are the ones who need to be careful...you both look like you are about to explode in an abundance of love and that's a good thing." "You better believe that man, I can wait until tomorrow. Thanks again for your time man, we'll see you at the wedding." "Couldn't think of anywhere else I rather be, take care man."

"Where is the guy who was driving the limo?" Oh you mean Charles, he's was in the Police car with Vincent. Immediately he signaled Charles to take me back to the hotel. Then he explained what happened. "When Vincent got off duty about an hour ago he showed up in his uniform, then the girls came in and crashed the party. Right after that the guys told me we had to think of a way to get you back. So this is what we came up with, We decided to play this little trick on you for crashing our party. Angell, I just couldn't help myself, it sounded like a real good idea, all my boys put me up to it. I had to carry it through or they would never let me live it down." "I just bet they wouldn't." "Come on baby, we were just joking around." "Honey, I know it, I'm not upset it was pretty funny." "Baby, let's get back to the hotel, so we can pick up your friends, can I ride with you back to the Hotel?" "Well I guess so." "Can I put my arms around you when we get inside?" "I don't know, that was an awfully cruel trick you played on me." Deep down inside I couldn't wait to sit close to him, so we got inside the limo and enjoyed our own level of imtimacy all the way back to the Hotel. It was almost midnight when we got back to the Hotel and we both decided to depart company knowing we would see each other before we knew it for the rest of our lives. We ended the night with a sweet tender kisses. "Thank you for waiting on me and for being the man I want to spend the rest of my life with." "I wouldn't have it any other way. Until then...I love you, baby." "Honey, would you please send my posse' back down, I need to get my beauty rest, after being placed under your arrest and almost going to jail, I really need it." "Don't tell me you really need it like that, those words are turning me on." "Come on boy, it's almost midnight, don't you get me started again." He got on his cell phone and asked William to send everybody down stairs. "PJ, tell them if they want to stay I'm okay, I can send the driver back for them. Honey, have fun that's a pretty wild combination you got up there." "Baby we'll be fine, they are in good hands. Looks like a few of your girlfrieinds are headed this way. Ladies, take care of my baby in there." Jackie, Linda and Rinda got inside the limo smiling from ear to ear. "Those are some bad boys up there, who really know how to throw a party." The driver, Charles, made a joke about the BB Crash which is what he called the Batchelors crashing with the Batchelorettes, which was kind of funny, then he teased me about the hand cuffs, we both started laughing at PJ's wild and crazy sense of humor. Charles went on his way and said his good nights after he dropped us off. The next day our replacement driver's name was Thomas he would be picking us up in the morning for our spa day wedding package to get massages, waxes, manicures and pedicures. Then we would be off to our next stop getting our hair done.

When we finally got back to my place my girlfriends spent the rest of the night telling me about the stock of men that were there and how nice the party was. As soon as I got a shower and my head hit the pillow I began to fall asleep. We tried to wait up for the other girls to make it back but I couldn't help it; my eyes were ready to close out on me. All of my closest friends, were in town and wanted to spend the night at my house as a farewell to the single life. I was sure the girls who lingered on at the batchelor party probably had too much too drink and just crashed out at the Hotel. The Hotel Suite was paid for, for the night and knowing PJ he probably just let them have the room. And God was I thankful, for him because he was so thoughtful and always took everything into consideration. I loved him, but I loved God so much more than anything. "Sweet dreams, I said to my self then I drifted off. It's the morning of the first day of spring, where promises of love is about to begin. I can hear the birds chirping, and the beauty of flowers coming into bloom, everything is beginning to turn green, the trees, the grass, outside the windows of love you can hear the birds chirping and humming birds singing.

We planned to have a light breakfast but woke up too late. Rinda fixed a pot of hot cofee and tea, and we pulled out some of the left over food from the wedding shower. I was so excited and refreshed. My girlfriend Jackie made me a light breakfast in bed from the left over fruit salad and other little appetizers that were just as good the morning after as they were last night. I noticed all the girls hadn't make it back which meant they must have had huge hangovers. We were all too tired anyway, if we didn't eat something now, it would'nt happen until later that evening. It was our pamper day, everybody had to go to the salon, we were getting the works. Linda owned the shop and was my personal hairdresser as well as one of my dearest friends, she was giving us the works. She booked the entire wedding party at her shop for the day.

As we were getting into the limo my phone ranged, I reached over and answered it, "Good morning, baby, I just called to tell you how much I love you, and that we had a blast last night, several of the ladies are still at the hotel. I had to book them another suite last night; the guys were knocked out all over the place, I didn't want double jeopordy on my hands. So I made sure the women were in one suite and the men were in the other. I think they all had a pretty good time. Janae wanted me to tell you that if for some reason you couldn't marry me, just let the girls know and they would take a stand and may the best woman win. I told him I hope he let her know that wouldn't be necessary, because the best woman had already won not once but twice." "Honey, you paid for another room?" "Yes baby, I had to, because they were totally lit up; I didn't want them parading through the hotel waiting on a cab, there were four or five guys staying in the suite for the guys, they were all full of it everything. I didn't think it would be a good idea for all of them to stay in the same room. Remember, I didn't have to pay for either one of the suites they were compliments of my best man William and Gerald they also took care of everything nothing came out of my pocket." "Thank you baby, I love you, yea for William and Gerald, no wonder they are both your best men, I can't wait to get you all to my self tonight." "I just bet you can't, I'm looking forward to having you all to myself every night." "Honey, please remind the girls that they need to be at the Spa by 10:00 this morning. By the way you better get a little extra rest this morning because you are going to need it, and then some, tonight you belong to me." He laughed, and said, "Baby I can't wait, I have some special moves you haven't even seen yet, I got plans for you. I'll meet you at the alter." Mark is driving us around today, I can have him drop the ladies off at your place if you like, so they can change. That's fine you have the key right, give it to Janae and I'll get it from her at the salon." "Okay baby, I know you ladies have to go and get beautiful." "Absolutely, thank you for everything, I'll see you later okay, honey don't forget our new marriage license the pastor has to sign them remember, and make sure William puts the rings in his tux this morning." "Baby I got this, thanks for reminding me about the license especially since I have both of them. I'll take care of that right now. Until then Angell."

Everything went according to plan it was the most beautiful day. The sun was shining with its rays of brilliance, the sky was lovely and blue, it was clear with the most magnificent white puffy clouds. What a gorgeous Friday God had made for us, the time went by quickly, before I knew it, it was time for me to get dressed. My Mother was coming over to meet me at my place to help me get dressed. Jacqueline had all of our gowns shipped to my place two weeks before the wedding in case anybody needed any alterations. The limousine picked us up from the salon, and took us straight to my place. I thank God that I had just enough space for all of us to roam around without getting in each other's way. It was hard to get past the tears, but we made it and finally it was almost four o'clock; time for us to go to the church. We all gathered together and my Mother said a prayer for our union and prayed for the whole occasion to be blessed and thanked God for every thing he had done so far.

The Wedding Tradition Blessings

My Mom was first, she gave me her special blessing and then I received **My Something Old,** which was the most beautiful diamond bracelet that belonged to my grandmother, it was so fragile vintage but sparkled just like new, it gave me a feeling of sentiment that she was there with us. **My Something New** was the most gorgeous diamond teardrop necklace from PJ's Mother and Grandmother which meant so much to me as I reminised about the love I was fortunate enough to share with her and the honor to marry her son, I whispered a prayer of love and told her that I missed her presence and would always treasure her love in my heart forever. **My Something Borrowed,** were teardrop earrings from my mom, and my best friend Daphine had already given me a beautiful blue lace garter with ice blue rinestones around it, the first time around with a matching hankerchief which was **My Most Sentimental Something Blue.** As I shed a few teardrops about my best friend, her three year old niece walked up to me and gave me the sweetest kiss and my blue hankerchief as joy filled my heart I began to marvel at the wonderment of God's love. The wedding traditions were covered, I was so thankful before we left the house the photographer was there taking all the before and after pictures. We all finished off the pictures and did one of those giant group hugs and were on our way a little before four-thirty. When we made it to the church, everything was so beautiful and just divine, the church was full of people all over, lots of pictures were being taken, before I knew it the wedding coordinator was coming in to get me as my favorite Uncle Jesse stood in the wings of the church waiting to escort me down the aisle we smiled at each other and proceeded to walk done to the middle of the isle to meet the man I had dreamed of marrying and spending the rest of my life with Jon Paul Morgan who was the love of my life. The ceremony was magnificent then God gave him to me, and me to him in front of more than a hundred witnesses. It was extraordinary, the photographers and videographers captured our dreams in that short expanse of time, every one there seem to have enjoyed the whole ceremony. PJ and I received so many gifts, our wedding reception was being held at the Ritz Carlton Hotel. Everyone was given directions in their wedding invitations and our coordinator directed our guest to the hotel after the pictures were about to wrap up. When we arrived at the Hotel the food was like a work of art; PJ and I knew several chef's that worked at the hotel; it was absolutely ravishing almost too delectable to eat, just extraordinary. It was a dream come true for both of us, we went from the first dance to trying to eat a bit in between; everyone came by to pay their respect to us, to the toast; to the cutting of the cake, to our first dance finally it was time for the garter toss and the wedding bouquet. Finally it was time to head for our honeymoon suite which was in the penthouse suite of the hotel; that was given to us by the company he worked for when we met. We didn't want to be traveling the night of our wedding, so we were scheduled for a cruise to a private Island in Hawaii, we would be leaving out first thing Monday morning. Our honeymoon suite was incredible, we had the most wonderful encounters that one could ever imagine, but now I was his wife and I truly belonged to him. It was beautiful to finally understand that scripture, "He that findeth a wife, findeth a good thing and obtains favor of the Lord." We were both so thankful that God gave us back to each other; in spite of our shortcomings we both recognized and understood that we all fall short of his glory. Our re-union was worth more than treasure at the end of a rainbow. Our hearts were filled with so many levels of passion for each other, our sensuality was incredible it was more than I had dreamed of; filled with love and tears of joy. I closed my eyes and let it all go, as the art of creativity of love for him took over. Jon Paul Morgan was definitely the most pleasurable man that I had ever been with, no matter what we experienced he was worth spending the rest of my life with. This was the man that my soul longed to love who had captured my heart with the very essence of his love for me, God could not have chosen a better man for me than him.

As grateful as I was, I reminisced of how blessed I was to understand that as my heart ached to finally discover the search for my soul mate, I thought it was a man, but it was God. His love always restored my love right back to his, as he taught me the true meaning of real love. It is unconditional love, respect, honor, understanding, a caring heart, forgiveness, sacrifices, laughter, new beginnings, to heartache, joy and pain. Allowing him to restore our hearts like a surgeon through the beauty of forgiveness and leaving room for repairing the yoke that makes us equal to the one he has prepared and chosen for us; the inner joy is endless as we stay true to love. So if you are waiting; keep waiting, if you are trusting; keep trusting, if you are believing; keep believing one day soon, he or she will be here. But know this, that God is always there ordering and directing our steps. As we take our time to open up, allowing him to search our hearts as we delight ourselves in him, He will reveal to us what we truly desire in our heart, mind, soul and spirit.

Take delight in the LORD and he will give you the desires of your heart. (NIV)

Delight yourself also in the Lord, and He will give you the desires and secret petitions of your heart. (AMP)

Delight thyself also in the LORD: and he shall give thee the desires of thine heart. (KJV)

Psalms 37:4

*In Search Of My Soul Mate, I Thought It
Was A Man, But It Was GOD
This is an Inspirational Love Story,
filled with words of enlightenment
to invigorate your Belief in the Power of Love.
It reflects on The Highest Level of Love that's possible to focus on
which instills satisfaction, comfort and strength.
It centers around a story of true love
held in the hearts of two people,
Manifested and Confirmed through the Spirit
of God's Unconditional Love.*